SOCIOLOGY OF WORLD TERRORISM

SOCIOLOGY OF WORLD TERRORISM
(Origin, Growth, Cause and Suggestions)

Edited by
Paras Kumar Choudhary

GYAN

ISBN: 978-81-212-1191-8

Price: ₹ 885

First Published, 2014

Published by

Gyan Publishing House
23, Main Ansari Road
Daryaganj, New Delhi-110002
Phones: 23282060, 23261060
Fax : 91-11-23285914
E-mail: books@gyanbooks.com

Laser Typesetting: Gyan print (AB-I), Delhi

Printed at: Chawla Offset Printers, Delhi

Cataloging in Publication Data—DK

Courtesy: D.K. Agencies (P) Ltd. <docinfo@dkagencies.com>

Sociology of world terrorism : origin, growth, cause and suggestions / edited by Paras Kumar Choudhary.

p. cm.

Contributed articles.

Includes bibliographical references.

ISBN 9788121211918

1. Terrorism—Social aspects. 2. Terrorism—Social aspects—India. I. Choudhary, Paras Kumar, 1964-

DDC 303.625 23

Dedicated to

Late Asha Devi (Beloved mother of editor)
and
Late B.C. Choudhary (Right Revered father of editor)
who have been my great source of inspiration
and invaluable strength.

Contents

Foreword

Terrorism has acquired a global shape, through its roots are contextually specific to the given situations and societies. India, Sri Lanka, Pakistan and Nepal in South Asia have been infested with terrorism. The reasons are varied, ranging from agrarian hierarchy, ethnic divides and prejudices, historical and cultural downfall and ideological differences. The champions of terrorism generally plead that they are fighting for the poor and against their oppressors. The plea of terrorist organisations against the developed countries is that their hegemony is such that all other countries remain at the receiving end. Political superiority over the underdeveloped and less developed parts of the world.

Dr. Paras Kumar Choudhary, Editor of the Book, has put together twenty-one papers covering different dimensions and magnitudes of terrorism. Understanding of terrorism with an inter-disciplinary perspective, drawing inputs from different parts of India and neighbouring countries, like Pakistan, Afghanistan, etc., is really a noble attempt made by the editor. Further, to see the menace of terrorism in terms of its structural and cultural counters on the one hand, and also as a coexistent phenomenon with democracy and globalisation on the other, is, in fact, an admirable venture. Dr. Choudhary looks at wider implications of terrorism and specially in the contexts of health, women and young people.

Terrorism is not restricted to create a sense of fear among the oppressors for the good of the deprived and oppressed people. It has resulted into real physical violence, killing, rapes, loot and brutalities. Pleasure becomes a distant dream. Generally, terrorism is a one-sided action. But there are also examples of counter-terrorism by the entrenched echelons, landlords and political heavyweights. An oppressive system has a tendency to dehumanise its "masses", as the "classes" control the state and society.

Is terrorism the only way to establish an egalitarian social order? Does it ensure more positive results compared to other ways and means for amicable solutions to human pathos? How to heal the latent wounds even after cessation of terrorism? Who are the people behind terrorist activities? Are they themselves sufferer or genuine and concerned fighters against oppressive indignities or a band of ruthless people, having the motto of self-aggrandisement?

The readers of the volume may find clues for answers to some of these questions. The merit of the volume lies in the new debate that it generates on the menace of terrorism. I am sure it has some fire to ignite our minds.

K.L. SHARMA
Vice-Chancellor
Jaipur National University,
Jaipur - 302017 (India).

Acknowledgements

First of all I express my deep sense of gratitude and respect to Goddess *Maa Durga* for her spiritual blessings to come out with this volume.

I wish to express my gratefulness to all those, who helped me in completion of this volume. The list of such persons is indeed a very comprehensive one, but a few persons need a special mention.

I am happy to express my obligation to all those who have contributed their valuable articles for this volume.

I am very much obliged to Mr. Baijnath Ram Honourable, H.R.D. Minister, Jharkhand, for his intellectual guidance.

I am very much obliged to Prof. L.N. Bhagat, Vice-Chancellor, Ranchi University, Ranchi for his intellectual guidance and affectionate encouragement.

I am very much obliged to renowned Prof. K.L. Sharma, Vice-Chancellor, Jaipur National University, Jaipur for his writing foreword and encouragement.

I express my gratitude to Mr. C.P. Singh, Honourable Speaker Jharkhand Vidhan Sabha, Jharkhand for his encouragement.

I express my gratitude to Dr. M. Rajiuddin, Prof. Vice-Chancellor, Ranchi University whose constant support helped me to complete the work on time.

I am very much obliged to Dr. Amar Choudhary, Registrar, Ranchi University, Ranchi for his support.

I wish to express my respect and gratefulness to all the faculty members and staff of Post-graduate Department of Sociology and Sociology Department of Colleges, Ranchi University, Ranchi, Jharkhand.

I am obliged to Prof. Anand Kumar, Prof. Noor Mohammed (Aligarh) Prof. Rabindra Sindhu (Amritsar) for their intellectual guidance.

I am also grateful to Prof. Sarfaraz Ahmed, Prof. Mustafa Hussain, Prof. V.K. Lal, Prof. R.N. Sharma, Prof. Ashish Das Gupta and Dr. Dharmsilla Prasad (Patna University) for their important suggestions.

I am very much obliged to Prof. Ravi Prakash Pandey, Prof. Girja Prasad, Deptt. of Sociology, Kashi Vidyapith, Varanasi for valuable suggestion and encouragement.

I express my respect to Prof. Jaykant Tiwari, Prof. Arbind Joshi, Prof. J.N. Singh Deptt. of Sociology B.H.U. Varanasi for his encouragement.

I should not forget to convey my best regards to Prof. K.N. Sahay, Ex H.O.D. Deptt. of Anthropology, R.U., Ranchi for his constant support and encouragement.

I express my gratitude to Prof. Pramod Sinha, H.O.D. Deptt. of Sociology, T.M. University, Bhagalpur, Bihar, Dr. Guni Shankar Singh, H.O.D., Veer Kunwar Singh, University, Ara, Dr. Daya Ram Yadav, H.O.D., B.P. Mandal University, Madhepura, Bihar and Dr. Birendra Singh, H.O.D. Bihar, University, Muzaffarpur, Bihar for encouragement.

I should not forget to convey my best regards to Shree Shree Ram Prasad Jee, Spiritual Guru for his blessings.

I want to convey my special thanks to Mr. Nirmal Kumar Ghosh, M.A. Sociology, Ranchi University.

I am indebted to my father Late Bhagwat Chandra Choudhary and mother Late Asha Devi for their blessings.

I express my special thanks to Miss Sonam ex-Research Asstt. P.G. Deptt. of Sociology, Ranchi University for their immense help an active co-operation to complete this work.

Last but not least, I express my thanks to my wife, Kanta Choudhary, son Raj Choudhary and daughter Pinkee for emotional support and for being my source of motivation all the time.

Paras Kumar Choudhary

List of Contributors

Aneesa Shafi, Ex. H.O.D. Deptt. of Sociology and Social Work, Kashmir University, Kashmir.

Anurag Ratan, Associate Professor and Head of the Deptt. of Political Science, G.S., P.O. College, Sultanpur, U.P.

B.N. Sahay, Associate Professor, University, Deptt of Anthropology, Ranchi University, Ranchi, Jharkhand.

Monika Sahay, A Lady Anthropologist, University Deptt. of Anthropology, Ranchi University, Ranchi, Jharkhand.

Eduardo M. Domingo, Associates Professor, Chair Theology and Religious Education Deptt. De La Salle University Manila, Philippines.

Hamid, Scholar, Social Work Deptt., Tata Institute of Social Sciences, Mumbai.

Hee Sook Lee Niinioja, Ph.D. Deptt. of Sociology, U.S.A.

Paras Kumar Choudhary, Head of the Deptt. University, Deptt. of Sociology, and Ex. Director Human Rights Education, Ranchi University, Ranchi, Jharkhand.

Jacquice Lewis, Deptt. of Sociology, Chicago, U.S.A.

Vijay Kumar, Professor, University, Deptt. of Political Science, Tilka Manjhi Bhagalpur University, Bhagalpur, Bihar.

Shailesh Anand, Assistant Professor, Deptt. of Political Science, Tilka Manjhi Bhagalpur University, Bhagalpur, Bihar.

Purabi Nandi, A Lady Sociologist, Currently School Inspector, Govt. of West Bengal.

Ravi Prakash Pandey, H.O.D. Deptt. of Sociology M.G. Kashi Vidyapith Varanasi, U.P.

Sovnath Yadav, Associate Professor, Dr. R.M. Lohia Awadh University, Faizabad.

Pramod Kumar Choudhary, Assistant Professor, University, Deptt. of Sociology, Magadh University, Bodh Gaya, Bihar.

J.L. Oraon, Ex Pro - Vice Chancellor, and Member, Jharkhand Public Service Commission, Jharkhand.

K.G. Vasantha Madhava, Aradhana, Pavanje, Halengadi Dhaka, Bangladesh.

Mohmad Saleem Jahangir, Associate Professor, Deptt. of Sociology, Kashmir University, Kashmir.

R.E.S. Tanner, Professor, Deptt. of Sociology, U.S.A.

Randhir Kumar, Ph.D. Scholar of AISSR Amsterdam Institute of Social Science Research at University of Amsterdam, The Netherlands.

Syad Iqbal Imam Rizvi, Assistant Professor, Deptt. of Sociology, Oriental College, Patna City, Patna, Bihar.

Y. Nath Pandey, Assistant Professor, Deptt. of Anthropology, Ranchi University, Ranchi, Jharkhand.

Sabir Hussain, Research Scholar Deptt. of Anthropology, Ranch! University, Ranchi, Jharkhand.

Rajesh Roshan, Research Scholar, Deptt. of Anthropology, Ranchi University, Ranchi, Jharkhand.

S.M. Fahimuddin Pasha, Double M.A. and Ph.D. Scholar, Currently Assistant Manager at Computer Society of India.

Syed Jamil Ahmed, Professor Department of Theatre, University of Dhaka, Bangladesh.

Umesh Kumar Verma, Writer and Research Officer Tribal Research Institute, Ranchi, Jharkhand.

Editorial Notes

Fanaticism incite terrorist attacks. So, we can say that Islam as a religion is not responsible for the terrorism, but the fanaticism that emerges from this particular religion is liable for terrorism. Rathbone and Rowley (2002), proclaimed that dehumanisation is one of the vital factors for terrorism. According to them, terrorists are fighting for being heard, recognised and treated as equal human beings.

India ranked among the world's most terrorism-afflicted countries: The recent Sachchar Committee report asserted that in many cases minorities are not getting proper representation in various economic and political areas. It improves the unrest among the members of a particular religion and makes them deprived.

In the society where there is illiteracy, hunger and economic disparity, terrorism flourishes rapidly. All these factors lead to increase in poverty which itself is the mother of terrorism.

It is true that socio-economic backwardness are hampering the social harmony, but we should not consider that this is the only reason that is destroying the fabric of society. There are other factors also that cause insurgency in society. Even though, countries like USA. and Israel are economically developed, but still they are facing the same problems.

Democracy in the Age of Terrorism: The Basic Challenges and Future Prospects

–Vijay Kumar and Shailesh Anand

As a matter of facts. Democracy is an "Ideal". It is a "Utopian" concept. "It is a form of Government it is a kind of Economy, it is an order of society, it is a way of life, it is all these things together" and many things more.

Citizens in a Democracy enjoy an extensive array of freedoms.

The democratic community, totals about thirty per cent of the World's population, holds about seventy per cent of its wealth and is more stable, united and prosperous. But areas where conditions are not so good and progress is less rapid have begun to threaten the Democratic World. This is especially the case along the so-called "southern arc of instability" that stretches from the Middle East to the Asia littoral. This huge zone is rendered chaotic by a number of problems: absence of clear-cut boundaries, security vacuums, power imbalances, poverty, ineffective Governments, high unemployment and extremist Religious fundamentalism. The result is a fertile ground for breeding terrorist groups engaged in supporting rogue govts, ethnic rivalries, drug-trafficking, weapon smuggling and organised crime. So, much so that, Walter, Laqueur, with his lifetime of research in terrorism, has called this era, "The Age of Terrorism".

Terrorism has been a dark feature of human behaviour since first recorded history. It is an active confrontation, evidenced by the fact that the incidence of significant terrorist attacks often spikes, to several levels like 9/11, 12/13, 7/7 and 26/11.

These are no longer just number or dates but have become turning points for countries who have suffered bloody and ghastly terror attacks. It is a problem capable of destabilising not only national but also international politics.

Today, usually all states are expanding resources to combat terrorism setting up especially trained police squads, planning policies and programs and holding operations to track terrorist groups in their own countries. Amercia has in particular, been spending a lot of money since mid-1990's on counter-terrorist operations.

By uniting together in their fight against terrorism the democratic countries seek to build a more secure and economically prosperous world in which people can live freely and enjoy healthy and productive lives.

Terrorism has no end. It leads nowhere except to death and destruction. Indeed, the ultimate success in fight against terrorism requires concerted support of all Nations.

Contemporary Conflict Resolution among the Sukuma of Tanzania

–R.E.S. Tanner

In Central Tanzania to the South of Lake Victoria there are about five million Sukuma and their neighbouring two million Nyamwezi, the biggest tribal group in the country possessing similar culture, a mutually intelligible language, living by a combination of subsistence farming and pastorlism.

As their population has increased, they have moved out into previously unoccupied areas repeating the same pattern of dispersed settlements except towards the East where their expansion came upon against the pastoral age-graded warrier system of the Vaasai. There appear to be several types of conflicts which all have the characteristic of being on-going rather than bring aimed or involving solutions, Firstly, inter-tribal tensions with the Maasai to the East which swings backwards and forwards according to the irritations to the Sukuma ethnic pride building up so that young men to break out in raiding for cattle which is abetted by the older men whose status depends on supporting rather than objecting to such violence. Quarrels between neighbours over field boundaries, livestock entering fields, misuse of water and grazing cattle too early in dry season in reserved land where only those involved have any interest into solutions.

Quarrels over women which do not involve neighbours over issues of marriage payments, ownership of children and adultery.

Quarrels over communal issues such as maintenance of water holes protection from thieves. Then, quarrels involving suspicion of witchcraft which have increased enormously in the last decades and have involved the killing of 2347 suspected witches and wizards 1970-1984 of which the majority were women.

Sukuma custom regards dispute as similar to moving staircases onto which new issues can get on and other get off as the situation fluctuates over time. It is their basic assumption that disputes can only be ameliorated within the changing social context of those involved and this is done by the use of arbitrators who are accepted because of their personal reputations.

The basis of conflict resolution is binary. The first objective is to keep the community intact by accepting the plain fact that every community is split by real and potential conflicts, a dialectic for the continuation of a viable community. No community can survive by making membership untenable by one-sided solutions. It is a binary framework of thinking in which there are rarely if ever quarrels for which one-sided solutions are possible.

The second objective is keeping the community intact by systematic institutionalised oppositions.

We have to accept that the vast majority of contemporary human relationships whether in Bombay, Birmingham or Banaras are controlled by folklore which is largely outside the boundaries of literacy and written records.

So, we can expect the Sukuma folklore of disputes and their solutions to adjust itself to new situations and that this would possibly develop in response to two different social and Environmental Stimuli. Firstly, in the old core areas attached to the main roads and the one railway line with possibilities of working in townships while retaining a holding of cash value land kept under cultivation by women and their absentee men.

It is probably wrong to call any system of conflict resolution traditional as there are processes of settling differences by word of mouth in every society todays as was the case in history.

It is moreover, a process which is almost existential in the ways by which its methods of problem solving come to fit into the needs of those involved without much recourse to the benefits of literacy.

Peace with other Species

–Jackecie Lewis

Peace studies encompass a wide range of topics. Creation of a peaceful world needs to also include peace toward non-human animals. True peace is not possible unless it encompasses other species.

Albert Schweitzer, in his Nobel Peace Prize addresses. "The Problem of Peace in the world stated, 'The human spirit is not dead. It lives on in secret. It has come to believe that compassion, in which all ethics must take root, can only attain its full breath and depth if it embraces all living creatures and does not limit itself to mankind."

It stands to reason that if humankind is to truly create a global peace culture it must include other species. Peace with the animals can be accomplished on a personal level by individuals choosing to change their consumer behaviour patterns. Most people do not do this because they remain ignorant and apathetic and their personal decisions perpetuate animal abuse. However, individuals can live a cruelty free lifestyle, which means, choosing not to consume products that harm animals.

In the U.S. Millions of animals suffer and die annually in painful tests to determine the "safety" of household products and cosmetics, products ranging from lipstick and eye shadow, to soap, furniture polish, weed killer, and oven cleaner are tested on rabbits, rats, guinea pigs, dogs and other animals. This is all the more tragic in light of the fact that there are numerous alternative products available to consumers that are not tested on animals and that have been proven to be safe and effective.

If a peaceful world is to be accomplished this should include non-violent consumer choices, such as purchasing products not tested on animals. This cruelty-free lifestyle is already practiced by many animal advocates and it makes sense that it should also be adopted by those who care about peace.

The area where individuals can demonstrate their peace towards other species is with their food choices.

This paper addresses two issues that stress the relationship between consumer choices and animal welfare. As consumers, we can decide not to buy products tested on animals and refrain from meat, egg and dairy consumption. By making these choices, individuals can make peace with the animals : Love is the foundation of Peace Movement. It is at the core, wishing its members to push forward in their goal of peace. Only then can true love be realised in its fullness.

Naxalism—Causes and Remedies with Special Reference to Tribal of Jharkhand

–Sabir Hussain and Rajesh Roshan

Naxalism is an informal name given to communist groups that were born out of the Sino-Soviet split in the communist movement in India. Ideologically they belong to various trends of Maosim. Initially, the movement had its centre in West Bengal. In recent years, they have spread into less developed areas of rural centre and eastern India, such as, Chhattisgarh, Andhra Pradesh, Jharkhand, Orissa, through the activities of underground Groups like the Communist Party of India (Maoist). They are conducting an insurgency, typically called the Naxalite Maoist Insurgency. They have now a presence in forty per cent of India's geographical area and are especially concentrated in an area known as the "Naxal Belt" comprising 92,000 square kilometres. Practically, all Naxalite groups trace their origin to the CPI(ML), MCC later fused with People's War Group to form Communist Party of India (Maoist). During 1970's the movement was fragmented into several disputing factions. By 1980, it was estimated that around thirty Naxalite groups were active, with a combined membership of 30,000.

The CPI (M) and some other Naxal factions are now considered terrorist by the Government of India. Poor employment prospects are major cause of Naxalism problem in Jharkhand. Unemployment is higher in rural areas. The present social structure of society in tribals is also a reason for Naxalism. Wherever, Maoist problems exists, there is a poor section of society, with no resources to meet their daily requirements. The failure of government to reach out to these areas is another major factor that aids the growth of Maoists in these areas. Popular schemes take long to devise but longer to implement on the contrary. Maoist groups have been collecting levies from the local population. They collect funds from individuals, groups and even government officials as commissions for letting them function in areas that are under their control. This money is used by them to buy arms.

Remedies for the Maoist Problems

1. The state will create an enabling environment for livelihood and employment opportunities. It will ensure that regional disparities are minimised for livelihood opportunities.
2. The state will work to ensure protection of its youth especially tribals from physical, mental, social and psychological abuse.
3. Deviant young will be re-oriented through positive engagement in social services. District level rehabilitation-cum-counselling centres will be constituted for deviant youth under public private partnership with civil societies.
4. The policy seeks to develop youth into responsible citizens of state and promote leadership among them for involvement in economic and social development. State will create opportunities possibilities and platforms for youth, especially rural and tribal youth for greater involvement in development programmes and reconstructions efforts.

Ethnic Conflicts: Perceptions and Counter Perceptions

–J.L. Oraon

The paper entitled "Ethnic - conflicts : Perceptions and Counter Perceptions" is basically a study of man and human condition and reflects the concerns of the fluid and very mixed societies of the world. Ethnicity is a connotative concept. The paper explores the aspects of ethnic separatism, forces of stability and change; trends of sociology and contemporary spiritual styles and international relations, the new ethnicity and social class religion and social group, ethnicity and race and above all, a word conscience along with the roots of perceived dangers with special reference to India and Pakistan. The paper reflects their ethnicity and ideology whereupon they draw deeply embedded cultural linguistic, religions or regionally significant symbols around which they can mobilise popular support, symbols that can generate a powerful political charge.

The term "ethnic" refers to a social group which consciously shared some aspects of a common culture and is defined primarily by descent. It is part of a family of terms of similar or related meaning such as, minority growth', 'race', and 'nation and it is not often easy to make sharp distinctions between them. Race refers to a group that is defined by common descent and has some typical physical characteristics. The ethnic group refers basically to vertical divisions. Horizontal divisions refer to class; vertical divisions to ethnicity. Thus, ethnicity becomes less and less coincident with state boundaries and ethnicity becomes a stronger basis for terminal loyalty than class ethnic groups, owing to migrations and economic inter-relationships, are less and less definable by physical boundaries. Ethnicity seems to have become a permanent force in modern world in its own capacity and multi-ethnic form is becoming increasingly common within each nation, wherein each group has guaranteed rights and guaranteed shares in the economy, polity, in social life. Ethnicity must now be placed at the very centre of our concern for the human condition.

More Challenges Threat Terrorism Poses to Public Health

–Syad Iqbal Imam Rizvi and Y. Nath Pandey

Terrorism can be defined as politically motivated violence or threat of violence, especially against civilians, with the intent to instil fear. Terrorism is perceived as a problem capable of destablising not only national but also international politics. It is a problem, we have been facing in India for more than two decades. In recent times, it has affected both developed and developing countries. Terrorism is an organised system of intimadation: Terrorism can cause injury, illness and death; create fear, anxiety and other psychological reactions destroying the physical infrastructure and social fabric of communities and cause profound adverse economic and political impacts on individuals, communities, nations and our global society. Terrorism appears in many forms - from planting a crude, home-made bomb, hand grenade or other explosive in a shopping centre, a railway station, a bus station or a bus, a train, or an aeroplane, to kidnapping and assassination of important personalities. The main aim of terrorists is to create havoc upon those whom they regard as obstacles or enemies or oppressors.

Major Challenges of Terrorism for Public Health Are

- Improving public health system capabilities to respond to health consequence of terrorist Acts.
- Controlling Terrorist Weapons.
- Addressing factors that may breed terrorism.

Taking Actions to Help Prevent Terrorism Are

- Advocating the control, reduction and elimination of weapons of mass destruction.
- Helping reduce access to biological agents that can be used as bio-terriorist groups.
- Promoting a balance between response to terrorism and to other public health concerns.
- Maintaining support for other public health priorities. Promoting the protection of Civil Rights and Human Rights.

Terrorism is a threat to Public Health and to society as a whole. Health professionals can do much to mitigate the health consequences of terrorists threat, acts and to help prevent them. At the same time, health professionals must maintain and promote a balanced perspective that gives terrorism preparedness an appropriate priority amidst many other health problems people suffer from as well as the underlying societal factors that contribute to the development of these health problems.

Terrorism Under the Shadow of Religion and World Peace

–B.N. Sahay and Monika Sahay

This is a social phenomena that a religion unites the people of one religion; whereas on the other hand, it creates communal differences and disputes among the people of other religions. In past, due to religious differences more people have been killed than in political wars. Today also, due to it different religious organisations are harming or killing people of other religions.

Globalisation has changed the World which has become like a small village. Man is linked throughout the world through different communication systems and easy conveyance of media. But globalisation has negative ·mpact also. It has favoured terrorism also, especially today's religious terrorism. Today it has become very easy to get information of any place sitting at far distance place. Due to easy availability of such facilities, terrorism has increased. In religious field, *Jehad* has been interpreted in two senses. In view of an evil desire, and Anti-socio-religious acts to control it. Also interpreted as the act of fighting, against followers of other religions to spread Islam. Almost in all Religions, different saints have realised and preached "God is one". Thus, the inherent supernatural power in all religions and their activities are the same. Religion's highest level of sacred performances is the self-realisation i.e., realisation of existence of God in one-self. Different Communities of the World developed their concepts of God (beliefs) and rituals according to their own experience and thinking. Due to this reason, we find differences in different religions. Now due to globalisation, all major religions could come nearer to each other and they agree that the Supreme Power 'God' is one and universal who is controlling life, births and death. Thus, we see there is unity in diversity of World Religions.

This shows religion does not cause social disturbance, it is caused by some miscreants who indulge in anti-social activities under the shadow of religion to create social disturbances.

Religious disputes are due to misunderstanding of religious truths. It can be avoided by teachings or preaching of religious truths.

To propagate such ideas, different committees should be formed at different levels in villages, blocks, district, states, National and International levels i.e. (U.N.O.) These committees will work for socio-religious harmony among different religions.

Such organisations will certainly help in bringing religious harmony and controlling religious extremists.

Globalisation—An Underpinnings of Terrorism

–Mohmad Saleem Jahangir

The term Globalisation is one of the most commonly employed phrases in contemporary society. Globalisation of the World has become the ultimate celebration of political, economic and social homogenisation of the global populations. It propounds a wide range of connotations in diverse disciplines, and to different individuals, making it a rather vague concept. Ascendance of Globalisation has opened up new dimensions of development and exploitation in developing societies. Globalisation focusses on the emergence of Super National Institutions in order to decide to shape up and constrain the policy options for any particular developing society. Although its wide connotation stands for the overwhelming impact of global economic processes including process of production, consumption, trade, capital flow, and monetary inter-dependence. It also signifies the rise of neo-liberalism as a hegemonic policy discourse, the emergence of new global cultural forms, media and technologies of communication which shape the relations of affiliation, identity, and interaction within and across local cultural settings. Globalisation has many definitions, but at its root it is about the planet getting smaller and free-flow of people, goods, capital and ideas across borders.

Globalisation as a process was facilitated by the liberalisation of transporter transactions by the dilution of sovereignty. It is essentially a measure of the ease with which labour, ideas, capital, technology and profits can move across borders with minimal governmental interference. This measure of liberalisation is also a surrogate measure for security.

Armed Conflict in Kashmir: Socio-psychological Consequences

–Aneesa Shafi

Armed conflict is the major source of sufferings affecting societies significantly. The socio-cultural strains of conflict bear a deep-rooted effect on human psychology. A society whose psyche is shaped under the shadow of conflict suffers serious disadvantages in its march towards progress. Widespread gender oppression, insurgency in Nepal, Sri Lanka, the border conflicts in Kashmir or the resources-based conflicts over land, forests, dams and mines have led to widespread displacements of population resulting in significant sense of insecurities. In such stressful situation, the impact of conflict on mental health is being recognised and addressed as being related to an inter-relationship of psychological and social problems which together constitute the disorder. Individuals being victims of terrorist situation suffer psychological stress and even proximity to such situations directly affects the mental well-being.

Terrorism in the state of Jammu and Kasmir has affected whole society directly or indirectly. The issues of livelihood and survival for the members of the society become critical due to presence of millions of troops and armed civil militia. As per the governments reports more than 30,000 people lost their lives in conflicts. More than 6,000 women widowed and more than 15,000 children rendered orphans. Daily exposure to variety of severe traumatic stress has led to an escalation in mental ailments as more than 40,000 patients visit the only Mental Hospital in Srinagar in a year, most of them suffering from post traumatic stress disorder. More than eighty five per cent of population takes anti-depressants medicine out of which seventy per cent are women. The state is witnessed to one of the highest rates of suicide in India. On an average day, two to three cases are registered in the city's two major hospitals which attribute the growing occurrences of depression to the turmoil in Kashmir.

Javanese Muslim's Tolerance and Flexibility Through Syncretic Ornamentation

–Hee Sook Lee Niinioja

Java located on the southern Indonesian archipelago, has a tropical climate, rich rainfall, and fertile soils, supplying abundant natural resources. Although Islam became the dominant religion in 16th Century, the basic patterns of ancestral, mythical belief and Hindu - Buddhism were integrated within Sufi-Islam which had much of its orthodoxy in its spread from Arab world. As Sufi believed mosques to be sacred, the holy pre-Islamic architecture and ornaments became a means for Islamisation, creating a combination of indigenous and Islamic ideas and forms as a distinct regionalism. The Political and Islamic movement in Java is divided into three periods according to political religious movements:

(i) continuation of pre-Islamic influence in the transitory period (15 century—1619)
(ii) European (1619-1945), and
(iii) a pure Islamic Movement in the contemporary period (1945 - to the present).

Islamic culture and Art have been influenced and remodelled by local traditions with countries which they come into contact, in order to comply with its religious and Philosophical ideas. Today, south east Asia (the Malay) including Java represents almost one-quarter of Islam's global community. Islamic Civilisation is inextricably linked to the message of the Prophet since its arrival to Java in the early 15th century. Islam not only altered local cultural landscapes, but also created a unique regional heritage.

Among many types of Pre-Islamic motifs which appeared in Javanese mosques, Kala-makra (fish and elephant trunk) and floral motifs seemed to continue the most, particularly Lotus flower.

Islamic poets describe flower as a book, where one can study the knowledge about God. And its combination with birds can be considered as the characteristic of Islamic Javanese decorative art, despite a ban by the hadith.

A Javanese term, *"Bhinneka Tunggal Ika"* (Unity in Diversity), was created by the Javanese people to emphasise their own identity and culture. Java has been a centre where mystical Animism, Hindu - Buddhism, and Islam co-existed together, moving towards a syncretic religion.

Javanese Muslims are greatly concerned with continuity of their cultural heritage, which was created by local genius (Wale's theory) across countries, beyond religions and faiths. Furthermore, Javanese Muslims emphasise importance of holy ornaments that were derived from Hindi-Buddism and try to link them with Islam.

Java is a peaceful melting pot; Javanese Islam is syncretic; Javanese descendants adore their cultural heritage; and Javanese Muslims are tolerant, inventing a beautiful amalgamation from many sources, beyond faiths and religions, in order to pay tribute to Allah.

Reasons and Suggestion of World Terrorism

–Purabi Nandi and Ravi Prakash Pandey

Terrorism has been the spontaneous outburst of intense feeling of Nationalism. One important cause of the growth of terrorism in India is the well advertised impotency of the government in dealing with any group, which could show its capacity for mischief and make the government simultaneously feel that enforcement of the law of the land will be bad for its electoral interests. The general image of the government is made up by the manner in which the lawless elements are dealt with everyday. The government officials, the nationalist leaders, and the Revolutionaries differences are regarded as the reasons for the rise of the Revolutionary movement.

As conceived by the *Times of India*, October 2007, Page No. 8, Pakistan is the most dangerous country in the worid and has become a safe heaven for terrorists, a media report says, "what is new, and more frightening, is the extent to which Taliban and Al Qaida elements have now turned much of the country, including some cities, into a base that gives militants more room to manoeuvre, both in Pakistan and beyond."

Reasons for World Terrorism:

(*a*) **Blatant corruption** : There is widespread corruption in all fields of administration and at all levels from the ministers down to peons. The situation is still not so bad as it was in declining years of the Turhigh Empire of Tsarist Russia or Chiang Kai - Shekh's Kuominatang in the years 1940-1948. In the higher rungs of the administration there are still honest and dedicated officers but their influence is just little because since 1970 or so, they have been unable to pass the test of 'loyalty' not to the country or the constitution - but due to their political loss. Dishonesty can not operate under set of rules, which permit corruption in all fields except in terrorism. It has been estimated that profits from smuggling on the Indo-Pak border in Punjab amount to about Rs 2,000 crore per year.

(*b*) Political movement in dealing with terrorism even when the government of India became serious, it failed because the civilian bureacucracy and police, meant to crush it, had become pretty useless instrument for this job. The principal reason for failure in both Assam and Punjab was political. The sum-total of all this was that deterioration in the law and order situation become rapid and Assam and Punjab situations were handled with a degree of incompetence which was truly amazing. It was obvious that even basic principle was not understood. Since early 1960's several factors were operating to make all the agencies responsible for maintaining law and order weaker and weaker.

Sign of lawlessness is the increase in gang wars. There are generally only two reasons for gang warfare—first is the dispute over sharing of elicit gains. The second reasons is revenge for murder or murders of one, of the gang members. Both reasons imply a poor state of police control and failure of police to bring the culprits to book.

There are socio-economic causes of rising lawlessness on which there is hardly much agreement. Moreover, this is a plea often taken by a lazy or motivated administration to divert the attention from its own failures.

The main instrument for combating terrorism is the police. The government of India, the State governments, the District Magistrate and even leadership of the Police have to depend mainly on the rank and file of the Police to maintain law and order.

Intelligence plays a vital role in combating terrorism. Its role in other law and order situations is also important. However, intelligence is not the remedy for all serious ills of the administration.

Violence, Terrorism and Religious Radicalism: Intertextuality as Sociological Paradigm

–Eduardo M. Domingo

Deplorable terrorism and religious radicalism is rapidly being excepted into the lives of very structure of religions and faith-based communities. Despite efforts, both of faith-based and government sponsored dialogues, kidnappings, massacres, and beheadings still besiege the media headlines. Consciously or unconsciously, people seemed to have started associating fundamentalism with the religious radicalism. After the famous 9/11, New York attack some Muslim scholars even think that the literal understanding and interpretation of Islamic Teachings is being taken as a reason by certain Muslim Radicals to justify their terrorist acts.

Generally understood as the shaping of the meanings of texts by other texts describes Intertextuality as a catch-all word that deals with contexts, cultures, periods, theories and frameworks. Carried out in the reader's reading. Intertextuality refers to the history of a prior text and how it is transformed. It is the complex relationship between a text and other texts taken as basic to the creation or interpretation of a text.

This paper illustrates the importance of (1) Vertical dialogue in intertextuality, i.e., the relation of the violence and terrorism to contexts these came from, and (2) the importance of horizontal dialogue in Intertextuality, i.e., texts on violence and terrorism interacting with the new contexts these are being applied to texts not only reflect what people think. These also carry the concrete culture, the preconceptions and the cultural - historical paradigms of writers. Understanding contexts can therefore shed light to the proper understanding of texts. Without an informed context, a text to be given many different meanings.

Rooted upon specific assumption, sociology of religion must look into the contexts of the texts on terrorism and violence. Political and religious context, among others, shape the texts of violence and terrorism. Thus, to understand better the texts and social theories implied by these texts, one may need to read their contexts and texts. Re-reading the different context on violence and terrorism is equally important. These may necessiate different attitudes, models and sources to measure research. In fact, recent researches show that contexts should not be overlooked and should be read accordingly. Globalisation, specially its heterogenising or homogenising tendencies, is transforming the texts and contexts of violence and terrorism. Globalisation has been evolving and has been developing its own socio-political categories, communication - language patterns, and its own value systems.

The vast and instantaneous information technology also invites the sociology of religion, and the study of violence and terrorism as well, to think globally and to think differently about religion itself. This 'new' power and influence of Information Technology to religion, cultures and entities are transforming the sociology of religion and its cognate discipline and are becoming new texts too.

Indeed, Horizontal Inter textuality challenges the sociology of religion to the possibilities of doing, new areas of inquiry of generations new ways of thinking and even of formulating radically different canons.

A serious study and analysis of terrorism today demands Inter-textuality. There is need for critical dialogue, more reflection, assessment, further discussions and research not only of the different texts on violence and terrorism.

Religion can play a positive role to combat or countrer act International Terrorism by establishing a framework for religious tolerance develop a culture of 'conflict prevention', rather than a culture of 'conflict resolution' by engaging Media as partners, establishing a framework of Inter-religious dialogue.

As we emphasise the faith or religious dimension of terrorism, we should equally reiterate, too, the importance of basic human dimensions of violence and terrorism.

Understanding terrorism today, therefore, needs a more holistic and total approach.

Like a coin, there is the real need to see not only its religious face or its faith dimension, but we should also see its human face.

After all, the human face of terrorism is not only real but it may even be more basic and essential to encounter and resolve terrorism more humanely.

In the Shadow of Liberal Democracy: Terrorism Intertwined Intricately with Globalisation

–Syed Jamil Ahmed

"A Liberal democratic state is founded on two principles: Individual rights and majority rule. Not only is the state run by "the rule of majority, as expressed through free and fair elections, but, it must also protect the rights of individuals and minorities, in other words, it must guarantee the freedom or liberty of its citizens. These guarantees are typically incorporated into a written constitution, and government is further limited and constrained by the rule of law."

For the liberal democratic system to function effectively, it is also necessary that the State guarantee a transparent system of Government, protection of property, administration of justice to resolve clashes of interest, defense of its territory and provision of essential public goods that cannot be availed by private means by the majority.

In the global normative regime, today, "human rights now constitute the basis on which the International legitimacy of a state is determined". The market in a liberal democratic system can never by restricted only to the domestic; it necessarily incorporates the international as well. Hence, a liberal democratic state cannot but attempt to ensure the freedom and well-being of its citizens by mobolising all its resources for promoting a "free" market the world over. In this "free" market, it is most profitable for the liberal democratic citizenry to pool individual resources to pursue large-scale projects in one or more "host countries" which promise to generate vast wealth. Globalisation is hardly 'natural' or even autonomous, as many of its ardent proponents claim. As Guttal argues persuasively, "It is the result of specifically conceived, planned and targetted neo-liberal policy and structural measures that sought to bring all aspects of social, economic and political life under the rubric of market capitalism". The dialectics of global capitalism, which is generating tension by the acceleration of "income concentration and the social exclusion of large masses of urban populations, is leading people in most countries at the periphery of capitalism to be trapped in societies where the level of violence is high. Ironically, globalisation has enabled the Islamic terrorists to function more efficiently. The use of information technologies such as the internet, mobile phones and instant messaging has extended the global reach of many terrorist groups.

Pakistani Action Against Terrorists An Analysis

–Anurag Ratna

It will be worthwhile to have an idea about the history of Talibans. The USA and Pakistan are equally responsible for the birth and growth of

Talibans. Both had jointly created the Army of students to fight the Soviet Union in Afghanistan and free it from latter's clutches.

To meet this purpose, they provided Talibans with modern weapons and other war equipments. These armed men became known as Talibans who had played great role in freeing Afghanistan from USSR Army. Even after the return of USSR Army, Talibans were not disarmed or compelled to surrender their weapons. Incidentally, they organised themselves into an armed force. Today, Talibans comprise many other groups other than orignal armed group. In this group, there are many Afghani migrants who were given shelter in Pakistan due to fear of Russian Army, but never returned to their country even after the withdrawal of Russain forces.

Pakistan's Army is strong trained and well-equipped with latest weaponary system. It is fully capable of defeating and destroying Talibans. And, yet, it has been so far unsuccessful in tackling Talibans who are neither organised and trained nor equipped with modern weapons. Army action is being taken against Talibans only half-heartedly. There are many reasons for it which are as follows:

(a) Helplessness of the Pakistani Government

Pakistani government is even today dictated and dominated by the Army which has great sympathy with the terrorists. Pakistan Government can not take any independent action ignoring army's dictates.

Even Mumbai attack of 26/11 was managed by Pak Army and ISI, but Pakistan government found itself helpless to take any action against them. Due to this factor, it has failed to operate fully and in determined manner against the terrorists. Again another reason behind it is that Government does not want to finish terrorism root and branch as Pakistan wants to use Terrorism as a tool to achieve its objective against foreign countries, particularly India.

(b) The soft-approach of Army towards Taliban

Pakistan army's position *vis-a-vis* Talibans has been highly controversial. One the one hand, it is posing itself to be under the Political Executive, is acting against Terrorists in Pakistan, but on the other hand, it is helping Pak-based Talibans via ISI, who are working in other countries specially in India to implement Islamic Agenda, Sponsored by Al-Qaida.

(c) Adverse effect of Army Action

Pak Government's action against Taliban with massive support from USA is proving costly for its common citizens, due to heavy loss of people's life and property. Many men and women, children are being killed in fiercest battle from both-sides Army as well as Taliban. It is due to this fact that Army is fast losing sympathy of the people of the area which may prove costly for this operation.

Due to above shortcomings, Pak Army will never succeed in its operation against terrorist. For achieving success it requires a change in its approach and strategy in certain important aspects.

On basis of above analysis, it is amply clear that present Government in Pakistan is not in a position to end terrorism. The Actions of USA and Pakistan are not adequate. They are taking Action against Talibans and Al-Quada militants. This does generate some hope. So, it is welcome and must be given full support and co-operation by the whole world.

Terrorism : Cause and Concern

– Sovnath Yadav and Parmod Kumar Choudhary

Almost all magazines, newspapers are flooded with information about terrorists, government's action and its impact on different sections of society.

Terrorism is an inter-disciplinary area of study. It can be seen and understood, from different perspectives: political science, psychology, sociology, history and law. In the present work, the psychological aspect of terrorism has been taken. Isolating terrorism from politics is difficult as present day terrorism has political implications. The word 'Terrorism' is defined as "the covert or secret resort to violence, or threat of violence, on the part of a group seeking to accomplish a purpose against some recognised authority". Terrorism may be classified in different ways, based on three geographical areas and motive :

1. Domestic — in own country against own people.
2. International — in which terrorists belonging to one nation attack citizens or property of another.
3. State sponsored — terrorism by groups, which are logistically or operationally aided by states.

Motives

(a)	Political	—	For ideological and political purposes-groups that focus on gaining power and supremacy.
(b)	Non-political	—	for private purpose and gain.
(c)	Quasi - terrorism	—	Skyjacking and hostage taking.
(d)	Official or state	—	used by nation against people.
(e)	Revolutionary	—	aims to overthrow or replace an existing government
(f)	Nationalist	—	Promotes interest of an ethnic or religious group that is seen as being persecuted by another.
(g)	Environmental	—	Groups dedicated to slowing down development that is harming animals.

In 20th Century, terrorism was increasingly used as the principal strategy or as an auxiliary instrument by groups which fought for national liberation, as well as by groups, which espoused social and ideological issues.

The late 1960's and the early 1970's were marked by the establishment of many terrorist groups. Since that time terrorism attracted more attention than ever before. It has become a frequent item on the agenda of international organisations, a subject of international accords, and generated much publicity and very recently it was a major issue in the SAARC summit held in Kathmandu, Nepal.

Causes of terrorism can be many. The first group are extremely self-centred individuals with little regard for the feelings of others. The second group resembles paranoid personalities. These individuals are suspicious and aggresive, sensitive and always ready to defend themselves.

According to some, rather, than analysing terrorism in terms of psychopathology, it should be seen in the context of culture, politics and religion. Terrorism is the product of its own time and place, there are no specific personality traits predicting one person more likely to become a terrorist than another.

The psychological study of terrorism is important to identify those who are or may become terrorists with a view of aiding prevention. As nobody is born terrorist. We should analyse the circumstances responsible for terrorism and individual vulnerability and to develop strategies to deal with it effectively and in reducing its impact.

Taliban Movement in Afghanistan

– Hamid

Afghanistan location is situated between Iran, Central Asia and the Arabian Sea and India. This has given these mountain passes a strategic significance for centruries. At certain times, Afghanistan was a buffer between competing empires at ideologies; at others it has served as a corridor through which armies marched in repeated efforts to colonise the country. Most recently, the British and Soviet have failed in the process to give the Afghans a sense of Independence and pride.

Civil war is a Revolution that may be used by those who want to bring about a change in a country. However, such change comes with a heavy price when existing structures are transformed drastically from one form to another.

The Taliban was one of the many groups that participated in the struggle against Soviet forces. When the Taliban launched their own movement across Afghanistan, they began to catch the attention of the international media, once they overran the country military so swiftly and yet so peacefully, they simply could not go unnoticed. A lot of theories started emerging about their origin, characteristics and objectives, nevertheless, they were and still are a complex phenomena. The Taliban leadership has been confused about the origins of the movement.

Historically, Afghanistan was deeply conservative Muslim country where Sharia, interpreted by Afghan tribal custom, prevailed for centuries, but Islam, traditionally practiced in Afghanistan was also immensely tolerant of other Muslims sects.

Kandahar has the symbolic importance of being the spiritual centre of the Taliban movement and also the place of its origin. The supreme Taliban leader, Mullah Mohammad Omar, made the city his strategic headquarters when the Taliban came to power in 1996.

One of the remarkable characteristics of Taliban leadership is that the top government official often switched from the battlefield to the ministry and back again, each time following orders from Mullah Omar.

The areas controlled by Taliban had been subjected to drastic changes to personal movement and behaviour. The Taliban had put a ban on wine and television, which is perceived to be immoral, there is also complete restriction on music, photography and the painting of living things, the sharing off one's beard or trimining it less than a fistful is prohibited, as is having a western hairstyle, gambling, betting, pigeon flying, dog rearing are also strictly forbidden. As time passed, and the

American military focus was diverted to the invasion and occupation of Iraq, the Taliban regrouped and began to extend its influence in the Southern part of Afghanistan. Their rise was assisted by a resurgent opium trade, which helped to fill the groups coffers, where observers say there is loose co-ordination between different Taliban factions and militant groups. Nevertheless, the Taliban in Afghanistan are still believed to be led by Mullah Omar.

Another Taliban stronghold is the Pakistan city of Quetta, where Taliban leaders in exile are believed to play a significant role in straight violence in Southern Afghanistan. From Quetta, Taliban leaders including Mullah' Muhammad Omar, a reclusive, one-eyed cleric, guides commanders in southern Afghanistan, raises money from wealthy Persian Gulf donors and deliver guns and ammunition to the battlefield.

The Talibans are not very clever, not very organised and it seems hard to argue that they have the best interests of the Afghan people at heart. They are able, through trial and error and perhaps through lucky co-incidence, exploit the problems of the government and international community to build support for themselves. Despite their horrendous attacks and oppression of the Afghan people, both currently and during their period as the government of the country, they are active.

A serious problem, the Taliban face and have faced over the past few years and which will definitely create problems for them in the long-term is their alliance with criminal elements they piously used to battle—drug-lords, criminals, kidnappers, corrupt businessman, corrupt politicians and foreign intelligence services (such as ISI—INTER SERVICES INTELLIGENCE (Pakistan) etc. They have joined with their own enemies to fight a common enemy. They thereby, pollute their own mission and agenda for the most part, the Taliban are also Afghans. They are both part of the problem and part of the solution.

Participation of Women in Terrorism: An Analysis

–Randhir Kumar

The concept of "terrorism" has over hundred definitions indicating that the essence of terrorism is basically, fluid and dynamic (Griset and Mahan, 2008).

At best one can understand the concept of terrorism from the commonalities that exist across the different interpretations of terrorism. Foster (2010), has noted the commonalities as "terrorism appears to be politically motivated, is generally systematic, deliberate or strategic; is directed toward non-combatant targets and uses violence and fear to achieve goals". Therefore, the term "terrorism" may evoke different perceptions for different persons.

The act of terrorism was being considered as the domain of males who played pivotal role, both in terms of planning and executing the violence. However, recently the role of women has been attracting much attention from the media. This instance, however, does not necessarily mean that earlier there was no involvement of women in the acts of terrorism. Women have always been in the supporting roles and recently they have been coerced or motivated to actively participate in the domain of terrorism.

The instances of women participation in terror activities can be found right from Gaza to Sri Lanka. Maoist movement in India all have cases of women participating in extreme violence, such as suicide bombing and killing.

The ideology of the terrorist organisation partly determines the level of participation of the women into the core activities of the group. This also means that the culture specific gendered perception would play an important role in assigning the tasks to a woman in a particular organisation.

In the Islamist radical group, Al-Qaeda the women are recruited but they are not assigned the tasks of suicide bombing. Here, the gender perception plays a vital role in type of work allotted to the female cadre.

Dr. Ali Khushailean, an expert on Islamist groups, has observed that females are primarily given the tasks pertaining to logistical duties, collecting donations and convincing mothers and wives to encourage their sons and husbands to join the holy war.

Different women have their own reasons for joining the terrorist organisations. The common way of recruiting women is by taking advantage of their personal and financial struggles. The widows of Chechen male fighters are often brain washed to avenge their husband or family member's death. Radical fundamentalist organisations like Al-Qaida forces women to obey their husband and often relate it with obeying God. Another motivating factor for joining the terrorist organisation is the creation of an image of martyrdom. Stem (2003) has noted that killing oneself is no loner an act of self-destruction, but rather divinely commanded martyrdom in defence of the faith.

However, blackmailing, coercion and prolonged conditioning by brain washing seems to be the major factors which are responsible for the extreme decision taken by the women to commit genocide.

A female involved in politics has a positive connotation while women indulging in any terror activity for whatsoever reason raises eyebrows and are often portayed as deviants. Terrorist organisations understand if an operation is carried out by their female counterpart, it would draw more of media attention and therefore strategise the terror activities accordingly.

The world is fast changing and witnessing a surge in number of females who are actively coerced. Terror and murder is no longer a domain of males anymore. Women play a number of roles in terms of combatant, human bomber, spy, sexual partner and domestic helper in terrorist organisations. Their participation in the terror activities can not be overlooked anymore. Sometimes women are exploited and used for terrorism and their participation is not of voluntary nature. Participation of women in terrorism throws new challenges in terms of counter terrorism agendas.

Socio-economic Factors of Naxalism in Jharkhand: A Sociological Analysis

- Paras Kumar Choudhary
(This article contributed by the editor)

The roots of Naxalism can be traced in the state of West Bengal. Naxal movement was started to oppose the atrocities over tribal peasants (agricultural) and was initially concentrated under jurisdiction of one particular "Police Station". However, today Naxalism has spread its tentacles in around fourteen states of India. The gravity of the situation can be analysed from the fact that in around 165 districts of India, 550 police station zones have been declared as Naxal-infested areas. Thus, it presents a great challenge to independent India.

At present in the name of 'movement' the various, factions of Naxals are competing fiercely to gain 'supremacy' over each other. The sole motive behind this friction is 'wealth' generated through levy. The source of this illegal ransom seeking can be for the construction of poor's house, installation of hand pumps, digging of ponds. Even the grocery shop owner's, petty contractors involved in business of coal, iron, opium etc. are not spared and have to pay levy to the Naxals for continuing their day to day business smoothly. The money involved in the 'levy' is one of the most important reasons behind the violent clashes among the Naxals.

The outspread of Naxalism was primarily due to socio-economic backwardness. At present, in Jharkhand there are atleast four organisations that have been declared as Naxal organiations BCP, TPC, JPC (Jharkhand Prastuti Committee) and SIMM (Sangharsh Jan Mukti Morcha). They are engaged in constant clash with each other for gaining supremacy.

BCP (Maoist) is the largest outfit and, therefore has its fight with all the others. This organisation has virtually taken the state under its influence. The second largest group is that of TPC. The stronghold of organisations is in the areas of Chatra, Hazaribagh, Palamu, Garhwa, Simdega, Gumla districts. The third largest is JPC. The area of their dominance is Latehar, Gumla, Chatra, Lohardaga and Hazaribagh districts.

Some of the socio-economic factors leading to Naxal Movement in Jharkhand are :

1. Disproportionate distribution of land and exploitation of landless peasants. Long pending cases related to land disputes in the court.
2. Exploitation of poor debtors by the landlords and money lenders.
3. Lack of employment opportunities among the youths leading to joining the movement.
4. Lack of education among the masses leading to easy prey to the brainwashing by Naxals.
5. Insensitiveness of the Government and terrorising the common people by police force.
6. Jharkhand's geographic location and mineral belts is not conducive for agriculture, leading to many people joining in this movement who do not have enough food grains to feed on.
7. No rights over the forest products for the tribal's of Jharkhand (though Central Government had passed a regulation, however it has not been implemented forcefully till now).
8. Poor law and order in the State.

The evolution of Naxalism in Jharkhand can be invariably attributed to the atrocities over the landless masses and government's apathy. When people found that they do not have a source of livelihood and are in the cycle of life long debt along with no provision of raising themselves higher into the economic status within the prevalent society, Naxalism provided an easy exit from these troubles. Utilising the poor socio-economic conditions of the masses, Naxals successfully proliferated themselves into various regions of Jharkhand and at times did some welfare activities for the masses.

The masses still obey Naxals in various places either due to their ignorance or fear factor.

It has been a common understanding among the Naxals group that the more violent activities they would carry out, the more influential they would be considered. The Government has also realised that utilising only armed forces against Naxal would be futile attempt to eradicate this dreaded menace. Therefore, systematically a broader framework has been implemented in which socio-economic improvement of the downtrodden along with provision of livelihood opportunities have been given due priority.

Terrorism—Its History and Observations upto 1947

– K.G. Vasantha Madhava

In recent years, Terrorism is gaining prominence among the public, thanks to the role of media. It is creating sense of fear among people. Terrorism can be defined in various ways. Among them, the easily understandable definition is that it is a calculative violence or threat of violence against the civilians in order to attain misdirected goals. These goals may be political, religious or ideological. To attain these goals, violence or intimidations are being used. The net result is creation of panic among common people. However, it should be noted that terrorism is the result of despair and resorted to by the people who have lost faith in regular method to achieve the goal.

We hear of terrorism of war, international, domestic, and revolutionary and sponsored by state.

Further, we also notice of the counter movement in terrorist in nature and cross-border terrorist movement.

History of Terrorism in Pre-colonial India: History of India provides instances of the nature of terrorism known by different names such as guerilla war and militant movement. All these movements resorted to terrorist technique to achieve their goals.

In support of these, we cite examples. In the middle of fourth century AD in Karnataka, Mayura Sharma resorted to tactis of terrorist after his humiliation in the court of Pallava at Kanchi. Mayura Sharma trained himself in war exercise and overpowered the frontier guards and established himself in the inaccessible forest at Sriparvata (Karnul district Andhra Pradesh). There he grew so powerful that he was able to challenge the authority of the Pallava by extracting tributes from the tributary rulers of the Pallava. Further he resorted to predatory excursions and caused havoc and fear among the resident of the area which was under the authority of the Pallava. The Pallava kings took the field against him but finally recognised Mayura Sharma as the king of his conquered territory. This led to the establishment of the Kadamba Kingdom with centre at Banavasi.

Similar instances occurred in the Deccan in the region of Ahmednagar in the first decade of the seventeenth century with the Mughal Emperor Jahangir. Thus, ended the first phase of terrorism. The terrorism has long history with its ups and down.

Naxal Terrorism in India with Special Reference to Jharkhand

–Umesh Kumar Verma

The Naxal movement took its name from Naxalbari village of Siliguri Tehsil of Darjeeling district of West Bengal, which came on the Indian scene in 1967. There was an armed upsurge of peasants and agricultural labourers against the local landlords under the leadership of Charu Mazumdar and Kanu Sanyal. The peasants stormed the grainaries of the landlords, forcibly harvested standing crops, burnt records of outstanding debts etc: This led to the formation in 1969 of the third major Communist Party of India (Marxist- Leninist). This party believed that the social equity in India will be only achieved by Marist-Leninist ideology and Mao-Tse -Tung's thoughts. The Naxal movement became popular among idealist youths and spread to rural and tribal parts of India, where people are poor and being exploited by landlords, contractors and Government personnel. This movement speaks the language of equality, justice, rights and asserts the need to fight to achieve. These aims, for which they are ready to die proves very attractive people to joint this movement. In the opinion of Indian Prime Minister Dr. Manmohan Singh Naxalite insurgency should not be viewed as a purely law, and order problem, rather it is a social and economic deprivation experienced by a significant part of India's population. Andhra Pradesh, Bihar, Jharkhand, Chhatisgarh, Karnataka, Madhya Pradesh, Orissa, Tamil Nadu, Uttar Pradesh and West Bengal are Naxalite affected states of India.

The origin of Naxalism in Jharkhand can be seen as expansion of Naxal Movement originality in West Bengal. The phenomenon of differentiation which had started in days of second World War, has also affected adversely the economic life of people of Jharkhand especially tribal population: mainly proverty, unemployment, economic disparity, corruption, displacement, migration, education system, inefficient governance etc. These have been responsible for origin and development of Naxalism in Jharkhand. The South West Part of Jharkhand has been mainly centre of Naxalism, which was previously governed by British administration. Naxals have created the posts of Commander and Zonal Commander in their administrative structure. They conducted training camps for using AK 47 Rifle, Land mines, Grenade, Hand Bomb, Cane Bomb, etc. Naxal forces are expert in Guerilla war. They collect levies from government employees related to conducting development programmes of State government like road, building, bridge construction, etc., which affected government development programmes adversely.

The education system is not less responsible for emergence of Naxal terrorism and violence. The education system has been unable to increase national feelings among students and forming National character.

Naxalism is an outcome of inadequate government and its structure since long in Jharkhand.

For eradication of Naxalism following steps can be taken:

1. Effective effort should be made for removal of poverty and unemployment in Jharkhand.
2. Population control policy should be implemented effectively in Jharkhand.
3. Different Governmental Development and Welfare Programmes should be implemented successfully.
4. The problem of corruption, exploitation, economic disparity, displacement, migration and youth dissatisfaction should be solved by political will power and good governance.
5. Naxal terrorism may be controlled by implementing appropriate strategies formulating by Gram Sabha and Urban Wards at local level.
6. The Administration and Police missionary should be sensitive and democratic towards Naxal problem.
7. There is need of analysis of Naxal problem by holistic approach to cover up all its aspects by conducting extensive research. Effective strategy should be formulated and implemented for its eradication.

Paras Kumar Choudhary
(Editor)

1

Ethnic Conflicts: Perceptions and Counter Perceptions

J. L. Oraon

The study of social patterns as an academic subject has been established widely but unevenly throughout the world. The study "Ethnic -conflicts: Perceptions and Counter perceptions" is basically a study of man and his human condition and reflects the concerns of the fluid and very mixed societies of the world. Ethnicity is a connotative concept. The world is all embracing and has been envisaged with heightened sensibility to the promises of life. The study explores the aspects of ethnic separatism, forces of stability and change; trends of sociology and contemporary spiritual styles and international relations, the new ethnicity and social class religion and social group, ethnicity and race and above all, a world conscience along with the roots of perceived dangers with special reference to India and Pakistan. It reflects their ethnicity and ideology whereupon they draw deeply from embedded cultural linguistic, religions or regionally significant symbols around which they can mobilise popular support, symbols that can generate a powerful political change. The appeal to ethnic identity draws upon more emotional layers of the human and social personality than does the appeal to class identity. Ethnicity has been conceived as a world phenomenon and placed in this study at the very center of our concern for the human condition.

Men, since Aristotle, 'have struggled to convince themselves that the capacity to reason, to draw up deductive syllogisms, is their distinguishing glory'. But admittedly, there are problems involved even in the exact determination of whether there is or is not an increase in "ethnic conflicts". We have the persisting conflict between the French and English speaking peoples in Canada. Shall we call it an "ethnic" conflict? Or is it a "language" conflict, or the struggle of a "suppressed nation" for independence? We have the division between "Indian" and "Spanish" elements in a number of Latin American countries. We have the tragic conflict between Protestant and Catholics in Northern Ireland. But isn't that an essentially "religious" conflict? Seemingly some large discernible trends in the world – political, social, economic are leading in general to our accentuation of ethnic conflicts.'

Let us consider the case of Pakistan and Islam – its ethnicity and ideology. There is an all too acceptable understanding that Pakistan like Israel and Iran is one of three confessional states in the world. Like Israel, its very origin was to fulfil a religions ideal, to create an Islamic state and an Islamic society for the Muslims of India. That has been the slogan of the Jamaat-i-Islami, the fundamentalist extreme Right-wing party, since Pakistan was created. Interestingly enough this was not their slogan before the creation of Pakistan, for they had opposed the Pakistan movement. The idea that the Pakistan movement was motivated by Islamic ideology is a misconception. Arguably the central driving force behind the Muslim movement was a class that has a distinct place in colonised societies, whose role needs to be recognised more fully and explicitly. This class is termed as *salariat,* the urban educated classes who qualify for employment in the colonial state. With them were associated the new professionals, who emerged in the context of the colonial transformation of Indian society, the lawyers, the journalists and urban intellectuals generally, who share many of the problems and aspirations of the salaried. In fine, the Pakistan movement was a movement of Muslims rather than of Islam. This was a movement in which diverse Muslim ethnic groups from different regions, representing different social strata and interests, were allied in pursuit of quite material objectives.

The Pakistan movement, in a sense, became a national movement, on the basis of the "Two-nation Theory" that Jinnah propounded, affirming that the Muslims of India were a separate nation from the Hindus. But, insofar as their politics entailed the establishment of "Pakistan" however they might have conceived it their objective was the creation of a "Muslim State" as a nation state. They did not seek an "Islamic state" as a theocratic conception. Thus, in Pakistan Muslim ethnic identity, once it had fulfilled its purpose for the *salariats*[2] of Bengal, Sind, Sarhad and Baluchistan, gave way to the respective regional ethnic identities. They draw on deeply embedded cultural, linguistic, religions or regionally significant symbols around which they can mobilise popular support, symbols that can generate a powerful political change.

Muslim ethnicity thus was only one stage in a process of ethnic definition and redefinition.[3] It represented a temporary alliance of various regional groups. However, there are clear patterns of conversions to Islam by different social strata in different regions. A paradox of the advent of Islam with Muslim rule was that at the heartland of Muslim empires of India, in the Gangetic plains, conversions to Islam were minimal. They were maximal in the two peripheries of the empire, namely the Indus plains (now Pakistan) and Bengal. The divergence in patterns of religious belief between the Gangetic plains and the two peripheries is paralleled by divergences in many other aspects of their respective social life. We, however, find that there is a fairly clear class pattern of Islamisation associated with the advent of Muslim rulers. Muslim rule installed expatriate Muslims brought from Arabia, Iran, Turkey, and Afghanistan as feudal lords at the foundations of their empires and many Hindus, especially Rajput chiefs, converted to Islam. Their dependent peasants 'Converted' *en masse* [4] likewise. Islam was established thereby as a predominantly rural religion.

In pre-colonial India Muslim Ulema and Hindu Pundits played a central role in the judicial system and held lucrative and influential positions. But soon after, the old feudal dispensations were no longer appropriate. Later, the Ulema were also being pushed out of the educational system.[5] Still another factor underlying the anti-Colonialism of the Ulema was the plight of Indian weavers, the *julahas* who were the most embittered opponents of colonialism. All these factors bound the Ulema to the Indian nationalist cause. They never argued for the setting up of an 'Islamic' state nor a Muslim state. Rather they called upon Muslims to join hands with their Hindu brothers in the patriotic cause against foreign rule. To rationalise that position they put forward a theory that constituted an essentially secular public philosophy. It was argued that faith was universal and could not be contained within national boundaries and that nationality was a matter of geography and Muslims were bound to the nation of their birth by obligation of loyalty along with their Muslim fellow citizens.[6]

Again, unlike the three Semitic religious of the Middle East namely, Judaism, Christianity and Islam the religions of South and East Asia, namely Hinduism, Jainism, Buddhism, Confucianism, Taoism, Shintoism, etc. do not have sharp boundaries.[7] Their followers can worship at more than one altar or accept more than one book or accept none. They have no revealed words of God and no Prophets. They have only the perceptions and sayings of the wise. Instead of creation, the broad Hindu group of religions believe in Cycles of evolution and in the reincarnation of the individual soul. Except for the Buddhist *sangha*, these religions have never believed in accepting an umbrella authority or organisation for enforcement. In the absence of a universal *Sangha* or Church, the unique envelope character of Hinduism has traditionally been maintained by a common elite language and ritual, an open-ended pantheon, and a highly stratified social structure. Hinduism has survived many centuries of dark ages, which have been marked by backwardness in social structure, technology, warfare and general welfare. The latest set of perceived dangers to Hinduism has evoked some move towards reform of the social structure. There is, however, no serious attempt to clearly define Hinduism or the parameters of a Hindu, or his ethnicity.[8]

Was the British India divided on the basis of religion? The answer is both yes and no. But it was not the intention at that time that all Hindus should migrate out of Pakistan or that all Muslims in India should migrate to Pakistan. While States in the neighbourhood have declared themselves Islamic or Buddhist, India is explicitly secular. On the national plane, we witness a curious interplay of increasing homogenisation of dress consumption and saving behaviour, spread of technology and of material aspirations generally.[9] On the other hand, there is a widely felt threat to separate or separable identities from the trends in politics, economic growth, education, technology, culture and crime. We can not afford to mix religion and politics. It would be ruinous for the minorities and even more ruinous for the Hindus. A victorious Hindu Communalism would, sooner rather than later, turn upon its own constituents, particularly by some castes, linguistic groups and regions against others. Quite for sometime past, our ethnicity has tended to compartmentalise growth by conferring a vested interest in claiming the status of or remaining small backward, weak – or a minority. While the handicaps are genuine and rampant, our efforts should be directed at removing or easing them, not at perpetuating or universalising them.[10]

Having a look at the world over, we have the movements for Scottish and Welsh autonomy in Great Britain, Breton and "South French" movements in France; the strain between Northern and Southern Italy. Some thinkers may define them as "regional" rather than "ethnic" movements. In each case an outline section of the country has not shared in the prosperity of the Center and this seems to have awakened some long dormant ethnic consciousness. We cannot discern whether the group pressing for autonomy or more Central Government funds feels deprived because of an ethnic difference or because of regional discrimination.[11] The group has a choice as to which basis of deprivation it will emphasise. Thus, in the world over we have a host of conflicts in which race, religion, region, and nationality are involved. We have Indonesia's involvement in that it dreamed of a "greater Malay empire" which included Malaysia and the Philippines.

All said and done, the term "ethnic" refers to a social group which consciously shared some aspects of a common culture and is defined primarily by descent. It is part of a family of terms of similar or related meaning such as "minority group", "race", and "nation" and it is not often easy to make sharp distinctions between them. "Race" refers to a group that is defined by common descent and has some typical physical characteristics. Where one decides that a "race" ends and an "ethnic group" begins is not easy. Swedes are physically somewhat different from French men or Italians; but we normally don't use the word 'race' to describe these differences. In European usage at least until the time of Hitler "race" was rather unself-consciously used to describe what we would call "nations" – such as in the term "the genius of the French race". Race tends to refer to the biological aspect of group difference, "ethnic" to a combination of the cultural aspect plus a putative biological element because of the assumption of common descent. So, it is possible for a race not to be an ethnic group. Brazilians of the predominantly Negro race do not appear as an ethnic group because they are not particularly aware of a common culture different from that of other Brazilians. This is also because they don't have a corporate self identity as a distinct group, even though individuals are aware of their physical characteristics and are aware that these physical differences tend to be associated with some common group characteristics such as a lower income level or particular occupation. In many countries, the ethnic group is tending to become a more significant basis for social organisation and for individual identification. "Race" then, refers to something more purely physical than ethnic group. "Religion", another significant basis of human organisation, seems on the face of it a very different matter from ethnic group. Religions are based on conversion and individual allegiance. The great religions – Christianity, Islam, Buddhism – include individuals of every race and ethnic group. Americans very often call a state "a nation" but in most European languages the nation refers very specially to the ethnic group, the state to the formal political organisation which grants citizenship.[12]

There is certainly a tension between ethnic groups and states. The problem is that both ethnic groups and states make claim to ultimate loyalty. At one time this competing claim was most strongly put forward by religion. With the decline of religion, these competing claims are most strongly put forward by the concept of ethnicity. States; then, are not ethnic groups, though the linking term "nation" can be taken as one or the other Nations are not necessarily ethnic groups. Though those are not coterminous with an ethnic group try to create a new national identity[13], which becomes a new ethnicity in case they succeed. Similarly, social classes are not ethnic groups. Social mobility refers specifically to movements between the strata of society, from one occupation, income level, education standard, to another social mobility is a term that cannot be used to refer to the shift from one ethnic group into another just as "social mobility" applies specifically to the class phenomena of society, so do "assimilation", "acculturation" and "conversion" apply to the ethnic phenomena.

Thus "ethnic group" refers basically to the vertical divisions of a society in contrast to the horizontal divisions. The horizontal divisions refer to class; the vertical divisions to ethnicity. As the Blacks rose socially to become doctors, professionals and white collar workers, their class changed. But their ethnic group remained the same. Even in India, 'the classic land of caste', the correlation between caste and class becomes somewhat weaker over time.[14] Here the caste groups may become "ethnic groups" where the castes are increasingly called "Communities" as the social positions of their members become more diverse.

But some new striking developments have made ethnicity a whole new force in domestic and international relations. [15] The efforts of States, new or old, to achieve "ethnic purity" are not leading to ethnically homogeneous states. The attempts of some nations to become "ethnically pure" only complicate the problems of others. Few Black African nations are ethnically homogeneous. The attempt to create homogeneity by the expulsion of Asians seems as futile as an effort to empty the sea. Despite efforts to make some states "ethnically pure," more and more states are becoming multi-ethnic old ethnic divisions emerge in old states and new ones are created in new states. In most countries, national interests and ethnic interests seem to dominate over class interests. Marxists try to interpret all conflicts as "class conflicts". Indeed in the ethnic conflicts of the post war world there is always a class component. Thus, ethnicity becomes less and less of a coincident with state boundaries and ethnicity becomes a stronger basis for "terminal loyalty" than class Ethnic groups, owing to migrations and economic interrelationships, which are less and less definable by physical boundaries. Creation of an International System of communications makes the spread of ideas and ideologies from one state to another even more rapid and effective. The new patterns of communications are one of the most potent forces in insuring that ethnic concerns and ethnic issues will remain serious forces and will indeed grow in seriousness. In the present circumstances, every ethnic group can develop a Diaspora. The Indian Pakistani struggle also has its international scope, as young Pakistanis are killed in the attempted seizure of Indian offices in London. Croatians, now settled in Sweden and Australia carry on their warfare against Yugoslavia.

All this boils down to the proposition that a number of factors are leading to the internationalisation of ethnic conflicts to a "Universalisation of ethnicity". It is difficult to make ethnicity and state coincide. Rapid growth of international communications has heightened ethnic consciousness everywhere. Thus, in the final analysis of things, the appeal to ethnic identity draws upon more emotional layers of the human and social personality than does the appeal to class identity. It touches on such primal things as one's language and religion, one's earliest family experiences, one's physical self image. Needless to say, ethnicity seems to have become a permanent force in the modern world[16] in its own capacity and the multi-ethnic form is becoming increasingly common within each nation wherein each group has guaranteed rights and guaranteed shares in the economy, the polity, in social life. Ethnicity must now be placed at the very center of our concern for the human condition.[17]

References

1. Ram Gopal, Indian Muslims London, 1959. Ch. XI for an Indian nationalist view and R. Palme Dutt, *India Today*, Bombay, 1970 pp. 453-9.
2. D.N. Pritt, *India in Labour Monthly*, XXIV, April 1942.
3. R. Palme Dutt. "India and Pakistan in *Labour Monthly*, XXVIII March 1949.
4. G. Adhikari, *'Pakistan and Indian National Unity'*, Bombay, 1943.
5. Y. Gankovsky and L. Gordon Polonskaya, *A History of Pakistan Labour.*
6. Edward Mortimer *'Faith and Power : The Politics of Islam'*, London, 1982.
7. H.A. Alavi, "The State in Post – Colonial Societies". *New Left Review*, 74 July – August, 1972.
8. H. Goulbourne, *Politics and the State in the Third World,* London, 1979.
9. B.T. McCully, *English Education and the Origins of Indian Nationality,* Williamsburg, 1940.
10. Aparna Basu, *The Growth of Education and Political Development in India*, Delhi, 1974.

11. Francis Robinson, *Separatism Among Indian Muslims*, Cambridge, 1974, p. 46.
12. H.N. Gardezi and J. Rashid (eds). *Pakistan. The Roots of Dictatorship*. The Political Economy of a Practorian State, London, 1983.
13. Adul Hamid, *Muslim Separatism in India*, Lahore, 1967.
14. McKim Marriott, *Caste Ranking and Community Structure in Five Regions of India and Pakistan*, Poona, 1960.
15. Seymour M. *Lipset Political Man, The First New Nation*, Harvard, 1975.
16. Martin E. Marty, *The Role of Religion in a Suddenly Changing World*, Doubleday, 1973. *Ibid.,* 10-14.
17. K.G. Vasantha Madhava, *Ibid.,* pp. 98, 111-112. 145-150.

2

In the Shadow of Liberal Democracy: Terrorism Intertwined Intricately with Globalisation

Syed Jamil Ahmed

We have dreamed of this event, everyone without exception has dreamt of it – because no one can avoid dreaming of the destruction of any power that has become hegemonic to that degree. At a pinch, we can say they did it, but we wished for it (Jean Baudrillard on 9/11 in *The Spirit of Terrorism*).

The point of departure of this essay is Baudrillard's contention that the spirit of terrorism, which is all about symbolic and sacrificial death, rises out of a fundamental antagonism that "points past the spectre of America [...] and the spectre of Islam [...], to triumphant globalisation battling against itself" (Baudrillard 2003a, 11). However, instead of pitting globalisation in opposition to human rights, as Baudrillard does in *The Violence of the Global* (2003b), this essay proceeds to argue that the discourse of human rights is but a Foucauldian normalisation technique of the liberal democratic order, which produces and necessitates globalisation for its survival.

In working towards this goal, the essay proceeds in three parts. The first draws on Foucault to trace the genealogy of disciplinary power invested in the liberal democratic States, and demonstrates how these States mobilise human rights in order to exercise the power on its own citizens and at the same time to normalise deviant States; the second argues that globalisation, pursued by liberal democratic States for their survival, generates tension by the acceleration of "income concentration and the social exclusion of large masses of urban populations" (Dupas 2001, 16) and incapacitates the State in most countries at the periphery of capitalism; and the third contends that contemporary terrorism of the Islamists has risen not only as a reaction to globalisation but is also facilitated by it, and is directed at the liberal democratic order. The essay concludes by arguing that a more ominous a threat than the Islamic terrorism appears to be looming in the horizon as the centres of global capital shift away from the West to China, India and Brazil. Such a shift may, in turn, accelerate the generation of tension in consequence of income concentration and the social exclusion, and breed multiple brands of terrorism as irreducible singularities that refuse to be 'regularised' and 'normalised' by the new global order.

Before proceeding further, it is necessary to insert a disclaimer. This essayist is a male, an academic and theatre practitioner by profession, a Muslim by birth, but one who is yet to see the necessity of submitting to the will of any divinity (Allah or otherwise), and a citizen of Bangladesh. The questions raised by the essay are relevant for him in his immediate social context, where Islamic intolerance against non-conforming Muslims (such as the Ahmediyas) as well as the Hindus has been on the rise. It reflects neither a legitimation of Islamism and the terror tactics that the Taliban clones mobilise, nor a virulent anti-Americanism despite the legacy of Abu Gharib and Guantánamo that the Junior Bush has lovingly bestowed on the humanity. As an act of criticism, this essay attempts to contribute to a form of praxis which eventually will "make harder those acts which are now too easy" (Foucault 2002a, 456). Hence, as the provocateur-scholar Baudrillard (2004) would say, "one should not confuse the messenger with the message."

Human Rights and Liberal Democratic Order

A liberal democratic state is founded on two principles: individual rights and majority rule.

Not only is the state run by "the rule of the majority, as expressed through free and fair elections," but "it must protect the rights of individuals and minorities – in other words, it must guarantee the freedom or liberty of its citizens. These guarantees are typically incorporated into a written constitution, and government is further limited and constrained by the rule of law" (Plattner 2010, 84). For the liberal democratic system to function effectively, it is also necessary that the State guarantee a transparent system of government, protection of property, administration of justice to resolve clashes of interest, defense of its territory (by force if necessary) and provision of essential public goods that cannot be availed by private means by the majority.

Liberal democratic States began to emerge in the Europe of the 18th century by appropriating, what Foucault (1982, 783) identifies as the 'pastoral power' of the Christian Church[1]. However, it changed the objective of the power. Hence, instead of leading the 'flock' to salvation in the next world, the States promised to ensure health, sufficient wealth, security and protection against accident in this world. Concurrently, the pastoral functions were devolved to institutions such as the family, private ventures, welfare societies, and public institutions such as hospitals (Foucault 1982, 784; 2002a, 125). As a result, a new mechanism of power was 'invented,' – the disciplinary power or governmentality, by which the subject is subjugated – a "tricky combination [...] of individualisation techniques and totalisation procedures" (Foucault 1982, 782). These techniques began to be applied to immediate everyday life, for example, in the family, medicine, psychiatry, education, and varied sectors of employment, and to make individuals subjects either as (i) "subject to someone else by control and dependence," or (ii) "tied to his [sic.] own identity by a conscience or self-knowledge" in a form of self-regulation (Foucault 1982, 781). In both cases, "a form of power which subjugates and makes subject to" (Foucault 1982, 781) underpins the notion of the subject.

In order to exercise disciplinary power by individualisation technique, but at the same time disguise its application, the liberal democratic State attempted to ensure the rule of law, equal rights for all citizens, free exchange of ideas, a market economy, free private enterprise, and a transparent system of government legitimised by the consent of the governed obtained through open and fair elections. Equal rights were ensured by weaving a corpus of legal instruments around the theory of sovereignty as the core – articulated as "a reorganisation of right that invests sovereignty" (Foucault 1980, 107). It came to be "superimposed upon the mechanisms of discipline in such a way as to conceal its actual procedures, the element of domination inherent in its techniques, and to guarantee to everyone, by virtue of the sovereignty of the State, the exercise of his [sic.] proper sovereign rights" (Foucault 1980, 105). As a result of these developments, a triangular formation of power, right, and truth came to be operative in the liberal-democratic society since the 19th century, in which disciplinary power can only be exercised by means of "two points of reference, two limits: on the one hand, to the rules of right that provide a formal delimitation of power; on the other, to the effects of truth that this power produces and transmits, and which in their turn reproduce this power" (Foucault 1980, 92-93).

In analysing the general principle involved in the relation between right and power, it is important to take into cognizance the historical fact that since the medieval times, the essential focus around which legal thought has developed is the power of the king. The juridical edifice of the European society was constructed "in response to the demands of royal power, for its profit and to serve as its instrument or justification" (Foucault 1980, 94), or to question it, put limits to it, and to challenge its prerogatives. Since the 18th century, however, when the latter role became predominant, juridical power of the sovereignty came to be equated with right, "which one is able to possess like a commodity, and which one can in consequence transfer or alienate, either wholly or partially, through a legal act or through some act that establishes a right, such as takes place through cession or contract" (Foucault 1980, 88). Theories of right current in the liberal-democratic societies continue to be obsessed with the person of the sovereign – the king's head is still not cut off since "right in the West is the King's right" (Foucault 1980, 94) – although power in the liberal-democratic social body is no longer "juridico-discursive" in conception (Foucault 1990, 82) nor anchored in a "juridical-political theory of sovereignty" (1980, 103). Here lies the first approximation of an 'un-said' hollow core that lurks beneath the surface of the supposedly self-evident and universal truth-claims exerted by the liberal democratic order regarding human rights. The hollow "undermines from within all that is said" (Foucault 2002b, 28) but liberal democratic citizenry are nevertheless caught inside the hollow as the order of liberal democracy ceaselessly renews it.

Human rights philosophers have attempted to fill the un-said hollow by turning to moral philosophy and building systemic arguments to answer to the question of philosophical validity of human rights. Nevertheless, the 'void' remains, as a consequence of which the 'un-said' hollow core concealed by the truth-claims of the liberal democratic order is unmasked quite easily, when the rights are claimed to be self-evident. Seizing this assertion Hunt (2007) observes, "self evidence is crucial to human rights" and the claim to self evidence is made in the oft-repeated 'whereas' in the preamble of UDHR (1948), which is a "legalistic way of asserting a given something as self-evident." As Hunt, however, pertinently asks, "[i]f equality of rights is self-evident, then why did this assertion have to be made and why was it made only at certain times and places?"

The hidden agenda that lurks behind the assertion of self-evidence, may be uncovered by going back to a curious anomaly in the contemporary history of human rights. In a volume compiled by UNESCO that collected together responses from philosophers on the philosophic bases of human rights, Jacques Maritain relates that at one of the meetings of UNESCO National Commission where human rights was being discussed, someone expressed astonishment that member States of violently opposing ideology could have agreed to a common list of rights. "Yes," was the response, "we agree about the rights but on condition that no one asks us why" (Maritain 1948, I). It is precisely at this juncture of 'why' that the discourse of human rights operates in inter-State relations.

In the global normative regime today, "human rights now constitute the basis on which the international legitimacy of a state is determined" (*Daði* 2001). Liberals have been justifying this assertion by arguing that "the rights of states are derived from individual rights and therefore have no autonomous moral standing" (*Daði* 2001). Claiming that ultimately a State can only justify its existence by protecting the natural rights of citizens, Teson (1988, 15) argues, "a government that engages in substantial violations of human rights betrays the very purpose for which it exists and so forfeits not only its domestic legitimacy, but its international legitimacy as well."

Hence, it is no surprise that Bush Jr. can brand the nonconforming states as "outlaw regimes" and can threaten to bring them down.

Those who deny freedom to others deserve it not for themselves; and, under the rule of a just God, cannot long retain it. The leaders of governments with long habits of control need to know: To serve your people, you must learn to trust them. Start on this journey of progress and justice and America will walk at your side (White House, 2005).

It is here that the discourse of human rights functions as a very useful tool to normalise the 'deviant' States such as Iran, China, North Korea, and Cuba, which refuse to conform to liberal-democratic norms.

Strictly on logical grounds, the insistence of the liberals that a State has no right to exist if it cannot ensure human rights, is well-founded because only a liberal-democratic State can ensure human rights. As the genealogy of human rights has shown, the discourse emerged as a masking device to serve the social body in Europe as it passed through the feudal order to that of liberal-democracy in the 19th century. "The essential function of the discourse and techniques of right has been to efface the domination intrinsic to power in order to present the latter at the level of appearance under two different aspects: on the one hand, as the legitimate rights of sovereignty, and on the other, as the legal obligation to obey it" (Foucault 1980, 94). In this system, legitimate rights of sovereignty cannot be expected in the absence of the legal obligation to obey the disciplinary power of the liberal democratic State. Hence, to implement human rights, it is necessary to establish a liberal democratic State.

Chris Brown (1999, 120) affirms this position by acknowledging that human rights "have no separate ontological status" because "they are a by-product of a particular kind of society, one in which the 'state' operates constitutionally, under the rule of law, is separated from 'civil society' and the 'family', and in which private and public realms are, in principle, clearly demarcated." Hass (2008, 179, n. 2) also agrees by pointing out that the countries where human rights are most likely to be respected have a "well-educated and homogenous population with a prosperous, stable, urbanised society in which there is relative income equality, considerable media development, and competitive multi-party systems," in other words, liberal-democracies.

So, this is the hidden agenda: a political 'double bind' for the non-conformist and 'deviant' States. Venerable Bush Jr. may launch as many Iraq Wars to destroy as many Saddam Hussein's WMDs; and if he fails to locate those WMDs, then he can always play the trump card of Saddam Hussein's abuse of human rights to provide his face-saving justification of his wars. On the other hand, when Iran tries at its own risk to match Israel's nuclear armoury, human rights organisations and the media clamour that Mahmoud Ahmadinejad's government has no right to rule. Yet, Hamid Karzai's right to rule Afghanistan is upheld despite, in Senator John Kerry's own words, "deeply flawed presidential election" (AFP 2009). Here lies one answer to Hunt's question as to why the discourse of human rights is evoked at certain times and places. For a more important answer, it is necessary to examine globalisation.

Globalisation and Liberal Democratic Order

To function efficiently, the liberal democratic order requires that the Sate be underpinned both ethically and practically by a functionally fluent relationship between human rights and market economy. The intertwining of the two determining factors is such that, in the words of Anwar Ibrahim (2010) speaking from his experience as the finance minister of Malaysia in the 1990s, "defending free markets has [sic.] at its core a conviction of the necessity to defend freedom."

The market in a liberal democratic system can never be restricted only to the domestic; it necessarily incorporates the international as well. Hence, a liberal democratic State cannot but attempt to ensure the freedom and well-being of its citizens by mobilising all its resources for promoting a 'free' market the world over. In this 'free' market, it is most profitable for the liberal democratic citizenry to pool individual resources to pursue large-scale projects in one or more 'host countries,' which promise to generate vast wealth. The embodiment of this desire for wealth is the multi-national corporation (MNC), whose corporeal presence as a legal personality is borne – in the last instance – not by the centralised management under a board structure at the 'home country' but by the shared ownership of capital by the liberal democratic citizenry, who are guaranteed minimal harm by limited liability and transferability of shares.

Within this parameter operate two invisible qualifiers, which are not to be lost sight of. Firstly, the shareholders "generally do not include workers, family farmers and fishermen, indigenous communities, the urban poor or even lower-middle-class families" (Guttal 2007, 529). Secondly, the corporations need the 'home' State "to act for them: to clear the ground for their entry into domestic arenas; to establish economic, financial, legal, and judicial frameworks that facilitate their operations; and, most important, to provide rational and ethical cover for their operations" (Guttal 2007, 529). This cover is easily evoked by equating the clearing of the ground for the MNCs with economic development for the host countries. In return for its effort, the 'home' State benefits by receiving a share of the corporate profits as tax. It is here, at this juncture where liberal democracies attempt to promulgate a world-embracing free market for the MNCs to harvest a rich profit that globalisation inevitably manifests itself.

Acknowledging a plethora of competing theoretical unpackings that have variously mapped globalisation as a condition, a phenomenon, a stage, or phase, a discourse, an ideology, a series of waves, a process, or many processes (Kumar 2003, 91-92), this essay locates itself in a clearing away from the maze by grounding itself on the premise that, in the last instance, globalisation is overdetermined by three factors: (1) the new communications technology and the information revolution, (2) galloping international trade, worldwide capital markets, and foreign investment, and (3) the MNCs that define the technological vectors, which in turn set the parameters for employability. In the inter-related operation of these three factors, the State is "the main conduit through which national (or indeed multi-national) capital is inserted into the global market" (Woods 2003, 4). Hence, "there is indeed no contradiction between the logic of globalisation and the self-interest of dominant nationalisms and nation-states" (Radhakrishnan 2001, 316).

Globalisation is hardly 'natural' or even autonomous, as many of its ardent proponents claim. "Rather," as Guttal (2007, 525) argues persuasively, "it is the result of specifically conceived, planned, and targetted neo-liberal policy and structural measures that sought to bring all aspects of social, economic, and political life under the rubric of market capitalism." Enabled by neo-liberal policies, globalisation is an integral companion of liberal democracy, "which cloaks neo-liberal policy prescriptions in the language of individualised rights, liberties, and choice. Neo-liberal, so-called 'democratic' states are both convenient and necessary for capitalism to expand its frontiers and reach" (Guttal 2007: 525).

However, arguing as a predictable economist, Martin Wolf (2004) offers a volume of statistics to bring home the 'glad' tidings that globalisation indeed works. With the ardent faith of a true believer he asserts that nothing but positive result can come from 'the market,' and if any problem does arise, the fault must lie with inept governments. Nevertheless, because his analysis is based primarily on aggregate statistics, he fails to take into account the far-reaching changes in the network of power relations that economic processes cause, and the profound impact of relative immobility of labour across national boundaries that arise from restrictions in immigration and cultural barriers (*Bryan* 2004). As Baudrillard (2003b) observes:

What is globalised is first and foremost the market, the profusion of exchanges and of all sorts of products, the perpetual flow of money. Culturally, globalisation gives way to a promiscuity of signs and values, to a form of pornography in fact. Indeed, the global spread of everything and nothing through networks is pornographic. No need for sexual obscenity anymore. All you have is a global interactive copulation.

The promiscuous market of globalisation gives rise to a constant homogenisation, an endless fragmentation, dislocation, discrimination and exclusion by means of the two dialectics within global capitalism: "concentration versus fragmentation and exclusion versus inclusion" (Dupas 2001, 11). The concentration-fragmentation dialectics is generated by the large-scale investments made by a restricted number of transnational corporations "to maintain the technological leadership in products and processes and [...] establish global networks" (Dupas 2001, 11). The investments set off the contrary process of "a wave of fragmentation – spin-offs, subcontracting, franchising and the growth of the informal economy, opening the way for a large number of small companies that can operate inside the production chain at lower costs" (Dupas 2001, 11). The rule of the game is simple: the corporations, driven by the sole motive of profit, are to decide "*what, how, when, how much* and *where* goods and services used by contemporary society will be produced" (Dupas 2001, 11); the small companies will receive a piece of the 'cake' so long as they can survive in the ferocious game of competition.

On the other hand, the inclusion-exclusion dialectic is engined by "the main actors of this new global economy" the MNCs that manoeuver "with the intention of maximising their competitive position (*i.e.*, regarding price and quality) and pursuing the maximum rate of return for their investors' resources" (Dupas 2001, 12). In this regard, it is important to remember that "the top 500 transnational corporations are responsible for thirty per cent of the world's gross product, seventy per cent of world trade, and eighty per cent of world investment" (Smith, Bolyard and Ippolito 1999, 212). This immense volume, in turn generates the possibility of harvesting substantial profit by the small and medium sized enterprises, given their capacity to integrate as subordinated entities into the production chains of the transnational corporations, and manoeuver within the framework of decisions taken by them. In consequence of the dialectic, the bottom "forty per cent of the world's population living on less than US$2 a day accounts for five per cent of global income" whereas "the richest twenty per cent accounts for three-quarters of world income" (UNDP 2007, 25).[2]

Consequently, in many countries situated at the periphery of global capitalism, the only options for being included in the global economy "are as passive consumers of 'global' trash, or providers of cheap labour or *materia prima.* Those excluded from these 'options' are forced to become part of a transnational economy of crime (sex, drug and organs trafficking, child labour, kidnappings, *fayuca* [smuggled goods], etc.)" (Gómez-Peña 2001, 10). The vulnerability of these people is considerably higher if one includes the threats they constantly face: structural unemployment that may be caused by "an increasing incapacity to generate formal jobs in an adequate quantity or of a certain quality" (Dupas 2001, 12); and the 'free' agency of capital that is released "from its national duty," to search anywhere "for investment opportunities and speculative profits" and "use its exit option as a threatened sanction" (Habermas 2003, 90).[3]

The exclusion versus inclusion dialectic affects not only people but also territories. The places that are not 'functional' within this new systemic logic will not find a role in the new global economy. Inside the city, this is reflected in the acceleration of the dualisation process of the city's social arrangements, producing a gap in the city's urban development (Dupas 2001, 12).

According to a UNDP (2007, 25) report, income differentials are widening in countries where over eighty per cent of the world's population lives.

The dialectics of global capitalism, which is generating tension by the acceleration of "income concentration and the social exclusion of large masses of urban populations," is leading people in most countries at the periphery of capitalism to be trapped in societies where the level of violence is high (Dupas 2001, 16). Agreeing with this assessment, Lindley (2007, 1) observes that "a fast-expanding gap between rich and poor" is one of the "six ways in which globalisation is tending to cause destructive violence."[4] Focussing on India, Chatterjee (2009, 156) studies Hindu–Muslim conflict in the neo-liberalising city of Ahmedabad, refutes "claims in some globalisation literature that ethnic conflicts occur because local spaces remain a 'nostalgic outside' [...] resisting secularising forces of globalisation," and shows "how neo-liberal policies of globalisation like industrial restructuring and urban renewal re-order community life and can aggravate situations of social unrest." Guerilla warfare in Nigeria against oil giants such as Shell Development Company by rebel group such as Movement for the Emancipation of the Niger Delta, increasing rate of school shootings (such as Virginia Tech and Columbine High School massacres) in the USA, inter- and intra-dominion religious violence in South Asia, beheadings in Mexico at the behest of drug cartels, and rising crime rates in European countries masterminded by international criminal gangs (Naím 2009, 32) are indicators that violence – or, borrowing from Baudrillard (2003b), "a wide variety of inhuman metastases" – has spread as a pandemic all over the world.

In this violence-infested globalising world, the State is increasingly being shorn of its capacity to manoeuver because (i) uncommitted capital globe-trotting in pursuit of profit mobilises the possibility of flight as a threat, and (ii) the necessity of implementing a tight budget for monetary stability significantly reduces allocations for social programs (Dupas 2001, 14). In such a complex situation, the States are demonstrating increasing unwillingness to be committed to the obligations of employment or social security for its citizens, leaving each person to fend for him/herself as "a responsible risk-taker" (Dupas 2001, 15). This, in turn, generates large-scale loss of legitimacy of the States situated in the margins of global capital.

As the dialectics of global capitalism generates tension in the context of increasing loss of legitimacy of the State, which, in turn, threatens the market – and hence, the process of globalisation – the discourse of human rights is mobilised to enable a liberal democratic order and remove the impediments to the market. It is thus, as Baudrillard (2003b) observes, "human rights circulate exactly like any other global product (oil or capital for example)." More ominously, terrorism emerges as a force intricately intertwined with globalisation. As Cronin (2002/03, 30) observes, "the current wave of international terrorism, [...] not only is a reaction to globalisation but is facilitated by it. She cautions, "analysing terrorism as something separate from globalisation is misleading and potentially dangerous" (2002/03, 52).

The Spirit of Terrorism

Acknowledging a plethora of competing theoretical unpackings that have variously traced the parameter of terrorism and consequently have turned it into an amazing maze "notoriously difficult to define" (Cronin 2002/03, 32),[5] four authoritative samples – two institutional and two individual – may be chosen for the purpose of this essay. The institutional definition emerging from the UN Security Council delineates terrorism as "criminal acts, including against civilians, committed with the intent to cause death or serious bodily injury, or taking of hostages, with the purpose to provoke a state of terror in the general public or in a group of persons or particular persons, intimidate a population or compel a government or an international organisation to do or to abstain from doing any act [...]" (Resolution 1566; UNSC 2004, 2). Not only does the resolution insist that acts of terrorism "are under no circumstances justifiable by considerations of a political, philosophical, ideological, racial, ethnic, religious or other similar nature" (UNSC 2004, 2), but implicitly assumes that it is limited to substate actors. However, the US Army acknowledges ideational underpinnings and implicitly concedes the possible implication of a State when it defines terrorism as "the calculated use of violence or threat of violence to attain goals that are political, religious, or ideological in nature [...] through intimidation, coercion, or instilling fear" (Chomsky 2002b, 128).[6] Nevertheless, the world's leading authority on terrorism Walter Laqueur (2001, 71), writing in the wake of 9/11, erases the implication of a State when he defines terrorism as "the substate application of violence or the threat of violence to sow panic and bring about political change." At the same time, he adds an important qualifier: "it is not an ideology or a political doctrine, but rather a method" (Laqueur 2001, 71).

All the three definitions discussed above are founded on a key perception: terrorism is that which generates panic/fear/terror. However, Noam Chomsky (2002a, 71) makes a crucial move when he does away with this foundational perception and observes, "it is a serious analytical error to describe terrorism as a 'weapon of the weak,' as is often done. In practice, terrorism is the violence they commit against us – whoever we happen to be." At this juncture, it becomes evident that if the events of 9/11 were acts of terror committed by the Al-Qaeda, the US military action in Afghanistan – as revealed by the Afghan War Diary 2004-2010 released by WikiLeaks – is as much an act of terror. If Al-Qaeda's action is "under no circumstances justifiable by considerations of a political, philosophical, ideological, racial, ethnic, religious or other similar nature" (UNSC 2004, 2), then the Iraq War declared by Bush Jr. is also not justifiable by claims to institute human rights. In sum, to overlook terrorism as "violence they commit against us – whoever we happen to be" Chomsky (2002a, 71) would be a germinal mistake. Cronin (2002/3, 33) is trapped in such a mistake to claim, "although states can terrorise, they cannot by definition be terrorists."

The second germinal mistake is to make a whole-scale equation of Islam with terrorism. This is not intended as an apology for Islam. Even a cursory glance at the EU list of persons, groups and entities involved in terrorist acts (EUR-Lex 2009, 37-42) reveals that only nine out of 47 groups and entities are Islamic. The current list of designated foreign terrorist organisations released by the US Department of State (2010) shows 29 Islamic organisations out of 45 as terrorists. The point is, as Cronin (2002/03, 39) shows, religious or 'sacred' terrorists (among which, the Islamists such as Al-Qaeda feature prominently) are but one of the "four types of terrorist organisations currently operating around the world." The other three types are left-wing terrorists (who are intertwined with the Communist movement), right-wing terrorists (who draw its inspiration from Fascism), and ethno-nationalist/separatist terrorists (who emerged in the wave of decolonisation especially in the immediate post–World War II years).

The problem with most of research on terrorism conducted in the Euro-American knowledge-production nodules is that they are bogged down in, as Baudrillard (2003a, 25) would say, in "typically Western form of calculation." In most cases, researches have been founded, implicitly or even explicitly, on the total misunderstanding inherent in Western philosophy since the Enlightenment – that civilisation is structured as a Manichaean struggle of Good against Evil, in which, "the progress of Good, its advance in all fields (the sciences, technology, democracy, human rights), correspond to a defeat of Evil" (Baudrillard 2003a, 13). Hence, it becomes impossible to explain the phenomenon of 9/11, which demonstrates "a crushing revisionism *vis-à-vis* modernity and progress, [and] a rejection not only of the global techno-structure, but also of the mental system of globalisation" (Baudrillard 2003b). It is as though, the researchers in the Euro-American knowledge-production nodules are at a loss to explain how such revisionism and rejection can arise when the liberal democratic order as the embodiment of the Good has already been proved to be the Truth of humankind's 'salvation.'

Baudrillard rises above this stupefaction by challenging the notion of civilisation perceived as a Manichaean struggle and the consequent triumph of Good. "No one seems to have understood," he observes, "that Good and Evil advance together, as part of the same movement" (Baudrillard 2003a, 13). Instead of envisioning the triumph of one and the eclipse of the other it is necessary to comprehend that the struggle between Good and Evil is illusory.

Good does not conquer Evil, nor does the reverse happen: they are at once both irreducible to each other and inextricably interrelated. Ultimately, Good could thwart Evil only by ceasing to be Good since, by seizing for itself global monopoly of power, it gives rise, by that very act, to a blowback of a proportionate violence (Baudrillard 2003a, 13-14).

In the political order of the Cold War period, the symmetrical relationship of the two superpowers insured tension and equilibrium of the Good and the Evil. With the fall of the Wall, when communism was erased and liberal democracy triumphed globally, the symmetry was broken and liberal democracy as the Good exerted a totalitarian control. At this juncture, the blowback of proportionate violence of globalisation made it possible for Evil to arise in exponential fashion and regain its invisible autonomy. Consequently, "a ghostly enemy emerged, infiltrating itself throughout the whole planet, slipping in everywhere like a virus, welling up from all the interstices of power: Islam. But Islam was merely the moving front along which the antagonism crystallised" (Baudrillard 2003a, 15).

Islam appeared as the moving front of antagonism because it is the most forceful contestation of all those values that are represented by liberal democracy in general and the discourse of human rights in particular. Citing the case of Afghanistan under Taliban regime, when all recognised forms of liberal democratic practice were forbidden, Baudrillard (2003b) observes:

> From the perspective of the West, of its consensual model, and of its unique way of thinking, it is a crime not to perceive modernity [of liberal democracy] as the obvious source of the Good or as the natural ideal of humankind. It is also a crime when the universality of [liberal democratic] values and [liberal democratic] practices are found suspect by some individuals who, when they reveal their doubts, are immediately pegged as fanatics.

The 'crime' of the Islamic terrorists "not to perceive modernity [of liberal democracy] as the obvious source of the Good" (Baudrillard 2003b) – for which it is branded as a threat to international security – leads it to a relentless drive for engagement "in a Manichaean struggle of good against evil, implying an open-ended set of human targets: Anyone who is not a member of their religion or religious sect may be 'evil' [...]" (Cronin 2002/03, 41). Further, it leads its adherents to engage "in violent behaviour directly or indirectly to please the perceived commands of a deity," recognise themselves "to be unconstrained by secular values or laws," and at the same time, display "a complete sense of alienation from the existing social system" of liberal democracy (Cronin 2002/03, 41). Their crime is intolerable to the liberal democratic order because they seek not "to correct the system, making it more just, more perfect, and more egalitarian," but "to replace it" (Cronin 2002/03, 41).

However, as already observed, beneath the surface of the supposedly self-evident and universal truth-claims exerted by liberal democracy – inside which liberal democratic citizenry are caught as the liberal democratic order ceaselessly renews it – lurks "a hollow that undermines from within all that is said" (Foucault 2002b, 28). The hollow masks that the liberal democratic citizenry have already been subjugated – made subject to – liberal democratic norms and values, "through the creation of liberal institutions, the establishment of a universal State-enforced legal framework, an increased role of civil society and the prioritisation of the means of social regulation through market mechanisms" (Ullah 2006, 68). There is no freedom to choose so far as the values are concerned. The State derives its power from the individuals who conform to the values and will serve them only after each individual has been made to conform to them. In other words, the crime of refusing "to perceive modernity [of liberal democracy] as the obvious source of the Good or as the natural ideal of humankind" (Baudrillard 2003b) is a fictive construct. The differentiation between Good and Evil in regards to Islamic terrorism and liberal democracy is illusory. The Good is that to which we subscribe – "whoever we happen to be" (Chomsky 2002a, 71).

Hence, it is no wonder that Islamic terrorism enjoys "dispersed popular support in civil society" (Cronin 2002/03, 41). The support is generated by, as Baudrillard argues, "the hatred of the rest of the world against the West [...]."

The hatred of non-Western people is not based on the fact that the West stole everything from them and never gave anything back. Rather, it is based on the fact that they received everything, but were never allowed to give anything back. This hatred is not caused by dispossession or exploitation, but rather by humiliation. And this is precisely the kind of hatred that explains the September 11 terrorist attacks. These were acts of humiliation responding to another humiliation (Baudrillard 2003b).

Instead of reducing the post-Cold War antagonism against the West into Huntington's thesis about 'clash of civilisations' – of the Western against the Islamic (and the Sinic) – it is necessary to see it as an almost anthropological confrontation between liberal democracy that promotes a homogenising universal culture in the form of globalisation, and all those alternatives dispersed in various domains that refuse to be 'regularised' and 'normalised' by submitting to liberal democracy, and dare to retain a quality of irreducible alterity or singularity, which, from the perspective of global power is heresy (Baudrillard 2003b).

Singularities [...] represent a different symbolic order. They do not abide by value judgements or political realities. [...] They defeat any uniquely dominant thought. Yet they do not present themselves as a unique counter-thought. Simply, they create their own game and impose their own rules. Not all singularities are violent. Some linguistic, artistic, corporeal, or cultural singularities are quite subtle. But others, like terrorism, can be violent (Baudrillard 2003b).

Faced with the irreducible alterities or singularities, the liberal democratic order has them seduced and/or assimilated into apathy and indifference,[7] or forces them to "attacking it into fighting on the ground of reality, which is always its own" (Baudrillard 2003a, 17).

The Islamic terrorism, as an irreducible alterity or singularity that refuse to be 'normalised' by submitting to liberal democracy, has learnt from the failure of the left-wing terrorism that it is futile to "attack the system in terms of relations of force," and have shifted "the struggle into the symbolic sphere,[8] where the rule is that of challenge, reversion and outbidding. So that death can be met only by equal or greater death" (Baudrillard 2003a, 17). The spirit of the adherents of Islamic terrorism must be understood as "all about death, not only about the violent irruption of death in real time – 'live', so to speak – but the irruption of a death which is far more than real: a death which is symbolic and sacrificial – that is to say, the absolute, irrevocable event" (Baudrillard 2003a, 16-17). Functioning according to the rule of symbolic exchange, they have defied the liberal democratic order by offering it with the gift of their own deaths, and thus turning their deaths "into an absolute weapon" against a zero-sum-game system "that operates on the basis of the exclusion of death" (2002a, 16). Because the terrorists' sacrificial death in the symbolic plane is something that liberal democracy cannot respond to, the foremost State in the liberal democratic order suffered on September 11, the "worst that can happen to global power," which "is not to be attacked or destroyed, but to suffer a humiliation" (Baudrillard 2003b). The secret of their success lies in the fact that they do not hold together by "an employment contract, but with a pact and a sacrificial obligation. Such obligation is immune to corruption" (Baudrillard 2003a, 22).

Ironically, globalisation has enabled the Islamic terrorists to function more efficiently. As Cronin (2002/03) shows, "the use of information technologies such as the internet, mobile phones, and instant messaging has extended the global reach of many terrorist groups" (46),[9] CBNR (chemical, biological, nuclear, or radiological) weapons are increasingly becoming easier for them to access, they are now able "to reach across international borders, in the same way (and often through the same channels) that commerce and business interests are linked" (48), and are able to broaden "their reach in gathering financial resources to fund their operations" (49). Thus enabled by globalisation, they demolished the twin towers that symbolised corporate globalisation by "the trait of reversion that effaces the remainder, just as a single ironic smile effaces a whole discourse, just as a single flash of denial in a slave effaces all the power and pleasure of the master" (Baudrillard 1994, 163). In consequence, not only did they succeed in triggering the recent economic, political, and psychological 'recessions' in the liberal democratic countries but also in erasing the notion of human rights in those countries, and in its place, succeeded in enforcing on them "a police-state globalisation, a total control, a terror-based on 'law-and-order' measures [...] akin to those of a fundamentalist society" (Baudrillard 2003a, 32). Undoubtedly, the symbolic victory of the war on terror has gone to the terrorists.

Conclusion

In spite of "the terrorists' successful attempt to put death back on stage in a symbolic exchange with 'the system,' the majority of Americans have by now assimilated its violence into the broader narrative of a war against terrorism and Evil, one of the many things on TV" (Butterfield 2002). At the same time, the terrorists' challenge to the liberal democratic order has moved from the domain of the symbolic to that of the real – from the US to Afghanistan – as a hugely superior force of 150,000 troops drafted from the US, the UK, and more than forty other countries and equipped with the most lethal technology of war that the West has at its command, find it impossible to contain – let alone root out – a tiny force of 20,000-strong Taliban and their allies (BBC 2010).[10] In sum, the war on terror is far from over, even when the West has pitted all its might.

Notwithstanding the ignominy of the West in Afghanistan, more ominous a threat than the Taliban appears to be looming on the horizon. As the current scenario of globalisation shows, "most of the world's largest TNCs have their home bases in France, Germany, the UK, and Japan, with the largest concentration in the USA" (Guttal 2007, 526). However, in the dynamic arena of globalisation, where capitalistic expansion enables new actors to compete for economic and strategic dominance, the First World TNCs are being increasingly challenged by the RDE 100, *i.e.*, the one hundred corporate bodies based in the Rapidly Developing Economy, whose "sales reached a combined 1.5 trillion dollars in 2007" (Aguiar *et. al.* 2009, 19). Of the 100, 36 are based in China, 20 in India, 14 in Brazil, seven in Mexico, six in Russia, four in UAE, two each in Chile, Indonesia, Malaysia, Thailand, and Turkey, and one each in Argentina, Hungary and Kuwait (Aguiar *et. al.* 2009, 18). To these corporate bodies, one must add the names of global Indian entrepreneurs such as K.M. Birla, L.N. Mittal and Ratan Tata (Srinivas 2007).[11] But the dynamics of global capital looks even murkier today in consequence of the financial crisis of 2008-2009, "which had been the result of normal business activity in a *laissez-faire* economic regime" (Posner 2009, 235). In consequence of the crisis, "governments around the world have spent almost $11 trillion bailing out failing banks and trying to repair the financial system" (BBC

2009). Capitalism may survive, as Posner (2009, 234) believes, "because there is no alternative that hasn't been thoroughly discredited," but the survival will be "only in a compromised form." In that compromised form, the centres of global capital may well shift away from the West to China, India and Brazil. Hence, the rule of the globalising game will soon cease to be the West versus the rest or the North against the South; it will be a case of anarchical *mātsyanāya* (lit., "justice in the world of fish") as described by the ancient political treatises of South Asia, where any 'big fish' (in this case, a dominant State) will devour or attempt to, those lesser to it in might at the periphery of capitalism. At the same time, the dialectics of global capital may accelerate the generation of tension, and breed multiple brands of terrorism as irreducible alterities or singularities dispersed in various domains that refuse to be 'regularised' and 'normalised' by the new global order. The future of the spirit of terrorism must be sought here, in the dialectics of global capitalism generating violence in the impending *mātsyanāya.*

References

1. The defining characteristics of this form of power are that it: (i) assures the salvation of the individual in the next world, (ii) does not only command but is also prepared to sacrifice itself for the life and salvation of the flock, (iii) looks after the entire community, and in particular, each individual for his/her entire life; and (iv) is exercised by knowing the inside of people's minds and exploring their soul by making them reveal their innermost secrets in confessions.
2. The Forbes World Billionaire list of 2010 showed 1,011 10-figure titans, whose combined net worth is $3.6 trillion. The US accounts for 40 per cent of these billionaires. In one way or the other, their wealth is married to the stock market (Miller and Kroll 2010; Housel 2010).
3. Because they have viable market competitors at the local level, large countries such as the United States and Brazil have been the most successful in overcoming threatened or actual withdrawal by multi-national corporations.
4. The other five ways are: "the public media making this gap widely evident; a disturbingly fast rate of cultural interpenetrations; worldwide availability of modern weapons; lack of effective laws to control ruthless international concomitants of mass production/distribution; and fear of macro-ecological catastrophes due to excessive increases in population and in per-capita consumption and waste" (Lindley 2007: 1).
5. For example, Lord Carlile of Berriew Q.C., Independent Reviewer of Terrorism Legislation acknowledges that "[t]here is no universally accepted definition of terrorism. It remains the subject of continuing debate in international bodies" (Carlile 2007: 3). Further, in *Political Terrorism: A New Guide to Actors, Authors, Concepts, Data Bases, Theories, and Literature,* authors Alex P. Schmid and Albert J. Jongman draw "heavily on the contributions of more than fifty

authors in the field of terrorism" (2005: xii) and after a lengthy deliberation acknowledges that "we need more knowledge of why terrorists, both state and non-state, choose terrorist tactics and strategies over other methods of waging conflict" if "a specific theory of terrorism [is to] come within reach" (2005: 135).

6. Cited from US Army Operational Concept for Terrorism Counteraction_ (TRADOC Pamphlet No. 525-37), 1984.
7. As Baudrillard (1994: 163) says, "the system is itself also nihilistic, in the sense that it has the power to pour everything, including what denies it, into indifference".
8. "The symbolic is neither a concept, an agency, a category, nor a "structure," but an act of exchange and a *social relation which puts an end to the real*, which resolves the real, and, at the same time, puts an end to the opposition between the real and the imaginary" (Baudrillard, 1993: 133). Derived "loosely from Mauss's analysis of the *Potlatch*, Bataille's theory of expenditure, and a deconstruction of Lacan's symbolic/real/imaginary triad," Baudrillard's symbolic sphere attempts to overcome "the biased distinctions of Western metaphysics – Cause/Effect, Being/Nothingness, Real/Imaginary, Normal/Abnormal, Good/Evil" (Butterfield).
9. This, in turn, has enhanced the efficiency of the terrorists in activities such as "administrative tasks, coordination of operations, recruitment of potential members, communication among adherents, and attraction of sympathisers" (Cronin 2002/03: 47).
10. The figure excludes the Afghan National Army, numbering about 94,000 in October 2009, and just above 80,000 Afghan police (BBC 2010).
11. Recently, "K.M. Birla's Hindalco acquired the world's largest producer of rolled aluminium products, Novelis, for $6bn. Before that, L. N. Mittal - who is based in London but holds an Indian passport - took over the world's largest steel-maker, Arcelor, and Ratan Tata gobbled up another steel manufacturer, Corus, to become the fifth largest producer" (Srinivas 2007).

Works Cited

1. AFP. 2009. Top US senator pleads for patience on Afghanistan. http://www.google.com/hostednews/afp/article/ALeqM5i-ND1wGIRzFKVd2SrBCzb_nMGlg (accessed 07 August 2010).
2. Aguiar, Marcos, Cameron Baily, Arindam Bhattacharya *et al.* 2009. The 2009 BCG 100 New Global Challengers: How Companies from Rapidly Developing Economies are Contending for Global Leadership. The Boston Consulting Group (GCG). http://www.bcg.com.cn/export/sites/default/en/files/publications/reports_pdf/The_2009_BCG_100_New_Global_Challengers_Jan_2009.pdf (accessed 06 August 2010).
3. Baudrillard, Jean, 1993. *Symbolic Exchange and Death.* Trans. Iain Hamilton. London: Sage.
4. Baudrillard, Jean, 1994. *Simulacra and Simulation*. Trans. Sheila Faria Glaser. Ann Arbor: University of Michigan Press.
5. Baudrillard, Jean, 2003a. The Spirit of terrorism. In *The Spirit of Terrorism and Other Essays*. Trans. Chris Turner, 1-34. London: Verso.

6. Baudrillard, Jean, 2003b. *The Violence of the Global.* Trans. François Debrix. http://www.ctheory.net/text_file.asp?pick=385 (accessed 07 July 2010).
7. Baudrillard, Jean, 2004. This is the Fourth World War: The *Der Spiegel* Interview with Jean Baudrillard. Trans. Samir Gandesha. *International Journal of Baudrullard Studies*, 1:1. http://www.ubishops.ca/baudrillardstudies/spiegel.htm (accessed 07 July 2010).
8. BBC. 2009. Follow the money. http://news.bbc.co.uk/2/hi/business/8249411.stm (accessed 06 August 2010).
9. ———. 2010. Q & A: Foreign forces in Afghanistan. http://news.bbc.co.uk/2/hi/south_asia/8388711.stm (accessed 06 August 2010).
10. Brown, Chris. 1999. Universal human rights: a critique. In *Human Rights in Global Politics.* Eds. Tim Dunne and Nicholas J. Wheeler. Cambridge: Cambridge University Press.
11. Bryan, Felicity. 2004. Rev. of *Why Globalisation Works* by Martin Wolf. Publishers Weekly 04/12/2004 (PW Review 2004 April #2). http://www.publishersweekly.com/pw/reviews/search/index.html (accessed 14 July 2010).
12. Butterfield, Bradley. 2002. The Baudrillardian Symbolic, 9/11, and the War of Good and Evil. *Postmodern Culture* 13:1. http://muse.jhu.edu/journals/postmodern_culture/v013/13.1butterfield.html (accessed 06 August 2010).
13. Carlile, Lord of Berriew. 2007. The Definition of Terrorism, A Report by Lord Carlile of Berriew Q.C., Independent Reviewer of Terrorism Legislation, Presented to Parliament by the Secretary of State for the Home Department, by Command of Her Majesty. http://www.icj.org/IMG/UK-Carlile-DefTer.pdf (accessed 02 August 2010).
14. Chatterjee, Ipsita. 2009. Social conflict and the neoliberal city: A case of Hindu–Muslim violence in India. *Transactions of the Institute of British Geographers,* 34:2, 143-160.
15. Chomsky, Noam. 2002a. September 11 Aftermath: Where is the World Heading. In *Beyond September 11: An Anthology of Dissent,* ed. Phil Scraton, 66-71. London: Pluto Press.
16. ——— . 2002b. Who are the Global Terrorists? In *Worlds in Collision: Terror and the Future of Global Order*, eds. Ken Booth and Tim Dunne, 128-138. New York: Palgrave Macmillan.
17. Cmiel, Kenneth. 2004. Recent History of Human Rights. *The American Historical Review*, 109: 117-135.
18. Cronin, Audrey Kurth. 2002/03. Behind the Curve: Globalisation and International Terrorism. *International Security,* 27: 3, pp. 30-58.
19. *Daði, Ýhsan.* 2001. Human Rights, Foreign Policy and the Question Of Intervention. *Perceptions: Journal Of International Affairs,* VI: 2. http://www.sam.gov.tr/perceptions/Volume6/June-July2001/dagi8.PDF (accessed 7 July 2010).
20. Dupas, Gilberto. 2001. The Logic of Globalisation: Tensions and Governability in Contemporary Society, Management of Social Transformations (MOST) Discussion Paper No 52, United Nations

Educational, Scientific and Cultural Organisation. http://unesdoc.unesco.org/images/0012/001220/122036eo.pdf (accessed 16 July 2010).

21. EUR-Lex. 2009. Council Common Position 2009/67/CFSP of 26th January 2009 updating Common Position 2001/931/CFSP on the application of specific measures to combat terrorism and repealing Common Position 2008/586/CFSP. *Official Journal of the European Union,* 52: L 032, 37-42. http://eur-lex.europa.eu/LexUriServ/LexUriServ.do?uri=OJ:L:2009:023:0037:0042:EN:PDF (accessed 02 August 2010).
22. Foucault, Michel. 1980. Two Lectures. In *Power/Knowledge: Selected Interviews and Other Writings 1972-1977*, ed. Colin Gordon. New York: Pantheon, pp. 78-108.
23. ——— . 1982. The Subject and Power. Trans. Leslie Sawyer. *Critical Inquiry,* 8:4, 777-795.
24. ——— . 2002a. Truth and Power. In *Michel Foucault Power: Essential works of Foucault 1954-1984* (Vol. 3), ed. J. D. Faubion, pp. 111-133. London: Penguin Books.
25. ——— . 2002b. *The Archaeology of Knowledge.* Trans. A. M. Sheridan Smith. London: Routledge.
26. Gómez-Peña, Guillermo. 2001. The New Global Culture, *TDR: The Drama Review* 45:1, 7-30.
27. Guttal, Shalmali. 2007. Globalisation, *Development in Practice,* 17: 4–5, 523-531.
28. Habermas, Jürgen. 2003. Making Sense of the EU: Toward a Cosmopolitan Europe. *Journal of Democracy,* 14: 4, 86-100.
29. Housel, Morgan. 2010. Why They're Billionaires, and You're Not. The Money Times. http://www.themoneytimes.com/featured/20100313/why-they039re-billionaires-and-you039re-not-id-10103544.html (accessed 17 July 2010).
30. Hunt, Lynn. 2007. "Inventing Human Rights: A History," Wade Clark Roof lecture on Human Rights at UC Santa Barbara. http://www.youtube.com/watch?v=YZVD1G4q0bA (accessed 8 May 2010).
31. Ibrahim, Anwar. 2010. Universal Values of Democracy and the Market Economy, a lecture delivered at the Centre for International Private Enterprise Development Institute. http://developmentinstitute.org/Member/ibrahim/ibrahim_universal-values/Desktop%20Flash/index.html (accessed 14 July 2010).
32. Kumar, Vidya S. A. 2003. A Critical Methodology of Globalisation: Politics of the 21st Century? *Indiana Journal of Global Legal Studies* 10:2, 87-111.
33. Laqueur, Walter. 2001. Left, Right, and Beyond: The Changing Face of Terror. In *How Did This Happen? Terrorism and the New War 71*, eds. James F. Hodge Jr. and Gideon Rose, 71-82. New York: Public Affairs.
34. Lindley, Mark. 2007. Current Links between Globalisation and Violence. *Journal of American Science,* 3:1, 1-4.

35. Maritain, Jacques. 1948. Introduction. In *Human Rights: Comments and Interpretations,* ed. UNESCO, I-IX. http://unesdoc.unesco.org/images/0015/001550/155042eb.pdf (accessed 1 August 2010).
36. Miller, Matthew and Luisa Kroll. 2010. World's Richest People: Bill Gates No Longer World's Richest Man. Forbes.com. http://www.forbes.com/2010/03/09/worlds-richest-people-slim-gates-buffett-billionaires-2010-intro_2.html (accessed 29 July 2010).
37. Naím, Moisés. 2009. Globalisation. *Foreign Policy,* 171, 28-34.
38. Plattner, Marc F. 2010. Populism, Pluralism, and Liberal Democracy. *Journal of Democracy,* 21:1, 81-92.
39. Posner, Richard A. 2009. *A Failure of Capitalism: The Crisis of '08 and the Descent into Depression.* Cambridge MA: Harvard University Press.
40. Radhakrishnan, R. 2001. Globalisation, Desire, and the Politics of Representation. *Comparative Literature,* 53: 4, 315–32.
41. Schmid, Alex P. and Albert J. Jongman. 2005. *Political Terrorism: A New Guide to Actors, Authors, Concepts, Data Bases, Theories, & Literature.* Piscataway, N. J.: Transaction Publishers.
42. Smith, Jackie, Melissa Bolyard and Anna Ippolito. 1999. Human Rights and the Global Economy: A Response to Meyer. *Human Rights Quarterly,* 21:1, 207-219.
43. Srinivas, Alam. 2007. India's Rise as a Manufacturing Giant. BBC. http://news.bbc.co.uk/2/hi/south_asia/6356767.stm (accessed 07 July 2007).
44. Teson, Feranado. 1988. *Humanitarian Intervention.* New York: Transnational Publications.
45. Ullah, Samina. 2006. Gender and Liberal Democracy: The Deconstruction of Liberal Imperialism in Afghanistan, *Undercurrent,* III: 2, 67-74.
46. UNDP. 2007. *Human Development Report 2007/2008: Fighting climate change: Human solidarity in a divided world.* Houndmills, Basingstoke: Palgrave Macmillan.
47. UNSC. 2004. Resolution 1566 (2004) adopted by the Security Council at its 5053rd meeting, on 8 October 2004. http://www.ustreas.gov/offices enforcement/pdf/unscr1566.pdf (accessed 30 July 2010).
48. US Department of State. 2010. Foreign Terrorist Organisations. http://www.state.gov/s/ct/rls/other/des/123085.htm (accessed 2 August 2010).
49. Wolf, Martin. 2004. *Why Globalisation Works.* New Haven, Conn.: Yale University Press.
50. Woods, Ellen Meiksins. 2003. *The Empire of Capital.* London: Verso.
51. White House, The. 2005. President Sworn-In to Second Term. http://georgewbush-whitehouse.archives.gov/news/releases/2005/01/20050120-1.html (accessed 07 August 2007).

3

Naxal Terrorism in India with Special Reference to Jharkhand

Umesh Kumar Verma

Introduction

The Naxal movement took its name from Naxalbari village of Siliguri Tahsil of Darjeeling district of West Bengal, which came on the Indian scene in 1967, when there was an armed upsurge of peasants and agricultural labourers against the local landlords under the leadership of Charu Mazumdar and Kanu Sanyal. The peasants stormed the granaries of the landlords, forcibly harvested standing crops, burnt records of outstanding debts, etc. This led to the formation in 1969 of the third major Communist Party of India (Marxist-Leninist). This party believed that the social equity in India will be only achieved by Marxist-Leninist ideology and Mao-Tse-tung's thought. The Naxal movement became popular among idealist youths and spread to rural and tribal parts of India, where people are poor and being exploited by landlords, contractors and government personnels. This movement speaks the language of equality, justice and rights and asserts the need to fight to achieve. These aims, for which they are ready to die-proves very attractive for people to join this movement. The Home Ministry of India observed in 2005 that ninety one per cent of violence and eighty-nine per cent of deaths arising from violence, are the result of Naxalite action in India.

In the opinion of Indian Prime Minister Dr. Manmohan Singh, Naxalite insurgency should not be viewed as a purely law and order problem, rather it is a social and economic deprivation experienced by a significant part of India's population. Andhra Pradesh, Bihar, Chhattisgarh, Jharkhand, Karnataka, Madhya Pradesh, Orissa, Tamil Nadu, Uttar Pradesh and West

Bengal are Naxalite affected states of India. The intensively Naxalite affected districts identified in these states are as below :

1. Andhra Pradesh - Adilabad, Anantapur, East Godwani, Guntur, Karimanagar, Khamman, Kumool, Mahbubnagar, Medak, Nalgonda, Nizamabad, Srikakulam, Vishakhapatnam, Vizianagram and Warangal.
2. Bihar - Auranagabad, Banka, Dharbhanga, Gaya, Jamui, Jahanabad, Kaimur (Bhabhua), Khagaria, Muzaffarpur, Patna, Rohtas and Sitamarhi.
3. Chhattisgarh - Bastar, Dantewara, Jashpur, Kankar, Kawardha, Rajnandgaon and Surguja.
4. Jharkhand - Bokaro, Chatra, Dhanbad, Garhawa, Giridih, Gumla, Hazaribag, Koderma, Lohardaga, Palamu, West Singhbhum, East Singhbhum, Ranchi.
5. Karnataka - Bellary, Bidar, Chikmagalur, Gulbarga, Kolar, Raichur, Shimoga, Tumkur, Udupi.
6. Madhya Pradesh - Balaghat, Dondori, Mandla, Aurangabad, Bhandra, Chandrapur, Gadchiroli, Gondia Nanded and Yavatmal.
7. Orissa - Gajapati, Ganjam, Kandhamal, Kendujhar, Koraput, Malkangiri, Mayurbahanj, Nabarangpur, Raygada and Sundergarh.
8. Tamil Nadu - Dharmpuri and Viluppuram.
9. Uttar Pradesh - Chandauli, Mirzapur and Sonbhadra.
10. West Bengal - Bankura, Bardhaman, Hugli, Medinipur, Purulia and South 24-Parganas.

During the last three decades since 1980, the two main groups involved in violent activities, besides many factions and smaller outfits, are the People's War Group (PWG) and the Maoist centre (MCC). They have also extended their operation area from their old pocket in West Bengal, Bihar and Andhra Pradesh in 1970s to new guerilla zones in other states like Jharkhand, Chhattisgarh, Madhya Pradesh, Eastern Maharashtra and Western Orissa. These eight states comprise a large chunk of the Indian land mass and account for half of the Indian population. The People's War Group is active mainly in Andhra Pradesh, Western Orissa and Eastern Maharashtra and MCC is active in Bihar, Jharkhand and Chhattisgarh. Their main support base in these states are the poorest and the most deprived classes, the landless and the tribal people, who are ousted from their homes by upcoming Industrial projects, are being denied access to their traditional forest resources, regularly exploited by land owners and money-lenders and persecuted by the police and who continue to suffer from non-availability of education and health facilities in their far-flung and inaccessible villages.

Apart from expending their guerilla zones within India, the PWG, MCC and other smaller armed communist groups have been able to build a network with similar communist revolutionary organisations in the neighbouring states of Bangladesh, Sri Lanka, Bhutan and Nepal.

At present 200 districts of sixteen states of India are affected by Naxalites in which eighty-one districts are seriously affected. Geographically, in adjoining areas of Andhra Pradesh and Maharashtra Naxalities are more active. About 90 thousand kilometre area of India are in the effect of Naxalites, which is expanded from Tamil Nadu to Nepal known as Red Corridor. Now-a-days there are about 15,000 Maoists in India in which 10,000 are armoured.

Naxalism in Jharkhand

The origin of Naxalism in Jharkhand can be seen as expansion of Naxal Movement revived in West Bengal. Present Jharkhand, which was a part of Integrated Bihar before 15th November, 2000, had been the prey of negligence of Contemporary Government of Bihar, which resulted in poverty and unemployment here. The geographical condition and monsoon-based agricultural system of Jharkhand affect rural economic life adversely. During the lean period, the landless rural folks have to migrate to other parts of the country in search of their livelihood. This phenomenon has been continued in Jharkhand since 1921. The phenomenon of differentiation, which had started in days of second World War, has also affected adversely the economic life of the people of Jharkhand especially tribal population : mainly poverty, unemployment, economic disparity, corruption, displacement, migration, youth unsatisfaction, education system, lack of political will, inefficient governance, etc. have been responsible for the origin and development of Naxalism in Jharkhand. Today Naxalism is a serious challenge for the internal security not only in Jharkhand rather in the whole country. All districts of Jharkhand are under the impact of Naxalism at any level. Dumka Division of Jharkhand, which was deprived of Naxalism previously, now-a-days has not segregated from it. Today Naxal activities are on climax in Palamu Division (Garwhawa, Latehar and Palamu district) of state, for which mainly feudal culture has been responsible. The south west part of Jharkhand has been mainly centre of Naxalism, which was previously governed by British administration. During British period, feudal culture came into existence, which could not be completely abolished even till date. Naxalites are not only cultivating terror and violence using ruinous arms but, they also rule parallel administration to State Government. They rule over with help of their own people's police and people courts. The posts of Commander and Zonal Commander are created in their administrative structure. They conducted training camps for using AK-47 Rifles, Land mines, grenades, hand bombs, Cane bomb, Rocket launcher, Bomb tunnel, etc. Some girls and women are also annexed in their people's police. Naxal forces are expert in Guerilla warfare. They also collect levies while running their parallel government in remote villages of hilly and forestry areas. They collect levies from Government employees related to conducting development programmes of State Government like—road, buildings and bridge construction, etc., which affect Government development programmes adversely.

More than two thousand Naxal attacks had taken place in Jharkhand in which 354 polices 1,051 public and more than 200 Naxalites died (Prabha Khabar, Ranchi, 16th November, 2010).

Todays the Naxalites have deviated from fundamental theory and philosophy of Naxalism. Naxalites began to live luxurious life using collected levies. They stay in Five Star Hotels and enroll their children in English Medium Schools. The women attached with Naxal organisations are exploited by Naxalites. Different Newspapers reveals that Naxalites have relations with politicians and they play important role in winning elections by politicians. Due to lack of political will power Naxalites have not been controlled.

The education system is not less responsible for emergence of Naxal terrorism and violence. The First Education Minister of India Maulana Abul Kalam Azad had suggested UGC to follow education system as per need of socio-economic requirement of the country, which could not be applied uptil now. Present education system is cutting the students from the society, making them self-centered. This education system has been unable in creating national feelings among students and forming National Character. The education system of India has concentrated to make people only literate not qualitative educated. The educational level of the country is degrading day by day. According to a report of World Bank, ninety per cent of degree holders of India do not deserve their degrees. About 35 crore countrymen in India are illiterate. In one side, the world level super markets and food chains are available in Indian cities, where urban youth are spending freely on fast food and Junkfood like

Pizza and Burger, but on the other side fifty-one per cent children are malnourished. The leaders, bureaucrats and people of corporates are leading luxurious life on another side the earning of about thirty crore Indians is only Rs 545 per month (Narayan Murty, 2009:1).

Due to lack of employment-oriented education imparted by Indian Universities' the activities of Naxalism are growing. The feudal thought of elites and bureaucrats is a great barrier in development of poor (Ibid., 2009 : 17).

The black money is an acute problem in India, which is responsible for socio-economic disparity. The economic system of India is of about ten kharab and parallel economic system conducted by black money is of same. According to the report of Swiss Banking Association, India is on the apex of five countries in the matter of black wealth. About Rs. 70 crore lakh of Indians money is deposited in Swiss Banks. The black money of India deposited in Banks of outside the countries is equal to budget of 50 years of India (Lal, 2009 : 9). According to the latest report of United Nation World Food Programme, (World Food Programme) half of total hungers of world reside in India.

The longer and complex judicial process in courts also encourages the naxal activities because the judgements are not given in time.

Summing up

The Naxalism is an outcome of inadequate governance and its structure since pretty long time in Jharkhand. For rapid economic and human development, fundamental changes are required in the governance structure and government institutions. Decentralisation of power and public participation through Gram Sabhas are essential for implementation of government development and welfare programmes.

For the eradication of Naxalism following suggestions are given :

1. The effective effort should be done for removal of poverty and unemployment in Jharkhand.
2. The population control policy should be implemented effectively in Jharkhand.
3. Different Governmental Developmental and Welfare programme should be implemented successfully.
4. The problem of corruption, exploitation, economic disparity, displacement, migration and youth dissatisfaction should be solved by political will power and good governance.

5. There is need of good personality in politics so that the movement should be provided to all round and sustainable development in the state establishing co-ordination among capital, talent and technique on the basis of dexterous leadership.
6. For the all round development of women, a significant effort should be made by Government and Non-Government Organisations, because they are a prey of exploitation relating to gender inequality and economic disparity.
7. The course contents of educational institutions should be changed as per socio-economic requirements of the society, and the national character should be developed among citizens to eradicate corruption, economic disparity, poverty, feudal mentality and gender inequality.
8. Naxal terrorism may be controlled by implementing appropriate strategies formulated by Gram Sabha and Urban wards at local level.
9. The administration and police missionary should be sensitive and democratic towards Naxal problem.
10. The judicial process of courts should be rapid and have transparency. Fast tract courts should be established for disposal of Naxal cases.
11. Black money deposited in Swiss and other foreign banks should be brought in the country for conducting poverty alleviation programmes to control over Naxal terrorism.
12. The Naxalities should be invited by the Government for dialogue and their participation in the sovereignty as per the Constitution of the country on the basis of election.
13. There is need of analysis of Naxal problem by holistic approach to cover up all its aspects by conducting extensive research and effective strategy should be formulated and implemented for its eradication.

References

- Narayanmurty, N.R. (2009) : *Durdarshi Netritya Ki Jarurat*, *Prabhat Khabar*, 15th April.
- Lal, B.R. (2009) : Kale Dhan Ka Such, *Prabhat Khabar*, 4th April.

4

Naxalism Causes and Remedies with Special Reference to Tribals of Jharkhand

Sabir Hussain and Rajesh Roshan

Maoist/Naxalism is an informal name given to communist groups that were born out of the Sino-Soviet split in the communist movement in India. Ideologically, they belong to various trends of Maosim. Initially, the movement had its centre in West Bengal. In recent years, they have spread into less developed areas of rural centre and eastern India, such as Chhattisgarh, Andhra Pradesh, West Bengal, Jharkhand, Orissa, though the activities of underground groups like the Communist Party of India (Maoist). They are conducting an insurgency, typically called the Naxalite Maoist Insurgency. They now have a presence in forty per cent of India's geographical area and are especially concentrated in an area known as the "Naxal belt" comprising 92,000 square kilometers. According to India's intelligence agency the Research and Analysis Wing, 20,000 insurgents are currently in operation and their growing influence prompted Indian Prime Minister Manmohan Singh to declare them as the most serious threat to India's national security. The term Naxal comes from Naxalbari a small village in West Bengal where a section of Communist Party of India (Marxist) CPI(M) led by Charu Majumdar and Kanu Sanyal led a violent uprising in 1967, trying to develop a "Revolutionary Opposition" in opposition to the CPI (M) leadership. The insurrection started on May 25, 1967 in Naxalbari village when a peasant was attacked by Land Lords over a land dispute.

Local peasants retaliated by attacking the local Land Lords and the violence escalated. Majumdar greatly admired Mao Zedong of China and advocated that Indian peasants and lower classes must follow in his foot steps and overthrow the government and upper classes whom he held responsible for their plight. He engendered the Naxalite movement through his writings, the most famous being the "Historic Eight Documents" which formed the basis of Naxalite ideology. In 1967, Naxalites organised the All India Coordination Committee of Communist Revolutionaries (AICCCR) and later broke away from CPI (M). Uprisings were organised in several parts of the country. In 1969, AICCCR gave birth to Communist Party of India (Mairxist-Leninist).

Practically, all Naxalite groups trace their origin to the CPI(ML). A separate tendency from the beginning was the Maoist Communist Centre, which evolved out of the Dakshin Desh Group. MCC later fused with people's War Group to form Communist Party of India (Maoist). During the 1970s the movement was fragmented into several disputing factions. By 1980, it was estimated that around thirty Naxalite groups were active, with a combined membership of 30,000. A 2004 Home Ministry estimate puts numbers at that time as 9,300 hardcore underground cadre around 6,500 regular weapons beside a large number of unlicensed country made arms. According to Judith Hall (2006) more recent figures put the strength of the movement at 15,000 and claim the guerrillas control an estimated one fifth of India's forests, as well as being in 160 of the country's 604 administrative districts. India's Research and Analysis Wing believed in 2006 that 20,000 Naxals are currently involved in the growing insurgency.

The CPI(M) and some other Naxal factions are now considered terrorist by the government of India. In February 2009, Central Government announced its plans for simultaneous, co-ordinated counter operations in all left wing extremism hit states Chhattisgarh, Orissa, Andhra Pradesh, Maharashtra, Jharkhand, Bihar, Uttar Pradesh and West Bengal to plug all possible escape routes of Naxalites.

Today some groups have become legal organisations participating in Parliamentary elections, such as Communist Party of India (Marxist–Leninist) liberation others such as Communist Party of India (Maoist) and Communist Part of India (Marxist–Leninst) *Janashakti* are engaged in armed guerrilla struggles.

Objective of Study

(*a*) To highlight the causes, problem and need of the Maoist and the tribal villagers affected by them.

(*b*) To find out the movement/activities of the Maoist groups, and their causes and suggestion for their remedies are the main objective of the study.

Research Methodology

The research design of the study follow all standard Anthropological Research techniques:-

- For the study stratified random sampling is used.
- A detailed structured schedule, observation, focus group discussion, and case study methods also followed.
- The importance of establishing proper rapport with Maoist is adequately stressed. The Research Investigators advised to define their role clearly with the help of coping mechanisms.

Study Area

For the present study, the field work is done in the state of Jharkhand. In Jharkhand, Ranchi, Khunti, Lohardaga, Gumla, Simdega, West Singhbhum, East Singhbhum and Saraikela-Kharsawan are main focus area.

Result and Discussions

The state of Jharkhand came into existence as the 28th state of the Indian Republic in AD 2000. It accounts for 40 per cent of the mineral resources of the nations. It also has 2.38 million hectares of forest spread over nearly 29.0 per cent of land area. Cultivable land is about 37.5 per cent of land area. The net sown area measures 29.74 lakh hectares. Assured irrigation is available for over one tenth of the cultivable area. In spite of this bounty of natural resources the state remains underdeveloped. Above 12.5 per cent of households do not get two square meals a day and 46 per cent of the population lives below the poverty line. Only 75.4 per cent of households have safe drinking water and 16.8 per cent have toilet facility. Approximately, 15.2 per cent households have electricity connection and only 15 per cent of rural areas have electricity supply. The road network density is 21.40 km per 100 sq km. There is a shortage of 37 per cent health sub centres, 64 per cent primary health centres, and 82 per cent community health centers.

At the count of the census of India, 2001 the state had a population of 26945829 of which schedule tribe constituted 7087068 of them 3565960 male and 3521108 female. The literacy rate of the state is 53.6 per cent with 38.9 per cent female literacy and 67.3 per cent male literacy. In Schedule

Tribe the total literacy rate is 33.0 per cent with 43.8 per cent, male literacy and 22.1 per cent female literacy. Total work force participation in Schedule Tribe is 46.3 per cent. Total male work force is 51.9 per cent and female work force is 40.6 per cent. Schedule tribe employment in the state is 27.5 per cent of main workers to all workers. Conversely the share of marginal is 18.8 per cent and proportion of non workers is (53.7 per cent) highest in the state. In schedule tribe about 52.6 per cent of the employed persons are cultivators and 31.0 per cent agricultural labour as compared to 13.5 per cent of other workers.

Poor employment prospects are the major causes of Naxalism problem in Jharkhand. Unemployment is higher in rural areas. Most of the work force is engaged in agriculture, wage labour, major and minor forest produce based livelihood, animal husbandry, household industry, mining and quarrying. Some of the agriculture and non-timber forest produce (NIFP) are under threat because of considerable depletion of the resource base.

Unemployment Across Age Groups, 1999-2000

Age Group	*Jharkhand*	*India*
15 – 19	25.28	14.40
20 – 24	16.9	13.50
25 – 29	10.53	9.20
30 – 34	5.72	5.80
35 – 39	3.75	4.60
40 – 44	4.36	4.20
45 – 49	4.02	3.90
50 – 54	5.05	3.90
55 – 59	4.83	4.00
60 – above	—	3.50

Over one quarter of the youth population in the state belongs to the tribal communication. They have a close association with nature, hardworking lifestyle, distinct and wholesome cultural practices. Most of them reside in rural areas, some in very remote areas. The tribal youth today is disillusioned due to lack of basic amenities of life, unavailability of livelihood opportunities and long and continuing tradition of exploitation are main reasons for emergence of Naxalism problems.

The present social structure in tribal is also a reason for causes of Naxalism. Invariably, wherever the Maoist problems exists, there is a poor section of society. With no resource to meet their daily requirements. The poor include various tribal groups. However, their poverty and lack of ability to improve their lot due to financial constraints by accessing education, the government machinery or even legal remedies remains an important factor for their supporting the Maoist.

Through poverty limits there has been a limited exposure to these ideas of the younger generation, making the situation dangerous. The local adage is that little knowledge is more dangerous and embodies the problem in tribals. The younger generation wants to have the facilities that are available in urban areas, which remains a distant dream given the infrastrutural problems and the failure of governments to perform. Schooling is poor if not non-existent, hence the rural youth fight a losing battle against their urban youth counterparts. This forces them to return to rural areas, still aspiring for urban facilities.

The failure of the government to reach out of these areas is another major factor that aids the growth of Maoist in these areas. The governance is poor or worse, in certain places it is non-existent. Popular schemes take long to devise but longer to implement. Even while implementing the benefit always reach those who are the haves and not those who are in need. The failure in formulation and implementation of the right schemes at the right time, and targetting the right people is the major problem. Despite the rise of the Maosit problem the state failed to tackle it effectively by providing the needed economic and political measures. The state failed to perform its duties in short governance, or the lack of its, in these areas is a primary reason for growth of the Maoist causes problem.

On the contrary, the Maoist groups have been collecting levies from the local population. They collect funds from individuals, groups and even government officials as commissions for letting them function in areas that are under their control. This money is used by the Maoist group to buy arms and recruit new members, especially from the unemployed youth in tribal areas since Maoist provide a monthly salary and uniform, they have become popular amongst the unemployed youths. Thus, the growth of Maoist movement is due to various factors.

Remedies/Suggestion for Reducing Maoist Problems

- The state will create for an enabling environment for livelihood and employment opportunities. It will ensure that regional disparities are minimised for livelihood opportunities.
- Tribal youth will be provided greater access to banking facilities and savings mechanisms. The state will create avenues of diversification of agriculture for increasing the share of Gross

State Domestic Product of the primary sector. Irrigation facilities will be provided by promotion water conservation measures, watershed development and power supply. Departments concerned with agriculture and agro-based industries and institutions will promote warehouse, food processing, packing and branding of agricultural products. The tribal youth will be provided with technical skill through Self Help Groups and youth clubs. Animal husbandry, bee-keeping, lac culture, sericulture, fishery, bamboo product development, etc., will be strengthened by technical inputs. Credit and market linkages and value addition of the products.

- The state will also take protective measures through minimum support price for agricultural and major and minor forest produce and link with upcoming industries.
- The policy seeks to develop youth into responsible citizens of the state and promote leadership among them for involvement in economic and social development. The state will create opportunities possibilities and platforms for youth, especially rural and tribal youth for greater involvement in development programmes and reconstruction effort. Special programmes will be developed to involve youth in various national service schemes and campaigns related to education, health, environment and village development and reconstruction programmes. Youth development initiatives will build upon the strength of traditional tribal institutions such as Dhumkaria, Gitioria and Ghotuel. At the grassroots youth will be the *Vikas Prahari* to act as the key motivator.
- The state will work to ensure protection of its youth specially tribals from physical, mental, social and psychological abuse.
- Deviant youth will be reoriented through positive engagement in social services. District level rehabilitation-cum-counselling centers will be constituted for deviant youth under public-private partnership with civil societies. The highest priority will be accorded to faster socio-economic development in insurgent areas.
- In schedule areas the traditional Adivasi Social Organisations and leadership should be recognised as the implementing agency. This is a system that is based on collective leadership and consensus decision-making process. Therefore, it is ideally suited in identifying the real needs of the local community and

implement the schemes through community participation. Also because of the collective and community process, there is less space for corruption and more space for transparency.

References

- *Naxalite Politics in India,* by J.C. Johari, Institute of Constitutional and Parliamentary Studies, New Delhi, published by Research Publications, 1972.
- *The Naxalite Movement,* by Biplab Das Gupta, published in 1974.
- *The Naxalite Movement: A Maoist Experiment,* by Sankar Ghosh, published by Firma K.L. Mukhopadhaya, 1975.
- *The Naxalite Movement in India,* by Prakash Singh, published by Rupa, 1995.

5

Participation of Women in Terrorism: An Analysis

Randhir Kumar

Introduction

The concept of "terrorism" has over hundred definitions indicating that the essence of terrorism is basically fluid and dynamic (Griset and Mahan, 2008). Authors, government and organisations have attempted their own definitions for the term but no consensus has been built over a single definition of terrorism. At best one can understand the concept of terrorism from the commonalities that exist across the different interpretation of terrorism. Foster (2010), has noted the commonalities as *"...terrorism appears to be politically motivated; is generally systematic, deliberate or strategic; is directed toward non-combatant targets and uses violence and fear to achieve goals"*. An altogether different perspective of the term "terrorism" can be reflected in the saying that *"One person's freedom struggle can be an act of terrorism for another"*. Therefore, the term 'terrorism' may evoke different perception for different person. For this study, it has been narrowed down to the cases of violence which results in loss of human life.

The act of terrorism was being considered as domain of males, who played pivotal role, both in terms of planning and executing the violence. However, recently the role of women has been attracting much attention from the media. This instance, however, does not necessarily mean that earlier there was no involvement of women in the acts of terrorism. One possibility could be that women have always been in the supporting roles and only recently they have been coerced or motivated to take active participation into the domain of terrorism. This study would first give some instances of women participation in terror activities worldwide. Thereafter, it would attempt to explore and critically analyse the reasons for their participation in terrorist organisation. The study would conclude by documenting the probable consequences of such participation and the social and moral cost of terrorist activities.

The instances of women participation in terror activities can be found right from Gaza to Sri Lanka. Even Al-Qaida in Iraq, Lord's Resistance Army in Uganda, Sierra Leone and Mozambique, Chechen rebel in Russia, Maoist movement in India all have cases of women participating in extreme violence, such as suicide bombing and killing. All the above mentioned examples of terrorism widely differ from each other in terms of their specific micro-environment, gender perception and motives of the so-called terrorist groups. Therefore, a single explanation would be insufficient in satisfactorily explaining the complex phenomenon related to women's participation in different radical organisations. However, a few commonalities among them can be certainly found. The subsequent part of the article would attempt to throw some light on various aspects of women involvement in terror activities.

Women's Participation in Different Terrorist Organisations

The ideology of the terrorist organisation partly determines the level of participation of the women into the core activities of the group. This also means that the culture specific gendered perception would play an important role in assigning the tasks to a woman in a particular organisation. For example LTTE *(Liberation Tigers of Tamil Eelam)* of Sri Lankan and Naxals ideology of India would fall into the category of Nationalist movement while that of Al-Qaida can be categorised under radical organisation based on religious fundamentalist principles. Dugdale-Pointon has pointed out that "*In nationalist groups women often take part in suicide attacks as the group leaders exploit the women's desire to be seen as having equal status with the men. In the LTTE women were active in up to forty per cent of the group's suicide attacks and this level of participation is common amongst Kurdish and Syrian terror groups.*"

In the Islamist radical group Al-Qaeda the women are recruited but they are not assigned the tasks of suicide bombing. Here the gender perception plays a vital role in type of work allotted to the female cadre. Dr. Ali Khushaiban, an expert on Islamist groups, has observed that females are primarily given the task pertaining to logistical duties, collecting donations and convincing mothers and wives to encourage their sons and husbands to join the holy war. Melhem (2010) has further noted that the male dominated Al-Qaida do not treat women as equals *as* "They think that women do not deserve the honour of martyrdom and that is why they are not given suicide attack assignments."

However, a totally different set up can be found in the case of Palestine female suicide bombers. As per Israel Ministry of Foreign Affairs "Palestinian terrorist organisations, including Hamas, expressed support for the involvement of women in terrorism as part of the 'overall Palestinian war effort'." In view of legitimacy given by the Muslims religious leaders, women have been enabled to participate in the armed operations and suicide bombing.

Different women have their own reasons for joining the terrorist organisations. One common way of recruiting women is by taking advantage of their personal and financial struggles. The widows of Chechen male fighters are often brain-washed to avenge their husband or family member's death. Radical fundamentalist organisations like Al-Qaida forces women to obey their husband and often relate it with obeying God. Moreover, the image of their husbands being involved in holy war is reinforced in the minds of the women (Melhem, 2010). Another motivating factor for joining the terrorist organisation is the creation of an image of martyrdom. Stem (2003) has noted that killing oneself is no longer an act of self-destruction *(intihar)*, but rather divinely commanded martyrdom (*istishad)* in defense of the faith. A notion of female emancipation and attainment of an equal status with the men in combat activities often drives the women of Nationalist movement. However blackmailing, coercion and prolonged conditioning by brainwashing seems to be the major factors which are responsible for the extreme decision taken by the women to commit genocide.

Patkin (2004) has examined the rhetoric of emotions surrounded with the first female Palestinian suicide bombers. Suicide bombing redefines basic cultural relationships and merges private, psychological motivations with public, ideologically-charged actions. A deep sense of contributing to the cause of community or the ideology sometimes becomes a compelling reason to join the activity of terrorism. An Australian Psychologist mentions an instance where one of her clients, a female Palestinian woman studying in Cairo, confessed that she was having a feeling of guilt as she could not join the fight of her community in Palestine. She wanted to contribute by giving birth to a number of sons and groom them in such a way that they would be ready to sacrifice their life for the sake of Palestinian Islamic Jihad (Lindner, E. G. 2001). These kinds of guilt feelings are common among the women who witness their male counterpart taking leads in the fight for a cause.

A totally different scenario exists in the terrorist group in Africa. Forster (2010) has documented the participation of women in the terrorist organisations of Africa, viz., in Lords' Republican Army (LRA) of Uganda and Revolutionary United Front (RUF) in Sierra Leone. In case of LRA, women as well as young girls are abducted and are forced to join the service. In case of denial they are threatened with their lives. Additionally many women and girls are forced to be sex slaves and the future child of the pregnant women would be trained to become a part of LRA. In case of RUF some girls and women voluntarily join the organisation because they saw it as the only way to survive. Here too abducting the women and coercing them into terrorism is a common phenomenon. The women in RUF would mostly marry with a common soldier so that they get better share in terms of food and loot. Moreover being single in such situation would mean that she is a communal property for sex (Bah, 1997).

One important dimension here is to understand the strategic advantage for the terrorist organisations to incorporate female combatants. A probable gain in carrying out operations related to suicide bombing by female comrades is that they are subjected to a lesser degree of security check. In opinion of Melhem (2010), "Terrorists take advantage of the way men and women are treated differently in our society. Women generally enjoy a kind of amnesty in society that would enable them to take part in terrorist activities without being noticed." Former Indian Prime Minister Rajiv Gandhi was assassinated by a female suicide bomber of LTTE and the plot was successful partly due to less degree of scrutiny for the females. However, taking lessons from the previous incidences the females now are subjected to advanced level of security checks in countries like Israel.

Other than suicide bomb mission, women in terrorist organisations serve a variety of supporting activities that are vital to the existence for such groups. For example, women in Sri Lankan *Liberation Tigers of Tamil Eelam* (LTTE) and Naxals of Jharkhand have their duties in the battlefield, kitchen and medical camps. In Gaza, old Palestinian women apparently worked for Hamas to carry food, water, and ammunition to the resistance at the front line (Broadwell 2006). Some women in RUF camps are assigned the task of managing small boys and girls units. These units prime focus is on the mutilation and murder of civilians (Mazurana, D and Carlson, K. 2004). Additionally, women take in charge of food distribution in the camps and even decide on deployment of the child soldiers. Some women even reach to positions of commanding a group of men under her authority.

Female Terrorist – Media and Conflicting Perspectives

Females have always been portrayed as considerate, compassionate and as life givers to human race. It has been somewhat assumed that women are less likely to indulge in insensitive killing or causing blatant physical and emotional pains. Therefore, when it comes to brutal killing such as execution of school children in Russia, it receives a mass media attention. Media sometimes acts on biasedness by stereotyping the activities of the women in different arena (Nacos, 2005). A women involved in politics has a positive connotation while women indulging in any terror activity for whatsoever reason raises the eyebrow and are often portrayed as deviants. Terrorist organisations too understand that if an operation is carried out by their female counterpart, it would gather more of media attention and therefore strategise the terror activities accordingly.

Now here come the conflicting perspectives on the women participation in the terror activities. On one side, there are arguments that participation of women shows the intensity of passion behind the cause. The Kurdish separatist struggle attracts large number of female participants. In yet another instance, it has been pointed out that when injustice crosses its limits, women too shift to the activity of violence and work hand in hand with their male counterpart. The personal loss of dear ones and sense of seeking revenge sometimes becomes too strong urge which convince at least the women perpetrators about the killing or violence. If a terrorist is killed, the western media may represent it as a feat, while the other side perspective is ignored. It might become a cause for further attacks or increased participation of the deceased terrorist family members which may include both women and children.

There might always be a conflict in the human society and the reasons for the same can be innumerable. The groups who are in conflict may have their own justifications and arguments for defending their position and tactic. It can draw support from their female counterpart in the acts of violence and further justify their struggle. But the bottomline is that, whether the act of terrorism is committed on whatsoever pretext and executed either by male or female members, it has the same ghastly outcome. Such attacks lead to loss of human life, property and prosperity. Furthermore, it spreads a shockwave of agony and emotional trauma among the target population who may not have been even directly related with any of the conflict. For example killing of Russian school children by the Chechens can't be justified with any argument. On humanitarian grounds killing in any form is a moral hazard and should be avoided. Acts like suicide bombing not only leads to the death of the perpetrators but it also inflicts an irreversible damage of human life and on survivor's psychology.

Conclusion

The world is fast changing and witnessing a surge in number of females who are actively participating in terror activities. It may be voluntary or coerced, but the fact that terror and murder is no longer a domain of male sex anymore. Women play a number of roles in terms of combatant, human bomber, spy, sexual partner and domestic helper in terrorist organisations. Their participation in the terror activities can't be overlooked anymore. Sometimes women are exploited and used for terrorism and their participation is not of voluntary nature. Participation of women in terrorism throws new challenges in terms of counter-terrorism agendas.

The world has some other alternatives for the social change. Lindner (2001) has described "Moderates are those who have to curb extremism and invite their representatives back into the camp of moderation, of patient change, and long-term solutions." Lindner cites the example of Nelson Mandela who showed great personal strength and maturity in transforming his feelings of humiliation and distancing himself from the urge of revenge. He did not become a Hitler and contributed to social and societal change. Similarly, there is a need of maturity in the terrorist organisations and the concerned stakeholders to show some maturity. In the whole process of conflict resolution the gender perspective needs to be integrated with strategies framed for disarmament, demobilisation and reintegration process (Foster, 2010).

References

- Broadwell, P. (2006). *The Growing Role of Women in Terrorism* (1st Edition), Boston Globe, Boston.
- Cunningham, K.J. (2003). *Cross-Regional Trends in Female Terrorism. Studies in Conflict and Terrorism.* Volume 26, Issue 3, pp. 171-195.

- Dugdale-Pointon, TDP., Suicide Attacks — Terrorist. Accessed on 5th October 2010 via http://www.historyofwar.org/articles/weapons_suicide.html.
- Forster, C. (2010). Terrorism in Africa: The Role of Women in Terrorist Groups. Africa Intelligence's Gender Issues Unit.
- Griset, P. and Mahan. S. (2008). *Terrorism in Perspective* (Second Edition). USA: Sage Publications. p. 35.
- Lindner, Evelin Gerda (2001). Women and Terrorism: The Lessons of Humiliation. In *New Routes: A Journal for Peace Research and Action. Special Issue: Targetting Women*, Volume 6 Issue 3, pp. 10-12.
- Melhem, B. (2010). More women recruited for Al-Qaida terrorist attacks. Prince Naif Chair for Intellectual Security. Retrieved on 5th October 2010 from http://www.alarabiya.net/articles/2010/02/11/100088.html
- Nacos, B.L. (2005). The Portrayal of Female Terrorists in the Media: Similar Framing Patterns in the News Coverage of Women in Politics and in Terrorism. *Studies in Conflict and Terrorism*, Volume 28, Issue 5, pp. 435-451.
- Patkin T.T. (2004). Explosive Baggage: Female Palestinian Suicide Bombers and the Rhetoric of Emotion. *Women and Language*, Vol. 27.

6

Socio-economic Factors of Naxalism in Jharkhand: A Sociological Analysis

P.K. Choudhary

The roots of Naxalism can be traced in the state of West Bengal. Naxal movement was started to oppose the atrocities over tribal peasants (agricultural) and was initially concentrated under jurisdiction of one particular "Police Station". However, today Naxalism has spread its outreach in around fourteen states of India. The gravity of the situation can be analysed from the fact that in around 165 districts of India, 550 Police Station zones have been declared as Naxal-infested areas. Thus, as it presents a great challenge to independent India. Due to Naxal operations not only the development work of the affected states have been hampered but it also has resulted in amplifying the on-going social discontent among masses.

Naxal movement today has lost its sight from the fundamental issue of bringing a change in the economic conditions. The historical development of the movement can be broadly sub-divided into two phases: first was from its inception to 1980, and second from 1980 to present day. Naxalism fundamental premise were to create a movement to oppose *Zamindari* (A form of landlordship) system and safeguards the land of farmers (original tenants). However, once the violence was incorporated as a means, its focus from the primary issue was lost and end targets were also diversified. Additionally, it also resulted in relationship with other illegal organisations. In order to strengthen the organisation unscrupulous means of ransom seeking became a key tool. At times due to their operations many innocents are being killed. Every now and then media would report the blowing of railway stations or tracks and damaging the government property. Naxals have also posed a challenge to internal security of India. The state government of Chhattisgarh, Andhra Pradesh, Bihar, and Jharkhand has being specifically worried about the Naxals development in their respective states.

At present in the name of 'movement', the various fractions of Naxals are competing with each other to gain 'primacy' over each other. The sole motive behind this friction is 'wealth' generated through levy. The source of this illegal ransom seeking can be from the construction of poor's house, installation of hand pumps, digging of ponds. Even the grocery shop owners, petty contractors involved in business of coal, iron, opium etc. are not spared and have to pay levy to the Naxals for continuing their day to day business smoothly. The money involved in 'levy' is one of the most important reasons behind the violent clashes among the Naxals. It is only due to levy, the Naxals considers police to be their enemy. The officers and political leaders are targetted when they do not oblige to the illegal demands of the Naxals (See, *"Aapsi Jang ka Akahada", Levy wasuli ekmatra udeyse"* {Wrestle among each other: Levy seeking is the main objective"} by Rajiv Kumar, *Sanvad Manthan*, 7th July 2007).

At the time of formation of Jharkhand state, twelve districts were under the influence of Naxals. At present there are twenty-four districts at Jharkhand out of which twenty two have been declared as Naxal affected regions (See, 157 areas do not have rule of law by Ajay Kumar, *Prabhat Khabar*, 15th November, 2006; 10 Police station areas under Naxal terror, by Surjeet Singh, *Prabhat Khabar*, 15th November, 2006)

The outspread of Naxalism was primarily due to socio-economic backwardness. After India gained independence the policies related to land reallocation remained somewhat impractical. Due to this many people were devoid of land and it lead to social anger among the masses (See, Genesis of Naxalism due to asymmetric distribution of land, by Dr. Surendra Paney, Special issue on occasion of 7th establishment day, Ranchi, 16th February 2007, *Hindustan*).

At present in Jharkhand there are at least four organisations that have being declared as Naxal organisations. BCP, TPC (Tritiya Prastuti Committee; old MCC), JPC (Jharkhand Prastuti Committee) and SJMM (Sangarsh Jan Mukti Morcha) are in constant clash with each other for gaining supremacy. BCP (Maoist) is the largest and therefore has its fight with all the others. This organisation has virtually taken the state under its influence. The second largest group is that of TPC. The stronghold of the organisation is in the areas of Chatra, Hazaribagh, Ranchi, Palamu,

Gadhwa, Simdega, Lohardaga and Gumla districts. The third largest is JPC. The area of their dominance is Latehar, Gumla, Chatra, Lohardaga and Hazaribagh districts. The fourth organisation's SJMM (Sangharsh Jan Mukti Morcha) influence is within three districts *i.e.* Latehar, Gumla and Lohardaga.

BCP has its stronghold in five blocks of Gumla districts viz., Bishunur, Chainpur, Raidih, Dumri and Palkot. In Koderma district earlier there was dominance of MCC and at present MCCI has greater influence. In Pakud district, Kisan Vikas Samiti has established its grip, while in the district of Bokaro MCC and other small organisations are active. In Giridih and Chatra districts, BCP supremacy can be observed, however, in Chatra TPC, JPC have marginal influence and Communist Party and Jharkhand Liberation Front are also attempting to get a foothold. In Latehar distrtict BCP, TPC, MCC and Jharkhand Sangharsh Morcha are active. In Hazaribagh region BCP and Jharkhand Sangharsh Janmukti Morcha are present and TPC is relatively new entrant in this region. In Eastern Singhbhum district initially Gudabandha and Dumaria police areas were having influence of Peoples War Group, however later Dumaria, Potka, Ghatshila, Chakulia, Patmada, Kamalpur and SGM police areas too were dominated by Naxals.

Incidents and deaths due to Naxalism in Jharkhand

2006		2007		2008		2009		2010	
Incidents	Deaths	Incidents	Deaths	Incidents	Deaths	Incidents	Deaths	Incidents	Deaths
310	124	482	157	484	207	742	208	448	142

Source: Ministry of Home Affairs Government of India.

The above incidents and deaths are evidence of insurgency in Jharkhand. Call for Bandh, blowing up rail tracks, murder of cops and political leaders including Sunil Mahto and Anup Marandi (Son of Babulal Marandi) were mishaps of Jharkhand.

The Role of Socio-economic Factors in Rise of Naxalism

Naxalites started as a force to liberlise downtrodden and in the name of social justice and development, started to run a parallel government of their own negating the existing laws and governance. Naxals have devised their own laws and using terror as an instrument to compel the masses to follow their decree. This phenomenon was well-observed in the instances where Naxals decided monetary penalties and redress the disputes among the people under their control area. In the district of Latehar a parallel government was run which comprised their own courts and taxation system. The settlement of dispute was on the basis of proverbial "An eye for an eye" strategy. The culprits were prosecuted in front of public and the verdict was given without any delay. If the Naxals fail to organise regular "public courts" at some places then just for the sake of registering their presence, they would definitely arrange it sporadically. As an exercise of confidence-building and increasing their mass support they even launched development activities. For instance, in the district of Hazaribagh, construction of several embankments, roads, schools and dams were undertaken by the Naxals. At places where the Naxals do not run any welfare projects, they would compel the officers or contractors to pay levy, which can be as high as twenty to forty per cent of the whole project.

The strategy of distributing free blankets and medicines along with cash among the poor people was adopted as a positive image-building exercise. In the district of Chatra, they also take care of small day to day necessities which also helped them to create a goodwill among the poor people of the area. At times large camps to distribute clothes (*dhoti* and *sari),* blankets, medicines and food grains are organised for people who do not have sufficient resources to buy even these basic necessities.

Some of the socio-economic factors leading to Naxals movement in Jharkhand have been summarised below:

1. Disproportionate distribution of land and exploitation of landless peasants. Long pending cases related to land disputes in the court.
2. Exploitation of poor debtors by the landlords and money-lenders.
3. Lack of employment opportunities among the youths leading to joining the movement.
4. Lack of education among the masses leading to easy prey to the brainwashing by Naxals.
5. Insensitiveness of the government and terrorising the common people by police force.
6. Jharkhand's geographic location and mineral belts do not support agriculture favourably, leading to many people who do not have enough food grains to feed on.
7. No rights over the forest products for the tribals of Jharkhand (though Central Government had passed a regulation, however it has not been implemented forcefully till now).
8. Poor law and order in the state.

Review of Literature

The practice of exploiting the masses, where Naxalism has witnessed its peak, has its roots in Indian culture which can be traced 2300 years back into the writing by Manu (in *Manusmriti*). It can be interpreted from the writings that exploiting and mistreating the *"dalits"* and tribals was legally recognised and claimed to be right. When India gained its independence and the Constitution was framed, then mistreatment of dalits and tribals was deemed to be illegal. However, as Dr. Ambedkar pointed out that unless the economic status of the dalits and tribals are not improved, the legal regulations to stop the atrocities would be meaningless.

M. Tung in his book *"Be concerned about the well-being of the masses"* has mentioned that for the welfare of masses we need to distribute land among the tenants. Furthermore, he stressed on the need of encouraging agriculture production and its trade, establishment of cooperative entity and formulating policies to safeguard the interests of the masses. The policies to be framed should be incorporating the dynamics related to day to day life of the masses which include health benefits, food safety, housing etc. Once we are able to address these concerns of public welfare then the masses would stand with governance and cooperate in nation building.

Mohan Ram in the articles published in *People's Daily* and *Peoples China* argues that in order to get rid of capitalist expansion and dominance, at times it becomes necessary to carry out an armed conflict. However, he also points out that the armed revolution should take into consideration "time" and "space" (location) factors to launch it. In case the revolution is targetted against non-relevant aspects and that too without sufficient preparedness, it is doomed to be a failure against the colonialism.

In *"The Communist Manifesto"* Marx-Engels have mentioned that the capitalists have adopted strategy of an outlook where they seem to be like a beggar for the "workforce". However, when the masses started to work under the capitalist mode of production they observed that behind the beggar face were the hardcore capitalists who seldom care about the welfare of the masses.

Lenin in his book *State and Revolution* has mentioned that the exploitation of working masses is exaggerated when the state join their hands with the capitalists institutions. For instance in India there was a decree passed by the government which mandated the banks to be nationalised. Parallely, a clause was also added saying that the bank workers would not be utilising the bank premise or an area of around thirty feet of the premise for staging protest. This clearly meant that due to nationalisation of banks, the workers were also alienated from voicing their concerns from the banks premise. In spite of this happening the Left parties of India welcomed this move whole-heartedly citing it as a progressive development.

Rakesh Pratap Singh did a sociological study on a Naxals dominated area called Bankatta village. He traced the whole evolution of Naxalism in the village. His findings suggested that due to socio-economic status of the villagers and subsequent brainwashing of people by the Naxals resulted in the uprising of Naxalism in the village.

D. Bandhopadhyay in his article published in *Prabhat Khabar* has mentioned that in order to root off the problem of Naxalism one should be looking at socio-economic indicators of that particular area. The Human Development Index would clearly denote the shortcomings in the area and relevant steps need to be undertaken to improve the conditions. Therefore, unless we are not able to pin-point the exact issues, we might not be able to frame an exact policy as a remedial measure. Same sentiments are expressed in an essay by sociologist Yogender Singh, in which he argues that the ever growing Naxalism is a direct by product of poor governance, who still is reluctant to proactively handle the issue. If one needs to end up the Naxalism, it would not require one single big operation, but several small operations in the form of societal welfare.

P.V. Ramanna (2007) in his article "Intellectual support to Naxalism: The most dangerous factor" argues that the way Naxals present their arguments to the masses reflects that they are genuinely interested in the well-being of the people. In addition, Naxals would highlight the poor governmental policies and landlord's atrocities and any segment of population who has been ever a victim of government negligence or landlord's mistreatment would become an easy prey.

Vrinda Karat (2007), a renowned politician negates the ideology of Naxalism to be an extended form of Leftist thinking. She points out that in form of Naxalism a whole set of violent teams have come up, which in no form even remotely touches the ideology of Leftist government. They are in fact a form of terrorism and any claim of being a Leftist is totally a farce. Prakash Singh (2007) has pointed out that the Naxals have strategic tie ups with anti-state elements of other countries. For instance, there were evidences that PWG activists were trained by LTTE (A rebel group in Sri Lanka) on carrying out armed operations and manufacturing of bombs.

Surender Pandey (2007) in his article has pointed out to a striking fact that percentage of cultivatable land in Jharkhand is very low and if one looks at the statistics it would be evident that several lakhs of families in Jharkhand might not even have land even for constructing their house, leave aside the possession of agriculture land. In spite of around ten years of Jharkhand formation, the irrigation facilities are still dismal. However, ex-chief minister of Jharkhand Mr. Babulal Marandi in one of his writings on "An appeal with the Naxals" has pointed out that the forces which led to uprise of Naxalism are no more existent in the region.

Conclusion

The evolution of Naxalism in Jharkhand can be invariably attributed to the atrocities over the landless masses and government's apathy. When people found that they do not have a source of livelihood and are in the cycle of life long debt along with no provision of raising themselves higher into the economic status within the prevalent society, Naxalism provided an easy exit from these troubles. Utilising the poor socio-economic conditions of the masses Naxals successfully proliferated themselves into various regions of Jharkhand and at times did some welfare activities for the masses.

However, with the passage of time the Naxals have become disoriented themselves. With several factions among themselves the people's welfare and needs are kept aside and the new focus has shifted to creating an area of dominance. Today Naxalism in Jharkhand is correlated with levy seeking from the rich people and contractors working on government project. The Jharkhand government along with Central government has launched several welfare programmes and infrastructure creation projects, but the Naxals, who once were pro-development seem to be the most disruptive force in nullifying the government initiatives. In a recent instance in the year 2011, around 40 trucks of GMR group, who were constructing super highway in the Hazaribagh district, were burnt off by Naxals over the issue of non-payment of levy. Other than that, there are several instances of burning down of power house and damaging public property which has been built for welfare of several remote villages. Therefore, the bottomline of these incidents clearly shows that the Naxals are no more interested in the socio-economic development of the masses and are concerned with their own benefits. Earlier they used to be voices for the common but now they have themselves turned into the exploiters of the masses.

The masses still follow Naxals in various places either due to their ignorance or fear factor. The fear factor is now playing a dominant role as the village folks know that if they deny their advances they would suffer from their violent repercussions. It has been a common understanding among the Naxals group that the more violent activities they would carry out, the more influential they would be considered. Therefore, the Naxals have become quite aggressive in their approach creating serious law and order problems. The government has also realised that utilising only armed forces against Naxals would be futile attempt to permanently eradicate this evil. Therefore, systematically a broader framework has been implemented in which the socio-economic improvement of the downtrodden along with provision of livelihood opportunities have been given priority. With the overall prosperity of Jharkhand, Naxalism is destined to be phased out, however it would directly depend upon the prosperity bough to the masses who are lured by them.

References

- Stalin, *The prospectus of the Communisat Party of Germany and the question of bolshevisation,* Part VII, p. 367.
- Mao Tse Tung, *Strategy in Chinese Revolutionary War,* Part 1, p. 192.
- 'A report on the situation in the tribal area of Bihar', Bihar Tribal Research Institute, Ranchi, 14 August 1968.
- A letter from Marx to Angles, Correspondence, p. 199.
- Mao Tse Tung: Be concerned with well-being of the masses, 1 pp. 147-148.
- Mohan Ram, *People's Daily*, June 16, 1950 and *People's China*, July 1, 1950.
- 'The manifesto of Communist Party' Marx Angles, pp. 79-80/ F L P Moscow, 1949.
- Singh, Rakesh Pratap, *Naxal Prabhawit Gaon Bankatta ka ek Samajshastriya Adhyan,* The Society, Mahatma Gandhi Kashi Vidyapeeth, Varanasi, Volume 4th December 2006.
- Tiwari, Jairam, *Naxaliyon ki Sarkar,* Social Audit, Hindpidhi, Ranchi, May 2007.
- Suman, Amrendra *'Vikhandit hote Maowadi'* Social Audit, Hindpidhi, Ranchi, May 2007.
- Bandhopadhyay. D. *'Naxalwad desk ke liye bada khatra' Prabhat Khabar*, 7th March 2007.

- Ramanna V.V. *'Naxaliyon ko milne wala baudhik samarthan zyada khatrnaak' Prabhat Khabar*, 11 March 2007.
- Karat Vrinda. *'Wampanth ke naam par Honewali Hinsa galat' Prabhat Khabar,* 11 March 2007.
- Singh Prakash, *'Bharat mein naxalwadi aandolan' Yojna*, February 2007.
- Pandye Surender, *'Bhoomi ke asaman vitran se utpan hua naxalwad' Hindustan*, 16 February 2007.
- Marandi Babulal, *'Ugrwadiyon se ek Apeel, Hay re ugarwaad' Prabhat Khabar*, Ranchi, 2005.
- Kumar Rajeev. *'Aapsi jung ka akhaada - Levi wasooli ek matra uddesh' Samwad Manthan*, 7 July 2007.
- Kunwar Ajay. *'57 kshetron mein kanoon ka raj nahin' Prabhat Khabar*, 15 November 2006.
- Singh Surjeet. *'10 Thanachetron mein naxaliyon ka khauf' Prabhat Khabar*, 15 November 2006.
- Banereji Sumanta, *In the Wake of Naxalbari, A history of the Naxalite Movement in India*, Subarnarekha, Calcutta, 1980.
- Dasgupta Biplab, *The Naxalite Movement, A Maoist Experiment,* Firma K. 1. Mukhopadhyay Calcutta, 1975.
- Johari, J.C., *Naxalite Politics in India*. Research Publications (The Institute of Constitutional and Parliamentary Studies), Delhi, 1972.
- Mohanty, Manoranjan, *Revolutionary Violence: A study of the Maoist Movement in India*, Sterling Publishers Pvt. Ltd., Delhi, 1977.
- Mukherji, Kalyan and Yadav, Rajendra Singh, *Bhojpur, Naxalism in the Plains of Bihar*, Radha Krishna Prakashan, Delhi, 1985.
- Ram, Mohan, *Maoism in India*, Vikas Publication, Delhi, 1971.
- Ray, Rabindra. *The Naxalite and their Ideology*, Oxford University Press, Delhi, 1988.
- Sinha, B.N. *The Naxalite movement in Bihar*.
- Singh, N.K. Naxalities in Bihar fight for Land, *Patriot*, Oct. 11.10.1969.
- Singh, N.K. Naxalities in Chotanagpur, *Fronties*, Feb. 13.1971.
- Tyler, Mary. *My Years in an Indian Prison*.
- Kumar, Ajay. *'Santavan Khatron mein Kanoon ka Raj nahin'*.

Newspapers and Magazines

1. Sanwad Manthan,
2. Prabhat Khabar,
3. Dainik Jagran,
4. Hindustan,
5. Ranchi Express,
6. Aaaj, and
7. Saptahik Samachar Patra.

7

Taliban Movement in Afghanistan

Hamid

The location of Afghanistan is between Iran, Central Asia and the Arabian Sea, and India has given these mountain passes a strategic significance for centuries. At certain times, Afghanistan has acted as a buffer between competing empires at ideologies; at others it has served as a corridor through which armies marched, repeated efforts to colonise the country, most recently by British and Soviet. Their failure in the process gave the Afghans a fierce sense of Independence and pride. (Rashid, Ahmad, "The Taliban").

Civil war and a revolution are instruments that may be used by those who want to bring about a change in a country. However, such change comes with a heavy price when existing structures are transformed drastically from one form to another. The use of these tools comes at a high cost as it entails great chaos and destruction. Usually, a revolution is followed by a civil war, as the change is not acceptable to some and strong resistance follows. But a civil war can occur without a revolution, because of its protracted nature. The Afghan civil war has passed through different phases. Afghanistan's case is unique because at first it was the Socialist revolution of 1978 that started the civil war, but the revolution did not bring about the change envisaged. The revolutionaries were not able to enlist the support of the Afghan masses, because they were not convinced about their program and ideals. The civil war that erupted then still continues.

According to Barbara Walter, Civil Wars can be divided into four based categories: (1) historical hatreds, namely, groups fight because they hate each other and have no desire to cooperate (2) conflicts of interest in which groups fighting for control of a single state inevitably encounter conflicts of interest that are difficult to reconcile; (3) greedy elites, that are stubborn, threatened, or self-interested leaders often with little to lose by continuing to fight, and (4) security dilemmas in which fear and uncertainty during the war can ultimately sabotage cooperation efforts and perpetuate violence.

The Taliban was one of the many groups that participated in the struggle against Soviet Forces. When the Taliban launched their own movement across Afghanistan, they began to catch the attention of the international media. Once they overran the country military so swiftly and yet so peacefully, they simply could not go unnoticed. A lot of theories started emerging about their origin, characteristics and objectives, nevertheless, they were and still are a complex phenomena. The Taliban leadership has been calculatedly mysterious about the origins of the movement.

Who are Taliban?

The nature of the Taliban- who they are and what they represent- has been difficult for outsiders to understand because of the excessive secrecy that surround their leaders and political structure. The Taliban do not issue political statements or hold regular press conferences. Historically, Afghanistan was deeply conservative Muslim country where Sharia, interpreted by Afghan tribal custom, prevailed for centuries, but Islam traditionally practiced in Afghanistan was also immensely tolerant, of other Muslims sects. (Ahmad Rashid)

Since 1992, however, the bloody civil war has destroyed this tolerance, setting sects/groups against one another in a way formerly unimaginable; the one-unifying factor of Islam has become a lethal weapons in the hands of extremists and a force for division and fragmentation.

The Taliban have created a new model of radical Islamic revolution—the Taliban began as reformers, following a well-worn tradition in Muslim history-based on the familiar notion of Jihad, the holy war against infidels. Jihad-however, does not sanction the killing of fellow Muslims on the basis of ethnicity or sect, yet the Taliban has used it to do just that. (Rashid, Ahmad, "The Taliban")

The Taliban version of Islam may be depicted as a mixture of Islamic puritanism that is observed in Saudi Arabia and Afghan tribal practices. However, it is important to make two relevant points. First, these tribal practices are not uniformly practiced by the entire afghan society, which is more nuanced in its approach to religion and social affairs especially as they involve in gender relations. Second, these characteristics transcend the formal border of Afghanistan and Pakistan and also prevail in the lower middle class Muslim families of the entire subcontinent. In this environment, all aspects of enlightened and secular education are perceived as antithetical to Islam. (Ansari M. Ehsan, *China, Pakistan and the Taliban "Syndrome"*).

The Talibans anomalous interpretation of Islam emerged from an extreme and perverse interpretation of Deobandism, preached by Pakistani *mullahs* (clerics) in Afghan refugee camps in Pakistan, Deobandism is a branch of Sunni Islam. It arose in British India as a reform movement that aimed to regenerate the Muslim society as it struggled to live within the confined state or colonised state. The Deobandis sought to harmonise the classical Islamic texts with current realities—an aim that Taliban had ignored. (Rashid Ahamd, The Taliban).

History of Taliban

The predominantly Pashtun Taliban emerged in the late 1994 as a messianic movement made up of Taliban (literally, student) from the Islamic *madrasas* (seminaries) who were living in refugee camps in Pakistan. They vowed to bring peace in Afghanistan, establish law and order, disarm the population and impose Sharia (Islamic Law). Welcomed by, a war-weary Pashtun, the Taliban were at first remarkably successful and captured, until they captured Kabul in 1996. They express no desire to rule the country, but, ever since then- abetted by their Pakistani and Saudi backers particularly Bin Laden acquired the ambition to capture the entire country. (Rashid Ahamd, The *Taliban*).

By the end of 1994, Mullah Omar had nearly 12,000 followers and was rolling up the warlords to the north and east. With his promise of restoring the centrality of Islam to daily life, he created a genuinely popular movement in a country weary of corruption and brutality.

Kandahar has the symbolic importance of being the spiritual centre of the Taliban movement and also the place of its origin. The supreme Taliban leader, Mullah Mohammad Omar, made the city his strategic headquarters when the Taliban came to power in 1996.

By 1997, the Taliban had accomplished major military success in the civil war. After the capture of Kabul, they also began to prove themselves in the political arena, and they felt the need of forming an alternative government to counter the legitimacy of Rabbani's (Northern Alliance) regime. Aware that peace and political stability in the country would ultimately make them a credible force, the Taliban instituted a framework *Shura* (consultative bodies) to achieve those aims. Mullah Mohammad

Omar Akhund, then asked the Shura/Counsel (is composed of ten ethnic members composition based in Kandahar all directives and policies were initiated from here and it virtually became a political capital for Taliban controlled areas, indeed Kandahar is the current Head-Quarter for Taliban Movement) to give some political shape to the movement.

One of the remarkable characteristics of Taliban Leadership is that the top government official often switch from the battlefield to the ministry and back again each time following orders from Mullah Omar. In one sense this produces remarkable flexibility among the Taliban hierarchy as they all act as both Administrator and military commanders. This flexibility in the military command has allowed the leadership to maintain better ties with the rank and file fighters than might otherwise would be the case. However, the Taliban administration in Kabul faced problems, when any minister is away, so the decision are not taking place until the minister comes, these ministers worked without pay, something unheard of in modern times, they do not use government properties for private use. Curtailing expenses and refraining from indulgence in squandering and extravagance, regular salaries are paid only to professional civil servants and trained soldiers drawn from the former communist army (Ghufran Nasreen).

The areas controlled by Taliban had been subjected to drastic changes to personal behaviour. The Taliban had put a ban on wine and television, which is perceived to be immoral. There is also complete restriction on music, photography, and the painting of living things. The shaving off one's beard or trimming it less than a fistful is prohibited, as is having a western hairstyle, gambling, betting, pigeon flying, dog- racing, and sodomy are also strictly forbidden. Women are obliged to observe strict *purda* (veiling, referring to cover all body) girls have been stopped from going to school nevertheless, they were allowed to attend Girls Madrassa/school. The Taliban had established a new security service "The Ministry of Enforcement of Virtue and Suppression of Vice" for eradicating corruption and other vices from Afghan society.

The year 2001 has seen universal outrage at the offensive launched by Taliban rulers against Afghanistan's Buddhist. Past condemnation has not remained to non-Muslim states, several Islamic countries including Pakistan have been appalled to by the destruction of Buddhist statue in the province of Bamiyan. The incident stirred dual controversies about both the character of Taliban regime and the culture, religion and national heritage in the Islamic state. In his characteristic style, Mullah Mohammad Omar Akhund shrugged off all objection to the planned destruction of

Buddhist statue saying "my job is the implementation of Islamic order" nonetheless, the destruction of the statues has further tarnished the Taliban image (Ghufran Nasreen).

In 2001, The United States, in particular, began their pressure on the Taliban to give up the Saudi exiled, Osama Bin Laden, whom the Taliban described as their "guest" in Afghanistan. Washington blamed Bin Laden for masterminding the terrorist and suicide attacks on the World Trade Centre in New York and Pentagon in Washington on 11 September 2001. The following month the US and its allies along with Afghan began on campaign the night of October 7, 2001 with a program of air strikes aimed initially at destroying the Taliban's limited air defenses and communications infrastructure. By October 15, Special Operation Forces designated to make contacts with the major Northern Alliance warlords and started operation from three Areas Mazar-e-sharif, Kandahar and subsequent battle against Taliban forces at Tora Bora and during operation Anaconda in the Shah-i- Kot Valley, Paktia Province by December 6, 2001. Mullah Omar fled Kandahar ending Taliban rule in Afghanistan. The US Army used to designate bombing targets actually death rays (used laser) since they apparently caused defenses to vanish whenever caught in their cross fire.

Re-emergence of Taliban

The Taliban were made welcome in Pakistan in 2001, when they retreated from Afghanistan and are still made welcome because of a certain logic put forward by the Pakistani army. Which mainly contains Indian involvement in the country and in the region and the army shifted stance to Pakistani Taliban. However, Afghan Taliban have been staying peacefully. Despite their defeat at the hands of the West in 2001, the Taliban continued to exist, living as a guerrilla warfare operation based in the mountainous and largely lawless tribal area on the Pakistan-Afghanistan border. As time passed, and the American military focus was diverted to the invasion and occupation of Iraq, the Taliban regrouped and began to extend its influence in the southern part of Afghanistan. Their rise was assisted by a resurgent opium trade, which helped to fill the group's coffers, where observers say there is loose co-ordination between different Taliban factions and militant groups. Nevertheless, The Taliban in Afghanistan are still believed to be led by Mullah Omar.

Dealing with vast areas and limited manpower, the American led - coalition continued to hold the cities and highways, but, faced with an increasingly vigorous insurgency, was forced to cede large parts of the countryside to the Taliban. As casualties among coalition forces mounted and conditions on the ground deteriorated, and the Taliban began to spill over into Pakistan, raising concerns about its stability, Afghanistan became once more a top foreign policy priority for the Western Allies.

Another Taliban stronghold is the Pakistani city of Quetta, where Taliban leaders in exile are believed to play a significant role in stirring violence in southern Afghanistan. From Quetta, Taliban leaders including Mullah Muhammad Omar, a reclusive, one-eyed cleric, guide commanders in southern Afghanistan, raise money from wealthy Persian Gulf donors and deliver guns and fresh fighters to the battlefield.

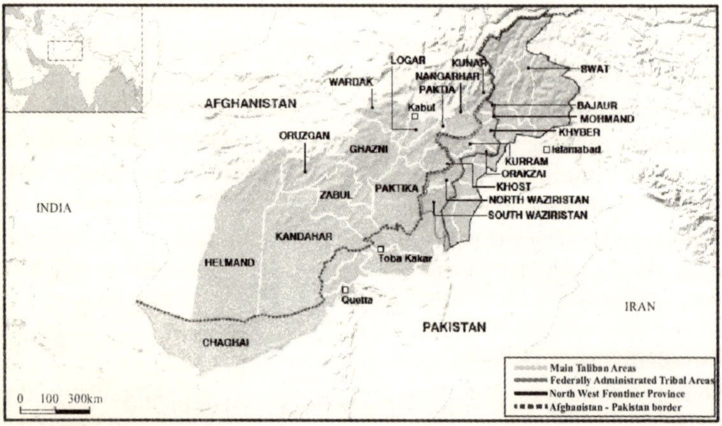

Recently, the president of United States of America announced a new strategy for Af-Pak and within the strategy there is clear indication that the Taliban and Al-Qaida pose an existential threat not only to Afghanistan but, for the whole world. Beside in the strategy there is an emphasis of international community participation to counter the terrorism (US department of Defense defined terrorism as: the calculated use of unlawful violence or the threat of unlawful violence to inculcate fear; intended to coerce or to intimidate governments or societies in the pursuit of the goals that are generally political, religious or ideological) and safe guard the human rights. As a result, the US plans to increase the US army in Afghanistan to 86,000, we hope it will not violate the human rights rather than bring security. "The strategy is not going to change in real terms," said one such former Western official. This is the concept of the three-legged stool—security, development and governance. It's called the 'comprehensive' or 'integrated approach' and it has been applied since 2002. However, there is a heated debate to increase the number of military force and provide incentives to tribal elders not to support the Taliban.

Reflection

I think it is a mistake to assume a religious mandate for the Taliban or even more of a mistake to think that the members of the Taliban are driven by real religious conviction. Of course, there's a quasi-religious leadership who may actually believe that what they're doing is driven by their beliefs in Islam, though it is far too easy to tear apart their rationale and definitely their methods of operation, which seem to go against many, many Islamic rules and laws — the biggest, in my opinion, is the targetting of innocents, both foreign and domestic, non-Muslim and Muslim. There is no justification for that tactic, but the Taliban leadership, despite occasionally putting out 'edicts' demanding their troops, try to limit the killing of innocents and civilians. But I don't believe the Taliban are basing their decisions on Qur'anic laws, rather trying to find 'laws' that fit their methods — a backward sort of logic, which is both dangerous and counter to true religious beliefs.

What I've seen over the years is that the core 'religious' group can keep itself more or less ideologically pure (at least pure to their own flawed interpretation of Islam) and, when they do that, they attract support and admiration from conservative Afghan populations, particularly in the South. With this support, they can win battles, either against foreign forces or corrupt government officials or others who prey on the Afghan population (and there are many who prey on the Afghan population). When they start winning, there's an Afghan mentality and culture that allows Afghans to switch sides easily and with few or no moral qualms. So, when the Taliban 'seem' to be winning and becoming stronger, Afghans cooperating with or working with the government in dangerous zones will often switch sides, thus swelling the ranks of the Taliban. Unfortunately for the Taliban, few of these new members actually have the same religious convictions as the core Taliban. Many are common criminals, people with grudges or the need for revenge against others, drug dealers and others. Some were fighters in previous battles and simply don't know how to do anything else. These new recruits start to 'pollute' the movement, leading to increased criminality, corruption and immorality in the group, which is noticed and resented by the population, who then start to turn against the Taliban. They start to lose power, the government /international forces start to win and people switch sides again away from the Taliban. The Taliban purge their ranks and become more ideologically pure again, and again start to attract more recruits. I've seen it happen again and again and it's very curious to watch.

However, there's a difference now. As the Karzai government proves itself to be incredibly corrupt, remarkably inefficient and ineffective and perhaps a worse enemy to the people of Afghanistan than the criminals and the Taliban itself; normal Afghans don't really see much alternatives. The government is horribly worse, so who else can protect them? Well, the Taliban. Even if you don't like them, they can protect you from the government and are seen to be fighting against foreigners. And let's be honest — there's a great deal of xenophobia amongst Afghans. Guests are fine, but when they overstay their welcome and are seen to be destructive or harmful or disrespectful, Afghans will rise up against them, very violently and very brutally.

These days, there are enormous grievances amongst the Afghan population. Development isn't working; money is not flowing to the people, but is being sucked up by greedy and corrupt government officials and foreigners; crime rates are huge; the normal person is perhaps as much or more in fear for his/her life than at any other time in recent history, certainly comparable to the Mujahedeen period leading to the taking of power by the Taliban in the first place. People are angry, frightened, confused and they're frustrated. Where can they vent these feelings? Who's giving them a voice or the ability to fight back against their oppression? These days, it seems to be only the Taliban. And the Taliban are increasingly good at appropriate propaganda to inflame these feelings and putting out exaggerated or completely false information to further enrage the people against government and foreigners.

The Taliban are not very clever, not very organised and it seems hard to argue that they have the best interests of the Afghan people at heart, but they are able, through trial and error and perhaps lucky coincidence, to exploit the problems of the government and international community to build support for themselves, despite their horrendous attacks and oppression of the Afghan people, both currently and during their period as the government of the country. There simply aren't other alternatives.

A serious problem the Taliban face and have faced over the past few years and which will definitely create problems for them in the long-term is their alliance with criminal elements they previously used to battle—drug lords, criminals, kidnappers, corrupt businessmen, corrupt politicians and foreign intelligence services (such as the ISI/Inter Services Intelligence Pakistan). They have joined with their own enemies to fight a common enemy. They thereby pollute their own mission and agenda. If the Taliban is ever successful, they will have to deal with these very powerful (and growing ever more powerful) forces who are now their allies. I do believe that the drug lords and larger criminals are aware that, if the Taliban comes to power again, they will very quickly be fighting one another, and they're most likely preparing for this. At that point, we'll see yet another civil war as we saw between the various Mujahedeen factions back during the Soviet and post-Soviet period. And I would argue that the criminal side is both better funded and much better organised than the Taliban. It will not be so easy for the Taliban to suppress and defeat these forces the next time they fight one another.

If this happens, who will suffer? Obviously, the people, the infrastructure, the development and the very fabric of the Afghan people and country. The Taliban are playing a very dangerous game and either don't care or are too stupid to realise it. Either way, it's bad news for the Afghan people.

In this, the Taliban have been destructively, horribly effective. As in the Pakistani Tribal Areas, the Taliban have threatened, bought off or killed traditional leaders across the South of the country and are trying very hard to do the same in other parts of the country. Without the traditional leadership, Afghans really do have nowhere else to turn. And without that leadership, there is no one to help them unite to stand up and say "Enough! No more!" Though always fighters and brave, they seem to be waiting for someone to come and help them see the truth and then to struggle for their common good.

In the past, Afghans have risen up to defeat those who oppress them. Yet now they are simply joining one of two sides equally guilty of the new oppression—government or Taliban. This is not in their self-interest. However, it is perhaps understandable. People do not spontaneously unite to free themselves. They need and crave leadership—someone with the power, moral authority and charisma to help unite them. They do not have this leadership now.

In the absence of that, they're being led astray by both sides, being fed misinformation and lies for political means and they are currently struggling against their own larger and long-term self interests. The Taliban, meanwhile, are operating a mafia-style operation. They threaten and kill, ally themselves with criminals and others to destabilise and terrorise the population, then tell the people how horrible things are with all the violence and if the people will support them, they'll make it all better. People are either afraid to say it or simply don't realise it, but the

Taliban are responsible for the violence and terror! Basically, the message is: 'Support us or we will continue to kill and terrorise you. But if you support us and bring us back to power, we'll stop killing you'. The Afghans' perception for Pakistan civil government and its Intelligence department is not good as they are perceived destructive elements for our country. On one side they help us in rebuilding our country and on the other side they provide safe shelter to the Taliban leaders and entice local Afghans to oppose the Afghan government. In south and Eastern Afghanistan our schools have been burning down in the name of Islam that the current government lead by Non-Muslim countries, spread anti Islamic literature and Christianity. What worries us (Afghans) being neighbour and sharing common culture, tradition and religion why they treat us as step brothers? We want to live peacefully and we are tired of war! There is no single family which is left without being hurt by this cold war, civil war and now Taliban insurgency.

But Afghans surely have the historical memory to realise that's simply not true. The Taliban have not learned their lessons and will continue to threaten and force and kill. They are not a better alternative, just one more very bad alternative facing the Afghan people. Currently, unfortunately, there is no good alternative and certainly not a local Afghan alternative. And this is a failure of the nation itself.

And let's not forget, for the most part, the Taliban are also Afghans. They are both part of the problem and part of the solution. But they are also Afghans' responsibility to deal with, not the international community. It is time to put the decision-making process and power back into the hands of Afghans, where it always rightfully belonged.

References

- Ghufran, Nasreen. The Taliban and the Civil War Entanglement in Afghanistan, *Asian Survey*, Vol. 41, No. 3, University of California.
- Mahmood Saba and Hrishchkind Charles. Feminism—The Taliban and Politics of Counter-Insurgency, *Anthropological Quarterly*, Vol. 75, No. 2, The George Washington University Institute of Ethnographic Research.
- Amr Sabet. (2003). Untitled Review, *British Journal of Middle Eastern Studies*, Vol. 30, No. 1, Taylor and Francis, Ltd.
- Biddle Stephen. (2003). Afghanistan and the Future of Warfare, *Foreign Affairs*, Vol. 82, No. 2, Council of Foreign Relations.
- Ansari M. Ehsan. (2000). *China, Pakistan and the Taliban "Syndrome"*, *Asian Survey*, Vol. 40, No. 4, University of California Press.

- Rashid Ahmad. (2000). The Taliban, Exporting Extremism.
- Drumbl A. Mark. (2002). The Taliban's 'Other' Crimes, *Third Quarterly,* Vol. 23, No. 6, Taylor and Francis, Ltd.
- Ghuran Nasreen. (2001). The Taliban and the Civil War Entanglement in Afghanistan, *Asian Survey,* Vol. 41, No. 3, University of California Press.

8

Terrorism its History and Observations up to 1947

K.G Vasantha Madhava

Introduction

In recent years Terrorism is gaining prominence among the public, thanks to the role of media. It is creating sense of fear among the people. The definitions of terrorism are many. Among these the easily understandable definition is that, it is a calculated violence or threat of violence against the civilians, in order to attain goals. These goals may be political, religious or ideological. To attain the goal, the violence or intimidations are used. The net result is the creation of panic among the common people. However, it should be noted that the terrorism is the result of despair and resorted by the persons who have lost faith in regular method to achieve the goal. In the course of study, we come across different types of terrorists methods. Very often we hear of terrorisms of war, international, domestic, the revolutionary and sponsored by state. Further we also notice the counter movement in terrorist in nature and cross-border terrorist movement. The last is unique because it is only in the Indian state of Kashmir. This has been a threat to the unity of India and its secular concepts according to the former Prime Minister Atal Bihari Vajapayee.

History of Terrorism in Pre-colonial India

History of India provides instances of the nature of terrorism known by different names such as guerrilla war and militant movement. All these movements resorted to terrorist techniques to achieve their goals. In support of these, we cite the following examples. In the middle of the fourth century AD in Karnataka, Mayura Sharma[1] resorted to the tactics of terrorist. After his humiliation in the court of Pallava at Kanchi, Mayura Sharma trained himself in war like exercise and overpowered the frontier guards and established himself in almost inaccessible forest at Sriparvata (Karnul district, Andhra Pradesh). There he grew so powerful that he was able to challenge the authority of the Pallava by extracting tributes from the tributary rulers of the Pallava. Further, he resorted to predatory excursions and caused havoc and created fear among the residents of the area which was under the authority of the Pallavas. The Pallava kings took the field against him but finally the Pallava ruler recognised Mayura Sharma as the king of his conquered territory. This led to the establishment of the Kadamba kingdom with centre at Banavasi.

Similar type of instance occurred in the Deccan region of Ahmednagar in the first decade of the seventeenth century. The Mughal emperor Jahangir truncated the Ahmednagar kingdom. Its Wazir, Malik Ambar[2] resorted to use of "terrorist tactics" against the imperial forces. In this context, he employed the local Mavalis, the Marathas who had thorough knowledge of the local situation. The Marathis under Malika Ambar evaded open battle. They had hung on the skirts of the Mughal army moved it on its way to a place of ambush, cut off its supplies and attacked convenient opportunity. These tactics to which the Mughals were not aware, wore them out and undermined their morale. The commanders indulged in mutual accusation and thwarted the plan of the general.[3]

After Malik Ambar, the Marathis under Sivaji adopted this type of warfare first against the Adil Shaha and then against the Mughals. By resorting to this type of war, the Marathas humbled the Adil Shaha and exhausted the Mughals under Aurangzeb. The latter chased the Marathas in different directions but ended in vain. It was by these tactics of warfare that the Marathas saved their kingdom which was in state of struggle for existence.[4] By using terrorist tactics against the imperial Mughals forces, the Marathas succeeded in breaking the back of the forces of Aurangzeb in the Deccan.

The use of terrorist activities by the Marathas were rarely used against their opponents after 1707 with the exception of Baje Rao second Peshwa. The striking achievement of the Peshwas was in the crushing defat of his arch enemy Nizam in the battles of Phalkhed and Bhopal in 1728 and 1738 respectively.

After this, the Marathas gave up these tactics of warfare and it was replaced by pitched battle. These tactics led to disaster in the battle of Panipat in 1761. The battle was not only a defeat but a catastrophe for the

Maratha cause.[5] The Marathas were too spirited to submit and they made their predominance in the Indian politics and twice collided with the East India Company in Fort William. In the second collision in 1803, the English commander Arthur Wellesley (future Duke Willington) broke the power of the Marathas at the battles of Assayes and Aragon. Further another English Commander, Col Lake subdued Scindia. Thus, the Marathas confederacy was shattered. However, the Holkar one of the confederates of the Marathas, was not easily subdued. He resorted to the guerrilla warfare against the English forces in 1804. By masterly guerrilla warfare, Holkar defeated the English troops near Kota (Rajasthan) and forced him to retreat to Agra. Further, the Holkar' force stalled Col Lake to storm Bharatpur.

All these broke the spell of Wellesley's magic. Hearing of these disasters in India, The East India Company headquarter in London immediately recalled Wellesley. Thus, ended the first phase of terrorism.[6]

The Terrorism in the Colonial India up to 1859

Between 1800 and 1859 India was under the authority of East India Company which was controlled in London. It witnessed a series of resistances and some of them resorted to armed struggles. These were mainly anti-British authority, local in nature and and these occurred in different parts of the country. The tribal risings were religo-political risings. Among these the prominent armed struggles against the English were the Pindaris and the Wahibis in central and North West India. These caused nuisance to the British. These open armed struggles became not only a nuisance to British authority but also emerged as a positive factor in power politics. They created mounting misery in Central India. They had intricate connections with the Marathas. The auxiliaries to the Maratha forces caused much damage to the Mughals army. In the course of the years these men known as Pindaris proved more ruthless more elusive and less coherent than the Marathas. They were "Jackals to the Maratha leopards". Their only object was plunder. They had no national pride. In the word of R.C. Dutt, the Pindaris, who offered their services to army chief who paid them, and plundered villages on their own account".[7]

They fed on social and political disintegration. They became a serious threat to the British India. Bundelakhand, the Nizamis dominion and the British territory Northern of sicar districts (Madras presidency now in Andhra state) became the victims of their raid and plunder. It was in this context the Governor General Fort William (Calcutta) took action against the Pindaris. After the successful conclusion of war with Nepal in 1816 and with grand design of military operations, Warren Hastings smashed the Pindaris once for all. The crushing of the Pindaris led to the third Maratha war. In the war the Marathas lost. They fell because they "were too divide to unite".[8]

The latter, the Wahabis, Muslim religious revival movement started by Sayid Ahmad in about 1820 and turned to violent movement against the non-Muslims. It evolved a definite plan to establish the rule of the Muslims throughout India after throwing away the *Kafirs*. The *Kafir* included the English and the non-Muslim Indians. They resorted to holy war known as the *Jehad*. Their presence as opponents to the established authority was felt in North West Frontier province. Its headquarter at Setana near Peshawar attracted attention of the Muslims far and wide in Patna and some places in Bengal, Hyderabad and in the Deccan. Its founder, Sayid Ahmad succeed in securing men and money from one end of India to other in spite of the Vigilance of the British police. Their *Jehad was* launched against the Sikh ruler Ranjit Singh. known for his liberal attitudes towards all religions. Sayid issued war proclamation against the Sikhs whom he described as oppressors of Muslims. Although he won initial success in the beginning, in the course of days the campaign turned into mad adventure. He failed to understand the military strength of Ranjit Singh. He crushed the Wahabis military adventure and killed its leader in 1831 in the battle of Balakot.[9] Although the *Dar-ul-Islam* met disaster, its legacy still inspires the militant Muslims in India. In other words, the Muslim terrorist moved in India owed much to the Wahabis.

There is strong opinion among the Historians that South India was passive to terrorist movements in the colonial period. There are many instances to refute the impression. There are violent movements against the British authority. Karnataka witnessed some such moments which turned into violent movements. These incidents are Dondi Wagh disturbance later spread to entire South India in1801-1802. Kittur rising 1829, Sangoli Raynna revolt 1830, the terrorist activities under Kalyana Swamy 1837 and the Bedas rebellion 1846 etc. Some of these rebellions turned into terrorist movements and caused headache to the British authority.[10] For instance the rebellion of Kalyanaswamy 1834-1837 became terrorist and closed the communications and public mails and took possession of the Government buildings. They were hard on the natives who supported the British. He was able to keep Mangalore within his possession for some days in the month of April 1837. But the British authority suppressed the rebellion. The rebellion of Kalyanaswamy is typical case of an early local protest against the British rule. The whole movements from the beginning to its end may be described as a primary resistance.[11]

1857-59 Uprising

All the above mentioned disturbances, agitations and armed rising reached their climax in the great rising of 1857 -1859. It was occurred by adequate causes and accumulation of adequate causes". In the course of the Uprising, the sepoys were fighting for their castes, the chiefs for their lost kingdom, the landed classes for their estates, the masses in certain areas for the fear of conversion to Christianity and the Muslims for the restoration of their old sway, yet all in their own way were fighting against the common enemy—the British. This fact gave the uprising of 1857 its own sweep and breadth. The end of the uprising was marked by the brilliant exploits of Tantia Tope. He resorted to guerrilla method against the English. He harassed the British for many months even when defeat stared him in the face. A man of great courage and a patriot of highest order, Tantia Tope proved to be the cleverest, the most troublesome and highly elusive enemy for the British in India.[12] In the end, he was betrayed by his own men and the British authority executed him in1859. With this, the rising ended in favour of the British in India.

The Terrorism after 1859 till 1947

The history of freedom movement in India is often coincided with the terrorist activities. They denounced the constitutional method to secure self-governments advocated by the Congress leaders. To achieve complete independence, the terrorists in different parts of India, resorted to armed struggle against the British. They advocated militant nationalism with firm belief in armed struggle. They were also called militant nationalists. They formed secret societies and gave physical training to their members. They manufactured or tried to secure arms and ammunitions. All were done in secret. Some of these societies set up vernacular Newspapers and these were used for transmitting their messages to their follower. They resorted to cause terror to the British officers in India. Their activities was confined to certain parts of India, but lacked in cohesion.[13]

Another outstanding terrorist movement after 1859 is led by Vasudevo Balwant Phadke–1845-1883. He represented the foremost frustration caused by the British policy in India. He was moved by the famine and inaction of the British government. It was the famine that moved Vasudevo to launch an armed struggle against the rulers. He was a courageous visionary who, for the sake of an ideal, gave no thought to himself. With a superhuman will and determination, he threw himself in to struggle for freeing India from the British yoke and intention of making his country a republic. In his own words "my mind was bent upon the downfall of the British power in India I thought nothing else. This idea haunted my mind". His intention was to paralyse the work of the Government. He further declared "If God will it we will be able to realise our ideal of establishing a free Republic in Bharat." For that he recruited armed forces mainly from the, tribal folks Kolis Bhils, and Dhangis. He attacked the money-lenders and the British officers. He struck terror in to the hearts of the Europeans. But reality was cruel to him. He was defeated. He was brought to Poona imprisoned and charged with waging war against the Queen. Despite this hardship Phadke delivered a roaring speech in the court room and utilised opportunity to expose the atrocity of the British. He was sentenced to transportation for life in Aden where he died after undergoing severe torture in 1883. But the legacy which he lelt behind inspired succeeding generations in their grim determination to liberate the country.

Phadke inspired several terrorists like Sarvarkar, Chapeau, Kanhere, Chandrashekhar Azad, Surya Sen (the leader of the Chittagong armoury raid 1930) and even Subhas Bose. Vasudevo Balwant Phadke was the first martyr of Indian freedom after 1857 revolution. He was also the first man to adopt guerrilla tactics of harassment of the government in the period after 1857 and let it not to be forgotten, that he was the first to proclaim the ideal of an Indian Republic. He was the pioneer of the armed revolutionary movement in India.[15]

In the course of the freedom movement in India, the terrorists played a significant role and contributed much to strengthen the freedom movement. The prominent among these are. Rampa rebellion or Gudem rebellion 1922-24. The Hindustan Republic association under the leadership of Bhagat Singh, Chandra Shekhar Azad, the role of Bahgat Singh the stir caused by his execution 1928; Chittagong Armoury raid under Surya Sen (1930), and the terrorist activities between the years 1942 and 1944 under Jayaprakash Narain (1902 -1907).[16] All these activities under the guise of terrorism became sources of inspiration. The leaders were sincere in their purpose although some of them disapproved the method of terrorism.

Observations

Terrorism has a long history with its ups and downs. The activities caused terror to their opponents. We know the activities of Indrajit in *the Ramayana* and Ghatodkatch in the *Mahabharata*.

(i) Some times the terrorists worked under a leader. But very often they worked without leader. For instance, the Marathas engaged in their guerrilla warfare against the Mughals between 1684 and 1707 without a single leader and even without proper capital. The Mughals chased them from place to place but they could not break the menace of the Marathas. In some cases, they worked and caused havoc with the collective leadership.

(ii) In the history of the Freedom movement, the terrorists exhibited daring courage and became intense nationalists.

(iii) All terrorists were militant nationalists but all militant nationalists were not terrorists.

(iv) The remarkable contribution of the terrorist is of the emergence of rich vernacular literatures. Their activities led to the compositions of ballads or lavanis in Karnataka.

(v) The terrorists despite their courage and heroism lacked practical outlook in implementing their programmes. Some times they worked at cross purpose. Their narrow base hindered their progress. It led to internal rivalry and squabbles. In many cases they lacked unity of command.

(vi) They were closed to the new ideas and techniques. Their activities were very often crude and outdated. Despite these defects, the leaders of the movement in the course of freedom struggle, won the admiration of the patriots.

References

1. Moraes G.M., *The Kadambakula, second ed.* 1, 1990 AES, pp. 1-2.
2. An abyssian by birth and rose to the power of Prime Minister of Ahmadnagar. As Prime Minister he had consolidated the truncated the state by good system of administration and liberal system of revenue and thus earned goodwill of the people. See Ashirbadhal Srivatsava, *History of India*, (Agra 1977) p. 576. Actually, the Marathis knew the tactics of guerrilla warfare but Malik Ambar utilised these tactics for his purpose.
3. *Ibid.,* p. 576.
4. Although the Marathas exhausted the Mughals, but with Aurangzeb on their side achieved the extinction of the Sivaji's compact and well-organised kingdom. In other words, he shattered the hope of centralised the Maraths Hindu empire by

breaking up Sivaji's kingdom. What emerged was the loose self destructive confederacy. After a century i.e., 1818, the Maratha confederacy collapsed through its own dissensions. See Percival Spear, *The Oxford History of Modern India* (second ed. 1979), pp. 44, 53.

5. *Ibid.,* p. 45. The catastrophe of the battle of Panipat was exaggerated by the British historians. But the Marathas soon recovered under the able guidance of Madhava R. whose force made advances in North and South India. It was only his death in 1772 has been regarded as the greatest Calamity which overtook the Marathas after the death of Sivaje. See R. Sathyanathaier, *A Political and Cultural History of India,* Vol. III Modern India (Madras 1972), pp. 67-70.
6. Spear, *Ibid.,* p. 112, 113.
7. Romesh Dutt, *The Economic History of India* Volume I, New Delhi 1976, p. 8.
8. Spear, Op.cit., pp. 118, 123-124 see also, Sachchidanada Bhattacharya, *A Dictionary* of *Indian History,* University of Calcutta 1976, p. 730.
9. R.C. Majumdar, *Three Phases of India 'Struggle for Freedom,* Bombay second 1967, pp. 9-11.
10. Spear *Ibid.,* pp. 288, 358. Suryanath U. Kamath, *A concise History of Karnataka, second ed. Bangalore* 1987, pp. 261-265.
11. *Ibid.,* 265 N. Shyam Bhat "*Rebellion of Kalyanaswamy,* 1834 - 1837, A case of local protest Against British Rule "*Studies in Karnataka History and Culture Proceeding* Volume II, Karnataka History Congress Mysore 1987, pp. 108-113.
12. Sen. S.P. *Dictionary of National Biography,* Calcutta 1974, iv p. 327, see K.G. Vasantha Madhava *History of Freedom Movement in India* 1857 -1947, New Delhi 1995, pp. 25.
13. K.G. Vasantha Madhava, *Ibid.,* p. 96, see Amithaba Mukherjee, ed. *Militant Nationalism in India* 1876 1947, Calcutta 1995, pp. 575-596.
14. Amithaba Mukherjee, *Ibid.,* p. 10.
15. *Ibid.,* pp. 10-14.
16. K.G. Vasantha Madhava, *Ibid.,* pp. 98, 111, 112, 145-150.

9

Terrorism Under the Shadow of Religion and World Peace: A Study of Unity in Religious Diversity

B.N. Sahay and Monika Sahay

This is a social phenomena that a religion unites the people of one religion; whereas on the other hand, it creates serious differences and disputes among the people of other religions. In the past due to religious differences, countless people have been killed than in political wars. Today also due to it, different religious organisations are harming or killing people of other religions. This has become a serious challenge before world's civilisations that how this socio-religious problem can be solved. In the present paper, the author has tried to analyse this problem and sought out its solutions on the basis of study of "Unity in Religious Diversity".

Today due to globalisation world has become like a small village. Man of one nation is linked with the man of other nation or nations through different communicational and conveyance media. Informations are being passed on to distance places through internet service. In connection with education, politics, commerce, health services, etc., man is visiting from one nation to other and as per their convenience and rules many of them are settling down there. Thus, communities of different religions are coming and living together. They are sharing their feelings and ideas including their religious ideas and faiths with one another. This is bringing social harmony among them (people of different nations). This is very important social change caused due to globalisation.

But globalisation has negative side also. It has favoured terrorism also specially in the context of religious terrorism. Today it has become very easy to get information of any place sitting at a distance place. Due to such facilities terrorism has also get increased.

In religious field, *Jehad* has been interpreted in two senses. In view of *Fakirs* (Islamic Saints with impact of Hinduism) *Jehad* is the act of fighting with own evil desires and acts (Anti-socio-religious acts) to control it. But some one has interpreted it as the act of fighting against the followers of other religions to spread Islam. In ancient time, when men were living in small *Kabilas* (Groups), such acts were considered in favour of their religion and society. At that time in different religions, their Gods and deities were considered different. But with civilisation development and globalisation, a drastic change has come in the world of religious thought. Now almost all religions' different saints have realised and preached "God is one". Thus, the inherent supernatural power in all religions and its activities is the same.

Sacred centers like church, mosque, temples, etc of different religions may be structurally different. The sacred performances within and outside these may be different; the performers of these sacred performances and the priests, father (religious) or *mullas* may be different; but the inherent supreme power 'God' within these aspects of religious life is the same. As per such thought if one condemns any other religion or its followers or harms or kills any person of any other religion is disregard to the same God (or *Allah/Khuda*). So considering this act we must always regard all religions and their followers.

Scientifically earth took birth from Sun about 5000 Million years ago. Then aquatic unicellular organisms came in existence from which multicellular invertebrates and vertebrates developed. Vertebrates includes different types of fishes, amphibians, reptiles, birds and mammals. Mammals includes goat, cow, pig, dog, tiger, lion, man, etc. Man's ancestor in early days lived in forests as animals. Then stone age, metal age, hunting and food gathering age and agricultural age came. Later on urbanisation and industrialisation took place. Thus, first of all physical evolution of the earth took place which was followed by biological evolution and it its later phase cultural evolution took place. In course of cultural evolution due to dangers of life and its fears, man developed the thought about the existence of supreme power 'God' controlling the whole universe. So, at the time of dangers of life, he surrendered to him and several times he got relief. Thus, beliefs and practices (actions of surrendering before God) unitedly gave birth to religions. Religion's highest level of sacred performance is the self-realisation, i.e., realisation of existence of God in one self. Different communities of the world developed their concepts of God (beliefs) and rituals according to their own experience and thinking. Due to this reason we find differences in different religions. Time to time followers of these religions did some modifications. Thus, religions are always changing. Now, due to globalisation all major religions could come nearer to each other and they agree that the supreme power 'God' is one and universal who is controlling the birth, life and death; in other words past, present and future of this world. Thus, we see a unity in diversities of world religions.

One saint Dr. Chaturbhuj Sahay of Mathura (U.P., India) on basis of his studies of different religions and realisation said that God has no certain name, shape or colour. According to him God is in form of light. The major religions of the world like Islam, Christianity, Buddhism, Sikhism and Hinduism (Vaidic) also believe accordingly. In some religions including Hinduism of later phase, anthropomorphisation of God took place and different deities in human forms came and are being worshipped. These deities are also considered as the incarnations of same God (*Brahma*). Thus, the same power being worshipped. So, there is always a unity in religious diversities.

Co-ordination by different great saints like Kabir Das, Tulsi Das, Hazarat Nizamuddin (New Delhi), Khwaja Moinuddin Chishti (Ajmer Sharif, Rajasthan), Sai Baba (Shirdi, Maharashtra), Langta Baba (Giridih, Jharkhand), etc., among different religions and their sects has brought major change in religious thought and brought socio-religious harmony among them.

Once upon a time, people of different sects were fighting among themselves for their own sects. Kashi Tirtha is known for Shaivites (followers of Shiva Sect). In ancient time, there were much differences in the ideologies of Shaiva and Sects. They used to fight frequently among themselves. Shaivities of Kashi did not like the entrance of Vaishnavites in the territory of Kashi. If they would see them in Kashi, they would beat or kill them. Their this act was not much different from present day religious terrorism. But above mentioned saints specially Kabir Das and Tulsi Das preached "God is One". All the deities are the incarnations of the same and single *Brahma* (God). There is no difference between Vishnu, Shiva, Rama, Krishna, Durga, Kali, Sita, Radha etc. Such religious ideologies brought unity and harmony among different Hindu Sects. Today all these sects' followers are not only living in harmony but in the same temple the deities of different sects like V*aishnava, Shaiva, Ganpatya, Sakta,* etc., are enshrined together and being worshipped. Today besides much differences among different Hindu Sects, there is a unique unity in sectarian diversity. All Hindus regard all the deities, their believes and performances of different sects without any discrimination. Hindus have 33 crores of deities. This shows the height of religious or sectarian differences among them. Besides, due to different saints a socio-religious harmony has been maintained.

Keeping in mind such religious modifications in multi-ethnic India where we see religious differences and communal disturbances including religious terrorism. Some religious co-ordination among different religions is urgently needed and it is hoped that such socio-religious effort will certainly bring social harmony and peace among them and if such idea is spread in the world it will bring world peace also in this regard.

In Indian politics a few decades earlier big political parties of the states and centre used to form government on their own capacity. But nowadays they are not getting majority of seats. So, they are compelled to form Government by making alignment with other political parties on common political agenda.

Time has come, similarly within the nation and world we should have some common religious points or agenda on which we people (of different religions) should agree, join hands and come on a common platform. For example we should agree on "God is one", the sacred centre, priest, rites and rituals and beliefs of different religions may vary but the inherent supernatural power in these religious aspects is the same. So, we all should regard one each other's religions and their followers; we should encourage participation in each others religious festivals and share in each other's feelings; in need we should cooperate with each other and help in eradicating poverty and fight against corruption; we should strengthen national unity and do so for the nation and world humanity etc.

There are a few such sacred centers scattered all over India, where multi-religious followers visit and do their religious activities. For example, we may take national level mosque of Hazrat Nizamuddin (New Delhi), Khwaja Moinuddin Chishti (Ajmer Sharif, Rajashthan), Sai Baba (Shirdi, Maharashtra). Besides, there are State level such sacred centers like Samadhi Asthal (grave) of Langta Baba (Kharagdiha, Giridih), Rishaldar Baba's Majhar (Doranda, Ranchi), both of Jharkhand, India etc. Such saints blessed and contributed for the welfare of all people irrespective of their caste and creed. So, they are popular among the people of different religions of the locality and the nation.

This shows religion does not cause social disturbance. It is caused by some miscreants who do such political activities under the shadow of religion, which creates social disturbances. It has been observed in several religious functions, that priests (*Maulvis, Pandits*, Fathers (in Christianity) or some senior religious followers or religious leaders generally condemn activities or beliefs of other religions. Such act create differences among the followers of different religions. By stopping such anti-social religious activities and propagating the message of one God and one religious goal of self-realisation, cooperation and national unity, etc., we may maintain social harmony among all the multi-religio-ethnic people. Besides, propagation of multi-ethnic sacred centers and their saints should be done in national and international interest. In long run, it will also help in bringing social harmony.

In metro-cities, people remain so busy in their earning of livelihood and other activities of their life that they do not have much time to think about their religion. Their outlook is also broad and scientific. So, we find social harmony and unity among them besides their different religions.

There are interior rural places, where life is very hard and nobody has so much time to think over own or other's religions. There is no social or political organisation to protect their religion or do any acts offence against other's religions. In such societies we find socio-religious harmony. For example, we may take the roadside village of Kargil (J&K and Laddakh). Here Muslim and Buddhists live together. It is surprising to note that here everybody is free to practice Islam or Buddhism according to their own choice. There is no pressure from their family or society in regard to choice of their religion. So, in the same family if one brother is following Islam religion, other is following Buddhist religion. If one brother being Muslim have married Buddhist girl, his brother being Buddhist married Muslim girl.

Such social situations give us a message that religions do not create socio-religious disturbance. But there are a few people who under shadow of religion, do anti socio-religious activities and create disturbances. Such activities should be controlled in favour of national unity, and as India is a secular country, we should have similar freedom as we found in Kargil, to follow any religion and marry any girl in any family irrespective of caste and creed. Such activities should be encouraged.

Several times impact of one religion is seen on the people of other religions. Recently, Salman Khan a popular actor of cinema world, Mumbai did the worship of the Hindu deity Ganesh. Several Muslims of Jharkhand and Bihar did Hindu *Chhat Vrata* (worship of Sun). One Hindu family of

Bihar celebrated Muslim Festival Muharram for the marriage of its daughter. Several Muslims are taking part in *Baidyanathdham Shrawan Bol-Bam Kanwar Yatra* (performed in July-August) for their fulfillment of desires. This shows religion is not a barrier in social unity.

Since ancient times urbanisation started in religious places. Due to different religious activities small industries also started there, which may be called sacred industry. Such sacred industries also started there, because in it people of different religions are found involved irrespective of their religion. For example, during *Baidyanathdham Shrawan Bol-Bam Kanwar Yatra* (Deoghar, Jharkhand, India) *Kanwar Yatra* (Pilgrimage) occupationally several Muslim families of Sultanganj are involved in preparing and selling the *Kanwar* (a dervice for carrying sacred Ganges water). It has nowadays taken the shape of a cottage industry here. In Kashi Tirtha, Vismillah Khan, a popular Shahnai (a type of musical instrument) player used to play Shahnai at Ganges Ghat (bank) and Vishwanath temple. During Chhath (Sun worship) festival several Muslims are found selling fruits. This shows unity in religious diversities.

Religious disputes are due to less understanding or mis-understanding of religious truth. It can be avoided by teachings or preachings of religious truths. For it, teachings of major religions should be started in schools, colleges and universities. It will give people better understanding of different religions and it will develop regards among them for other religions, their saints and prophets etc.

To propagate such ideas different committees should be formed at different levels like villages, blocks, districts, states and national and international levels (i.e. UNO). These committees will work for socio-religious harmony among different religions. As well as they will increase the number of members by making new members. Every member of such committee at different levels will make new four or five members every month. Thus, the number of such members will increase speedily in the nations and worlds. Within few years, it will be a vast socio-religious organisation on international level, which will certainly help in bringing religious harmony and controlling religious extremists (terrorists).

In this regard for further knowledge seminars may be organised and for it papers may be invited on following aspects:

1. Origin of religion and its changing forms in India and abroad.
2. Cultural-religious diversities and unity.
3. Sectorian diversities and unity among the Hindus.
4. Celebration of festivals of other's religions.
5. Disturbing and creating tension among people of different religions.

6. Politics behind the curtain of religion.
7. Marriage and other social affairs among people of different religions and social harmony.
8. Multi-ethnic sacred centers and their saints and deities.
9. Use of teachings of major religions and its future in India and abroad.
10. Other topics related to religion and peace.

References

- Betty R. Scharf: *The Sociological Study of Religion* (London, 1970).
- Caillois Roger: *Man and the Sacred,* (Illinois, 1959).
- Cohn, B.S.: Net works and centers in the Integration.
- Machim Marriott on Indian Civilisation, *The Journal of Social Research,* Vol. 1 No. 1 (Ranchi, 1958).
- Durkheim, E.: *The Elementary Forms of Religious Life* (New York, 1968).
- Eliade, Mircea: *The Sacred and the Profane* (New York, 1961).
- Hill Michael: *A Sociology of Religion* (London, 1973).
- Jindal Rajendra: *Culture of Sacred Town: A Soiological Study of Nathdwara* (Bombay, 1976).
- Kane, P.V.: *History of Dharmasastra,* Vol. IV (Poona, 1953).
- Mathur K.S.: *Caste and Ritual in a Malwa Village* (New York, 1974).
- Narain A.K.: "Varanasi" Souvenir 55th Session of Indian Science Congress (Varanasi, 1968).
- O'Ddea, Thomus F.: *The Sociology of Religion* (New Jersey, 1966).
- Saraswati: *Kashi Myth and Reality of a Classical Cultural Tradition.*
- Tylor, E.B.: Primitive Cultures, 2 Vols. (New York, 1874).
- Weber Max: *The Sociology of Religion* (London, 1966). *The Religion of India* (Illinois, 1956).

10

Armed Conflict in Kashmir: Socio-psychological Consequences

Aneesa Shafi

Abstract

The violence in the trouble torn state of Jammu and Kashmir has taken a heavy toll by influencing each and every member of society. Apart from resulting in the death of thousands, migration, economic instability, orphans, widows and half-widows...the violence has resulted in wide range of psychological and behavioural problems including suicidal behaviour. The issues of livelihood and survival for the members of the society become critical due to the presence of millions of troops and armed civil militia. The human rights violations recorded during the turmoil included political and extra-judicial killings, disappearance, custodial abuse, arbitrary arrests and denial of fair trial and destruction of property so on and so forth.

The broader objective of this study is to assess the impact of Armed Conflict on socio-psychological fabric of society. The universe of study is Kashmir province of Jammu and Kashmir state.

Armed conflict, terrorism is the major source of sufferings affecting societies significantly. The socio-cultural strains of conflict bear a deep-rooted effect on human psychology. A society whose psyche is shaped under the shadow of conflict suffers serious disadvantages in its march towards progress. In South Asia, political conflict and violence are on rise with persisting inequalities of the subsistence base of a majority of people and due to widespread political leadership destabilisation, widespread gender oppression, insecurity and violence are notable issues in many of these conflicts. The insurgency in Nepal, Sri Lanka, the border conflicts or state-conflicts such as Kashmir or the resources based conflicts over land, forests, dams and mines have led to widespread displacements of the populations resulting in significant sense of insecurities among the population.

In such stressful situation the impact of conflict on mental health is being recognised and addressed at as being related to an inter-relationship of psychological and social problems which together constitute the disorder.[1] Advances in behavioural sciences also point towards the interaction between biological, psychological and social factors shaping up individual mental framework.[2] Individuals being victim of terrorist situation suffer psychological stress and even proximity to such situations directly affects the mental well-being.

Death of a family member, arrest, disappearance, injury or sexual assault has long lasting psychological impact on survivors and dependents. Conditions prevailing in Pakistan, Nepal, Sri Lanka and North-east India and Kashmir serve as good examples of such communities which are suffering trauma in view of continued political and ethnic conflict.[3] Studies indicate that populations affected by conflict are not only affected by mental health problems but have associated dysfunction, which can last up to five years after the conflict.

This persistent dysfunction is linked to decreased productivity, poor nutrition, health and educational outcomes and decreased ability to participate in developmental efforts. While conflict has its impact on the entire communities, women became particularly affected because of their status and gender. Sexual exploitation, trafficking, transformation of roles and domestic abuse have a devastating effect on their physical and mental health. This has led to increased incidence of suicides particularly among women. The psychological trauma also becomes evident in disturbed and antisocial behaviour such as family conflict and aggression. Sleeplessness, fear, nervousness, depression, use of drugs are some more mental disorders aggravated by the conflict. The situation becomes grave when people become habitual to violence due to long exposure to conflict and availability of weapons.

Terrorism in the state of Jammu and Kashmir has affected whole society directly or indirectly. The issues of livelihood and survival for the members of the society become critical due to the presence of millions of troops and armed civil militia. As per government reports more than thirty thousand [30,000] people lost their lives in the conflict. More than 6,000 women widowed and more than 10-15,000 children rendered orphans. There are approximately 8,000 persons missing affecting nearly two lakh family members.[4] The human rights violations recorded during the conflict included political and extra-judicial killings, disappearance, torture, custodial abuse, arbitrary arrests and denial of fair trial, destruction of property, arbitrary interference into privacy, family and home affairs, suppression of freedom of speech and press.[5] The turmoil has led to a phenomenal increase in the psychological disorders among men, women and children. Daily exposure to variety of severe traumatic stress has led to an escalation in mental ailments as more than 40,000 patients visit the only mental hospital in Srinagar in a year, most of them suffering from post-traumatic stress disorder [PSTD]. More than eighty-five per cent of population takes anti-depressants medicine out of which seventy per cent are women.

The Study

The preliminary survey of Srinagar city showed an exceptional rise in the psychological diseases and associated mental ailments during the period of turmoil. The data for the study was drawn from a purposive random sample of 200 respondents who were either victims (if alive) or family members of victims. The study was carried out in Srinagar city. Srinagar has for long been the focus and attention of the international community mainly because it is the core political activity centre in the Jammu and Kashmir State. Srinagar city witnessed first armed conflict between the civil military and paramilitary forces which later on spread to other parts of Valley.

A majority of non-Muslims (Kashmiri Pandits) were concentrated in various parts of Srinagar who migrated to other parts of the country during prevailing conflict creating a vacuum in political and social life of Kashmir. The sufferings in the ongoing turmoil and the psychological disorders as its aftermath with killings, extortions, arson and custodial and other forms of torture became a daily routine and the rise in the mental disorders an exceptional outcome.

Objectives of the Study

The broader objective of the study is to analyse the impact of conflict on mental health of people in Srinagar city and also to assess the impact of mental illness on their socio-economic life.

Social and Psychological Disruption

The violence in the trouble torn valley of Kashmir has taken a heavy toll by influencing each and every individual of the society. Apart from resulting in the death of thousands, economic instability, changing roles, orphans and widows, half-widows, the violence and cruelty of conflict has resulted in wide range of psychological and behavioural problems including depression, anxiety, suicidal behaviour, post traumatic stress, nightmares and feelings of insecurity.

Daily exposure to a variety of severe traumatic stress has led to an escalation in mental ailments. Furthermore psychological trauma became evident in disturbed and anti-social behaviour, such as family conflict and aggression towards others. High degrees of psychological problems have affected the general health condition of people in the form of increase in the ratio of diseases like diabetes, hypertension and cardiac problems. Against the background of this continued insecurity, the uncommon psychological disorders form post-traumatic syndrome [PSTD] to dissociate disorders like hysteria, possessiveness to compulsive neurosis have shown an alarming increase when compared to pre-turmoil days.

The state is witness to one of the highest rates of suicide in India. Three cases of attempted or committed suicide are reported on an average day. Suicide cases accounted for only one per cent of admission in SKIMS before 1990s but presently the figures have changed drastically to eleven per cent of admission now.[6]

Suicides

The state is witness to one of the highest rates of suicide in India. On an average day, two to three cases are registered in the city's two major hospitals which attribute the growing occurrence of depression to the turmoil in Kashmir. This is very high compared to one or two cases a week, before the turmoil situation. It is estimated that around forty per cent of the cases are not reported as many casses in remote and mountainous rural parts go unreported. Experts believe that number of suicide cases has soared since the start of the conflict but the data is sketchy as the violence has made it difficult to do extensive and long term surveys. Suicide cases accounted for only one per cent admission in SKIMS before 1990s but presently the figures have changed drastically to eleven per cent of admission in the hospital.

In another major city hospital as compared to 368 attempted suicide cases in one year from April 2002, March 2003, an alarming number of 729 such cases were registered in the following year. The trend of suicide was more among females than the males. The stress has directly affected the tolerance level of people. A small domestic quarrel becomes reason for suicide.

Suicide has also become common among married men because of impotency which is attributed to mental trauma. A generation of youngsters suffering from depression and stress has led to psychological malfunction. Among 200 respondents the impact of terrorism in the nature of incident is tabulated as follows:

Table 10.1: Incidents Occurred in the Family

Sl. No.	*Incident*	*No. of Respondents*	*Percentage of the Respondents*
1.	Killed	109	54.5
2.	Missing	27	13.5
3.	Arrested	17	8.5
4.	Disabled Physically	7	3.5
5.	Injured	11	5.5
6.	Molested	13	6.5
7.	Physical torture	16	8
		200	100

As indicated in the table, a majority of 54.5 per cent of the respondents are witness to the killings followed by a high 13.5 per cent as missing in the conflict. The others have witnessed a detention of dear ones [8.5 per cent], physical disability [3.5 per cent], injury [5.5 per cent], molestation [6.5 per cent], physical torture [8 per cent]. The loss of life is an irrepairable damage and families of deceased persons undergoing bereavement are more prone to psychological stress.

The killing due to violent act in a family creates a sense of insecurity and fear in their daily life resulting in psychological problems. The study reveals that the family members of the disappeared suffer from mental ailments due to the fact that the situation does not allow them to come out of the trauma.

Due to uncertainty about the life/death of the victim, they live under the shadow of trauma and fear. The constant agony develops into a long duration of mental ailments.

Table 10.2: Persistence of Mental Illness after the Incident

Sl.No.	*Duration of Mental illness*	*No of Respondents*	*Percentage of Respondents*
1.	Less than one year	17	8.5
2.	1 to 4 years	36	18
3.	4 to 8 years	54	27
4.	8 to 12 years	58	29
5.	Above 12 years	35	17.5
		200	100

Mental disorders associated with the terrorism include a variety of stress related symptoms including behavioural changes affecting their physical condition.

Table 10.3: Psychological Problems Experienced after the Incident

Sl. No.	*Psychological Problems*	*Frequency of Responcess*	*Percentage of Respondents*
1.	Stress and Depression	172	86
2.	Nightmares	63	31.5
3.	Sleep disorders	174	87
4.	Aggressive behaviour	77	38
5.	Fearful	181	90.5
6.	Loss of interest in life	132	66
7.	Re-experiencing the incidence	119	59.5
8.	Vulnerable to Suicide	54	27

The study reveals that the majority of respondents 90.5 per cent have been fearful and experiencing insecurity in the sense that they are uncertain about their survival. Eighy-seven per cent experience sleeping disorders. They re-experience episodes of incident fearing to get victimised again and develop sleeping disorders. This is followed by 86 per cent respondents who experience stress and depression. They remain disturbed and prefer to remain alone. A large percentage 66 per cent of respondents has been experiencing behavioural changes in terms of loss in the interest in their life. 38.5 per cent developed aggressive behaviour. A substantial proportion of 27 per cent has developed suicidal tendencies. 31.5 per cent respondents also go through nightmares, they witness dreams full of violence and horror, 27 per cent respondents do not find life worth living and many times think of ending their life. However, fearing that it is a sin or for the sake of their family they do not actually end their life.

Psychological problems also have direct bearing on the general health. The study reveals that 100 per cent respondents suffer from other physical health problems.

Table 10.4: General Health Problems

Sl. No.	*General Health Problems*	*Frequency of Respondents*	*Percentage of Respondents*
1.	Hypertension	142	71
2.	Cardiac Problems	103	51.5
3.	Headache	49	24.5
4.	Gastroenterological Problems	115	57.5
5.	General Weakness	37	18.5
6.	Eating disorder	71	35.5
	Total number of Respondents	200	100

The data indicates a direct correlation between mental health trauma and general health problems like hypertension, which is rated highest [71 per cent], followed by gastroenterological problems [57.5 per cent], cardiac problems [51.5 per cent], eating disorder [35.5 per cent], headache [24.5 per cent] and general weakness [18.5 per cent].

Impact of Mental Illness on Social and Economic Life

A detailed analysis of the respondents' routines shows that mental illness has a large impact on the individuals, families and communities. Due to disorder the individuals are unable to participate in work and leisure activities. They do not shoulder their responsibilities towards their families. The family of the affected witnesses a strong impact of illness. They have to adjust and make compromises that prevent them from achieving their full potential, social relationship and entertainment. They set aside major part of their time to look after the mentally sick member. This leads to economic and social deprivation of the family. The impact of mental disorders in communities is manifest in the form of cost of providing care and the loss of productivity in quality of life. Mental disorder often leads to permanent disability, unhappiness and suffering. The data on the social life of the respondents reveal that 65.5 per cent respondents have got their social life affected due to mental illness. According to them, recurrent, intrusive and distressing collection of events, marked irritability, outburst of anger, sadness and disinterest in all social activities have affected their social relationships. They didn't like to join social gatherings like marriage functions etc. Most of the female respondents 61 per cent had stopped to attend all kinds of festive occasions after losing their dear ones.

The statistical figures while assessing the psychological problems experienced by respondents, displayed that turmoil has led to a strong impact on the life style of people as 60.5 per cent of respondents in the study revealed complete loss of interest in life in terms of not being conscious about their dresses, personal hygiene and bodily needs. Most of the times they didn't bathe, comb hair and even didn't change their old dresses. 51.5 per cent respondents have stopped watching TV, listening to music and didn't participate in anything which is entertaining. However 48.5 per cent respondents absorbed themselves more and more in TV entertainment programmes as a mechanism to divert their thoughts and forget their miseries. The findings indicate that out of total 101 married respondents, majority [72.5 per cent] found their spouses very supportive and caring towards them in their tough times resulting in the strengthening of their marital relationship. However 27.7 per cent respondents admitted that their mental ailment has weakened the bondage of their marital relationship.

Data shows that 61.2 per cent respondents with children (total number of with-children respondents is 31) admitted that their mental health problems had a strong impact on the physical and mental health of their children as they are not able to give proper etiquettes to their children. In most of the cases [36.7 per cent], their children remained sad and gloomy, showing lack of interest in studies [31.5 per cent], turning arrogant [15.7 per cent], adjustment problems with other children [5.2 per cent] and not taking part in sports and other extra-curricular activities [10.5 per cent]. Data on participation in economic activities and being economically productive do not augur well in conflict ridden valley of Kashmir.

Data reveals majority of the respondents [58.5 per cent] are not able to perform their job roles as a result of their mental instability. The findings reveal that hard fact that majority of the female respondents who normally were earning within their home from spinning, Gabba weaving and shawl making have altogether stopped their work because of their mental disturbances which has adversely affected the economic conditions of their families.

Changing Roles: New Challenges

The continuing conflict in Kashmir has imposed new and challenging roles on women leading to increasing numbers of female headed households. Responding to grave tragedies and emergencies in the family, women had to adopt themselves to these new roles as first generation bread earners, heads of households and craving publicity for justice, security and legal rights. Estimates put about 80 per cent of widows aged between 25-32 years with children below age of ten years. Majority of these women do not think of remarriage even if there is no taboo on remarriage in religion. The growing complexities expectedly add to circumstances of rendering these women vulnerable to mental health problems.

Disappearances and Disturbed Survivors

Official statistics put missing persons since 1990 at 13184. One per cent out of this has been declared dead by the Government. No satisfactory response to whereabouts of the disappeared persons have been given to family members of the missing who have been mounting enormous pressure for the settlement of the uncertainty surrounding the disappearances. The disappearances have a miserable impact on the survivors of the family of the missing. The impact is harsher on the economic well-being of the family incase the missing is the bread-earner of the family. The economic jolt is further augmented when the family members spend time and money in search of the missing visiting security officials, police stations, politicians, courts, prisons not only in their own state but also outside the state.

A few section of women called "half-widows", i.e., women who are unaware about the survival of their husbands has emerged as a consequence of the disappearances. Their number is estimated between 1500-2000. These half widows go through an identity crisis owing to the disappearance of their husbands, hoping falsely for their return in the absence of some proof of their death. They do not remarry for fear of social ostracism.

Social Stigma

Ninety per cent mental illness cases go unreported owing to social taboo besides ignorance and illiteracy. The family prefers to take such cases to physicians rather than psychiatrists. Most patients keep away from treatment owing to notion that anybody visiting a psychiatrist is insane. The treatment for the condition of psychiatric disorder due to stressful events is long term psycho-therapy. No one prefers long term treatments and go for short term remedies in anti-depressants, tranquilisers and sedatives which has shown alarming rise. Simultaneously, the society being traditional and religious oriented prefer to go to Sufi-saints for remedies.

References

1. *'Women, Human security and well-being in South Asia'* presentation session 19 Gender Issues, Wendy Harcourt, Society for International Development.
2. Syed Amin Tabish. 2005. Mental Health: Neglected for Too Long, JK *Practioner*, 2005; Vol. 12, No. (1).
3. *Op. cit* session 19, Harcourt Wendy.
4. Official statistics government of J & K.
5. Official record psychiatric hospital, Srinagar.
6. *Kashmir Conflict takes Suicide Toll.* 2004. <www jammu-kashmir.com>.

11

Pakistani Action Against Terrorists: An Analysis

Anurag Ratan

Pakistan was finally forced to take military action against Talibans. Today, Pak army is involved in strong action in those areas like Swat Valley. Waziristan, etc., where Talibans have been in command for many years. Nobody is able to predict the consequences of this battle because there is no clear indication or direction regarding it in sight. In this background, the purpose of this article is to analyse the status and direction of this battle and to give some suggestions for its success.

Background

It will be worthwhile to have an idea about the history of Talibans. The USA and Pakistan are equally responsible for the birth and growth of Talibans. Both had jointly created the army of students to fight the Soviet Union in Afghanistan and free it form latter's clutches to meet their purpose they provided them (Talibans) with modern weapons and other war equipments. These armed men became known as Talibans who had played great role in freeing Afghanistan from USSR army. Talibans were not disarmed or compelled to surrender their weapons. Incidentally, they organised themselves into an armed force.

Today, Talibans comprise many other groups other than original armed groups. In this group there are many Afghani migrants who were given shelter in Pakistan due to fear of Russian army but never returmed to their country, even after the withdrawal of Russian forces. There are certain Pakistani citizens who turned hardliner and there are certain people who were known for collecting money through their muscle power. Then there are certain foreigners, who migrated to Afghanistan following the fall of Soviet Union like Taziks, Uzbeqs, Kirgis etc., who had accepted the leadership of Osama Bin Laden in opposing the western countries and the puppet government of Riyadh. All these groups have no proper coordination among themselves. Nor have they any common agenda for their joint operation.[1] Pakistani Government was not able to understand the nature or ill-designs of the Talibans. Its sole motive was to divert these Talibans to Kashmir in a bid to destabilise India. But Pakistan found itself in trouble when these Talibans started attacking Pakistan and Afghanistan from their hideouts. These Talibans got stronger day-by-day. North-West Frontier Province (NWFP) and Pakistan's big cities became bloody targets of the Talibanies. Even the National capital of Islamabad was not spared and was attacked mercilessly by the Talibans many times.[2] It was an awakening call for both USA. and Pakistan. Now USA's Minister of State Hillary Clinton is holding both USA. and Pakistan responsible for the origin of Talibans and Pakistan's President Asif Ali Zardari honestly and categorically accepts the role of Pakistan for the birth of Talibans which is proving dangerous to its very existence.[3] USA provided Pakistan much economic assistance to fight against Talibans and pressurised it to control it with warning that if Pakistan failed to do so, the same would be done by USA. itself.[4] Taking serious note of the situation, Pakistan started taking, action against Talibans with the active support and cooperation of the USA. This started from the stronghold of the Talibans in Swat Valley situated in the North-West Fronticr Province (NWFP). Pakistan Air-Force is also assisting army in its operation against Talibans. Even USA's Pilot-less Drone Aircrafts are coordinating with the Pakistan's armed forces for the bombardment in remote and sensitive areas.

The fight against Talibans is in full swing. Pakistani army has been compelled to finish the Talibans which were created and brought up by it. This fight has provided some positive results. More than 2000 Talibans have been killed by Pak army and remaining six to seven thousands are hiding here and there to save their lives. It is proving a hard-task for Talibans to face the Pakistani army as they are no match to it neither in arms nor in training nor spying nor in organisation. They were like toys at the disposal of army which is itself bent upon destroying them. There is no place for them so they would not hesitate in showing their strength in cities like Karachi, Lahore, Islamabad, Peshawar etc. This is like a last cry before death.[5]

The action against Talibans has affected the lives of general citizens. Thousands of innocent citizens—young, old people and children—are killed alongwith Talibans. Thousands are wounded and more than one million people have been compelled to leave their places and forced to take shelter in other areas in Pakistan where they are living as refugees.

Analysis of Pakistan's Action

Pakistan's army is strong, trained and well-equipped with latest weaponary system. It is fully capable of defeating and destroying Talibans.[6] And yet it has been so far unsuccessful in tackling the Talibans who are neither organised nor trained nor equipped with modern weapons. Army action is being taken against Talibans only half-heartedly. It is not strong enough to wipe them out. This situation is highly frustrating as well as confusing.[7]

Mohsin Hamid categorically analysed this confused position of army in this fight against Talibans as it has to choose between Talibans and the democracy neither of which meet it. The hesitation of the army can be easily understood as it has been entrusted to fight those terrorists many of whom were trained by it and they firmly stood by the army itself and when Talibans declare, "We will decide your law, their voice is well-echoed by the Pakistan army's generals who have ruled Pakistan four times in its brief history."[8] It is well clear that the army action is being taken under the pressure of USA and not spontaneously by the army generals many of whom are fully supporting the goals of the Talibans and helping them indirectly. There is a lot of difference between army and the govermment over their priorities. The Government wants to take on the Talibans while the army stands up for anti-India campaign and invests its full energy to destabilise relations between New Delhi and Kabul.[9] The differences of priorities between the army and the government may lead to very dangerous consequences. The army may charge government for failure of its operation againt Talibans and topple the government to re-establish military rule once again. Pakistan and USA are not going to be much affected by it because Pakistani people have had long experience of military rule. The same position is of USA who are also habitual in dealing with dictators in Pakistan. But this situation may prove costly for India as the establishment of military rule in Pakistan has always been responsible for strained relations with India either in the form of war like 1965 and 1971 or the growth of terrorist activities during the regime of Gen Zia-ul-Haq. So, India is not in a position to welcome military rule in Pakistan.

Hence, India and USA both want the success of democratic government in Pakistan who could be successful in using its power and resources for the country's development by controlling or finishing the terrorists activities. The civill society of Pakistan and the democratic countries of the world are also supporting the Pakistani Government in its operation against terrorists. Even the Pakistani Government has not been so far successful in controlling Talibans. Pakistan's strong army, well equipped with modern weapons has spent more than nine months in its operation against terrorists but without success. There are many reasons behind it. The main among of them are as follows:

(a) Helplessness of the Pakistani Government

Pakistani Goverment is even today dictated and dominated by the army which has great sympathy with the terrorists. Pakistan Government cannot take any independent action ignoring army's dictates. Even Mumbai attack of 26/11 was managed by Pak army and ISI (Inter Services Intelligence) but Pakistan Government found itself helpless to take any action against them[10]. Due to this factor, it has failed to operate fully and in determined manner against the terrorists. Sometimes it differentiates between domestic and foreign-based terrorists, sometimes between the Afghani and Pakistani terrorists, sometime between the terrorists active in NWFP (North-West Frontier Province) and Baluchistan and in other parts of the country and sometimes between the terrorists active in POK (Pak Occupied Kashmir) and in other provinces. Another reason behind it is that the government does not want to finish terrorism root and a branch for Pakistan wants to use terrorism as a tool to achieve its objective against foreign countries, particularly India. The present situation is thus highly contradictory as the Pak Governments intention is not always clear about its action against terrorists. On the one hand, it takes action against them and on the other, it supports and promotes them. It takes action against terrorists under the pressure of US particularly exhange of military and economic assistance from the USA but it promotes and uses them against India and Afghanistan for settling its scores. Due to this contradictory position it has so far failed in its operation against terrorism and finds itself helpless in taking any action against Pakistan's terrorist outfits indulging in terrorist activities in India. That explains why Pakistan has been avoiding action against those responsible for 26/11 Mumbai attack.

Kami-a-Hayat is right when she says that the government lacks will and capacity to fight terrorism. Terorists, specially related to Al-Qaida. are very much, aware about the helplessness of the Pakistani governments.[11] Due to this factor they declare with self-confidence and boldness that the operation against Talibans would not be successful. It is very much clear that the Pakistan is not fully sincere in its operation against terrorists.

(b) The Soft Approach of Army Towards Talibans

Pakistan army's position *vis-a-vis* Talibans has been highly controversial. On the one-hand it is posing itself to be under the political executive, and is acting against terrorists in Pakistan but on the other hand it is helping Pak-based Talibans via ISI, who are working in other countries specially in India to implement Islamic agenda sponsored by Al-Qaida, Jaish-e-Mohammad, Hizbul Mujahideen, Lashkar-i-Toiba etc.,[12] dozens of such organisations have been identified and banned by Pakistan itself in recent times.

(c) Wrong Policies of USA

USA's policy towards Pakistan, India. Afghanistan terrorism etc is not in any way less responsible for the lukewarm attitude of Pakistani government as well as its army. During Cold War era USA considered the Pakistan its ally and India its enemy for achieving its objectives in South Asia, specially containment of Communism. For this purpose, it provided massive economic aid as well as military assistance to Pakistan. Pakistan exploiting this situation tried to match its military power with India and purchased such weapons as were not available to Indian army. In this way, it was successful in getting USA. aid in the name of containing communism and fighting with Russian army in Afghanistan. But it used this economic and military assistance in its military preparation against India. This fact is well-accepted by USA's diplomats, intellectuals and the spokesmen of foreign ministry. In spite of that this blunder is repeated by the present President Barrack Obama.[13] Recently, he has sanctioned 15 billion dollar to Pakistan for the fight against terrorism. India's apprehension is that Pakistan would misuse this assistance against India.

(d) Adverse Effect of Army Action

Pak Government's action against Talibans with the massive support from USA is proving costly for its common citizens, due to heavy loss of people's life and property. Many innocent people—men, women and children are being killed in massive battle between Army and Talibans. That is why common people suffer more than army or Talibans.[14] It is due to this factor that army is fast losing the sympathy of the people of the area which may prove costly for this operation.

Due to above shortcomings, Pakistan army will never succeed in its operation against terrorists. For achieving success, it requires to change its approach and strategy in certain important aspects. Here below are given a few suggestions for such a change:

(a) ***Pakistan's clear stand:*** Pakistan must specify the purpose of this operation. Honestly, speaking, Pakistan's intentions are not clear in this regard.[15] It should be made very clear to Pakistan that although the fight against terrorism is the concern of the whole world its final outcome would depend upon the role of Pakistan itself. There is no possibility of its end without destroying the basie ideological and power structure of terrorism which operates parallel to military operation.[16] For this, Pakistan must act against all terrorist organisations which are proving themselves as the enemies of mankind. V.P. Vedik is absolutely right when he points out that. "It is not enough to fight with its Talibans but also to prevent them from acting against neighbouring countries. If they are rooted out from Pakistan much would not be achieved. They would find their way in neighbouring countries. There is need to wipe them out by root."[17]

(b) ***Economic and social factors:*** The research conducted for the study of terrorism in Pakistan alongwith other countries clearly indicates that the socio-economic factors are the main causes behind the birth and growth of terrorism. Problems like illiteracy, poverty and unemployment provide ample fertile ground for the growth of terrorism. Most of terrorists are poor illiterate and unemployed youth. The growing poverty of Pakistan provides open ground for the growth and rise of terrorism. Due to failure of the political leadership and government. the recruitment agents affiliated to various terrorists group are successful in raising youth for their work. The agents of terrorists teach the lessons of gun-power and wrong aims of life at Dhabas and Tea-shops along roadside in Punjab and other provinces which often lead to death. It is better option

than the life of frustration.[18] So there is an urgency on the part of government not to resort to military action against Talibans but also to prevent terrorism on economic and social front and take immediate and firm steps against the problems like poverty, unemployment, illiteracy etc. As long as these problems exist, there will be no war to end terrorism from its root.

(c) ***The liability of people (Civil Society):*** There is a great responsibility for the civil society of Pakistan to oppose the extremism propounded by Al-Qaida and Talibans, based on the wrong interpretations of the teachings of Islam. If Pakistani civil society remains as inactive as earlier, it would have to face dictatorial regime again. There is no possibility of ending terrorism without the active cooperation of the people.

(d) ***Change of attitude towards terrorism:*** The attitude of both USA and Pakistan towards terrorism is based on false assumptions and double standings. USA is against AI-Qaida and Talibans but does not seem to worry about the growing and increasing terrorist organisations in Pakistan which are engaged in disruptive violent activities in different parts of India in their own style specially in J and K. The position of Pakistan is even worse. It is taking military action against the disruptive activities of Talibans and AI-Qaida in different areas of Pakistan (due to assistance of billion dollars from USA) but not taking any action against Pakistan-based terrorist groups which spread terrorism against other countries, specially in India: it is rather supporting them. Even it has opened way for communication with AI-Qaida and Talibans to seek their help or use them against India. It has so far not taken any action against the Pak terror groups encouraging terrorist activities in India. Dawood Ibrahim the man associated with many terrorist organisations and responsible for terrorist violence and disruption in Indian, has taken shelter in Pakistan, ignoring India's repeated requests. Pakistani Government has not so far taken any action against him but is treating him like an official guest. Pakistan is also hesitating in taking any action against Hafiz Saeed, the man responsible for 26/11 Mumbai attack sidetracking his criminal records. As long as Pakistan does not prevent terrorists from indulging in terrorist activities or desist from using them against India, there would be no hope left for the end of terrorists as a whole. Pakistan would have to change

its outlook against India. Ved Pratap Vaidik writes. "If Pakistan has a friendly approach towards India it must open way and wipe out the Punjabi and Kashmiri Talibans. Friendship towards neighbouring countries and the end of Talibans are the two sides of the same coin."[19]

USA also would have to change its attitude and approach towards terrorism. It must stop making any differentiation between the terrorism which concerns itself and the other which is causing destruction in India and other countries. Both terrorisms and Talibans are two sides of the same coin. By differentiating them USA is deceiving the whole world and itself. USA must realise that the terrorist organisations active in Pakistan are as opposed to USA as to any non-Muslim countries or persons or groups who are not convinced with their policy or aims and their motto which is to establish Islamic empire in the whole world. The Pakistani Taliban leader Baitullah Masud openly declared that the world peace could be achieved only through *Jihad*.[20] The enemies of these organisation are those countries and organisations who are aligned with USA or opposed to Islamic imperialism.[21] USA must revise its Pakistan policy to tackle the Islamic terrorists-based in Pakistan, For that it will have to persuade and convince Pakistani Government.[22] If USA really wants to overcome Talibans. it must radically change its outlook as well as its basic approach and policy towards terrorism.[23]

Conclusion

On the basis of above analysis, it is amply clear that the present government in Pakistan is not in a position to end terrorism. The actions of USA and Pakistan are not adequate. Still that they are taking action against Talibans and Al-Qaida militants, does generate some hope. So, it is welcome and must be given full support and co-operation by the whole world.

References

1. Peter Preston, 'Mushkil Nahin Hai Taliban Ko Harana'. *Hindustan* (Hindi). June 2, 2009. p. 12.
2. Sushil Sharma. 'Pados Mein Charontaraf Ashanti aur Asthiratha (Jhulasta Pakistan) *Hindustan* (Hindi), May 29, 2009. p. 9.

3. *Hindustan*. June 1, 2009.
4. Ved Pratap Vaidik. 'Lahore Hamle Se Sabak Sikhe Pakistan'. *Rashtriya Sahara* (Hindi). May 29, 2009, p. 16.
5. *Ibid.*
6. Mohsin Hamid. 'Pakistani Fauz Ko Had Pahachanni Hogi'. *Hindustan*. May 14, 2009. p. 12.
7. *Ibid.*
8. *Ibid.*
9. Peter Preston, *op. cit.*
10. Sushil Sharma, *op. cit.*
11. Kamilla Hayat. 'Ujadi Ummeedon Ka Desh'. *Dainik Jagaran* (Hindi). April 21, 2009, p. 6.
12. Mohsin I. Hamid. *op cit.*
13. Brahma Chellaney. 'Galti Doharate Obama'. *Dainik Jagran*. May 7, 2009. p. 8.
14. Kathy Gennan, 'Civilians Suffer Most as Taliban Wedges Jihad'. *The Pioneer*, May 29, 2009, p. 9.
15. Peter Preston. *op. cit.*
16. *Rashtriya Sahara* (Editional). May 29, 2009, p. 10.
17. Ved Pratap Vaidik. *op. cit.*
18. Kamilla Hayat. *op. cit.*
19. Ved Pratap Vaidik. *op. cit.*
20. *Times of India*, May 10, 2009.
21. K. Subrahmanyam. "Obama Ki Pakistan Niti". *Dainik Jagran*. April 5, 2009. p. 8.
22. Milton Bearden. *Afghan Chakravieu Ke Liye Nai Niti*. April 16, 2009. p. 12.
23. Brahma Chellaney. *op. cit.*

12

Violence, Terrorism and Religious Radicalism: Intertextuality as Sociological Paradigm

Eduardo M. Domingo, Ed.D.

Abstract

When people are beginning to believe that fundamentalism is the reason for the terror and havoc perpetuated by religious radicals, this study cautions that it may not be so. It intends to clarify the relationship between fundamentalism, religious radicalism and terrorism. Applying Intertextuality as a sociological paradigm, it suggests the re-reading of the different texts and contexts of violence and terrorism. It will try to demonstrate that the relationship of religion and terrorism is in fact ambivalent.

Rooted upon specific assumptions, sociology of religion must look into the contexts of the texts on violence and terrorism. Inappropriate reading and understanding of texts and contexts may readily lead to the misappropriations and misapplications not only of texts but also of implied sociological paradigms and theories. Re-reading the contexts of historical events, intellectual currents, cultural shifts and political events is therefore a must to bring new light to a better understanding and application of the sociology of violence and terrorism.

Although deplorable, terrorism and religious radicalism is rapidly creeping into the lives of the very structure; of religions and faith-based communities. Despite the efforts both of faith-based and government sponsored dialogues, kidnappings, massacres and beheadings still besiege the media headlines.[1] Consciously or unconsciously, people-seemed to have started associating fundamentalism with the religious radicalism. After the (in) famous 9/11 New York attack, some Muslim scholars even think that the-literal understanding and interpretation of Islamic Teachings is being taken as a ploy by certain Muslim Radicals to justify their terrorist acts.[2]

While Muslims have taken upon themselves the responsibility for terrorist attacks in these last few years,[3] commentators and columnists have also slowly subscribed these to fundamental Islam.[4] Some of the thoughts of Osama bin Ladin on the 9/11 strike indeed makes one to consider such links:

"According to their own admissions, the share of the; losses on Wall Street reached 16 per cent...a record...which has never happened since: the: market opened 230 years ago). The gross amount traded in that market reached US $4 trillion...so 16 per cent of 4 trillion is 640 billion dollars. This amount, for example, is the budget of Sudan for 640 years. They have lost this due to an attack that happened with the success of Allah lasting one hour only. The daily income of the American nation is 20 billion dollars. The first week they die! not work at all due to the psychological shock of the attack... so one week comes up to 140 billion...and if added to the 640 billion we've reached 880 billion. The cost of the building and construction losses; let us say more than 30 billion dollars. Then they have fired or terminated until today...from the airline companies more-than 170,000 employees...and American studies and analysis have mentioned that seventy per cent of the people until today, still suffer from depression and psychological trauma alter the incident of the two towers. One of the well-known American hotel companies, Intercontinental, has fired 20,000 employees...so watch as the amount reaches no less than one trillion dollars by the lowest estimate:, thanks to Allah's grace, due to these successful and blessed attacks. We implore: Allah to accept those brothers within the ranks of the martyrs, and to admit them to the highest levels of Paradise."[5]

Meanwhile, harassments against Muslims has been growing.[6]

Would it therefore be appropriate to conclude that religious fundamentalism is the perpetrator to the radicalism and violence we are all regrettably experiencing?

When people are beginning to believe that fundamentalism is the reason for the terror and havoc perpetuated by religious radicals, this stydy cautions that it may not be so. It intends to clarify the relationship between fundamentalism, religious radicalism and terrorism. Applying Intertextuality as a sociological paradigm, it suggests the understanding of the different texts and contexts of violence and terrorism. It will try to demonstrate that the relationship is in fact ambivalent.

2. Texts on Fundamentalism, Radicalism and Terrorism

Let us first take a look at the different texts on fundamentalism and religious radicalism being related to terrorism.

1. Some say that the Religious *Madrasas* or schools play an important role in relation to religious radicalism. *Madrasas* even serve as reservoirs for recruitment to violent and radical organisations. The fact is, however, that the relationship of *madrasas* to the mounting violence and terrorist activities is more often asserted than proven.[7]
2. Some think that the aggressive violence found in sacred texts justify fundamentalist radicals. The texts imply the correlation of violence to fundamentalism. Other scholars, however, read such violence as compensation for the feelings of powerlessness and despair of the people who recorded the sacred texts.[8]
3. Some radicals or religious fanatics take refuge in the very foundations of their religions. Openly claiming to be members, while in fact, they are not, they advocate principles that are contrary to the very tenets of the faith or religion they claim to belong.[9]
4. Studies show that Religious Fanaticism may breed religious radicalism, violence and terrorism. Other studies, however, also show that there are other principal breeding grounds for religious radicalism and terrorism which are socio-economic in nature.[10]
5. Based on an evolutionary perspective on the origin of religious violence, the religious moral psychology found in religion does not only generate pro-social and constructive morality but also prejudice and violence as well. The problem is to understand The conditions that trigger one or the other.[11]

All these texts truly indicate the ambivalence of the relation of religion to violence and to religious terrorism.

The Need for Intertextuality

Texts are born and coloured by the contexts these come from. Language, social-cultural contexts, political and religious contexts, among others, shape their texts and their meanings. Rooted upon specific assumptions, sociology of religion must look into the contexts of the texts on violence and terrorism. Inappropriate reading and understanding of contexts may readily lead to the misappropriations and misapplications not only of texts but also of implied sociological paradigms and theories.[12] Re-reading the contexts of historical events, intellectual currents, cultural shifts, and political events is therefore a must to bring new light to a better understanding and application of the sociology on violence and terrorism.[13]

The Meaning of Intertextuality

Generally understood as the shaping of the meanings of texts' by other texts, Orr describes intertextuality as a catch-all word that deals with contexts, cultures, periods, theories and frameworks. Carried out in the reader's reading, intertextuality refers to the history of a prior text and how it is transformed.[14] It is the complex relationship between a text and other texts taken as basic to the creation or interpretation of a text.

As introduced by Julia Kristeva, the theory of intertextuality assumes that texts need contexts and that the meanings found in the texts are based on presuppositions. Since texts are conditioned by contexts for possible meanings, intertextuality will involve a 'double-voiced critical dialogue' between two axes: the vertical (connecting the texts to contexts, Figure (1) and the horizontal (connecting the author/context and the reader/context of the text, figure (2) Involving mediation and critical dialogue, intertextuality leads towards the transformation of meaning where, at times, contexts become texts or texts become contexts, too.[15]

This study will illustrate the importance; of (1) vertical dialogue in intertextuality, i.e., the relation of the texts on violence and terrorism to the contexts these come from, and (2) the importance of horizontal dialogue in intertextuality, i.e., texts on violence and terrorism interacting with the new contexts these are being applied to.

Individually or as community, readers create meanings or interpretations to the texts of terrorism and violence. Recognising and differentiating today's new/different contexts, intertextuality may challenge us to depart from conventional frameworks, to reflect and to process.[16] Cases of inappropriate textual readings of historical-cultural contexts of violence and terrorism and their application to new contexts as texts simply indicate the need for intertextuality.

Texts not only reflect what people think. These also carry the concrete culture, the preconceptions and the cultural historical paradigms of writers. Understanding contexts can therefore shed light to the proper understanding of texts. Without an informed context, a text could be given many/different meanings. Vertical dialogue (the reciprocal and critical interaction of texts to their contexts) therefore becomes appropriate to the understanding of violence and terrorism as the proper understanding of contexts becomes pivotal too.[17]

Inter-multi Disciplinary Studies of Contexts

Sociology, anthropology, political science, history and religious studies may indeed help attain a comprehensive; contextual analysis of the texts and contexts. Understanding the contexts of violence and terrorism can in fact widen the interpretation and understanding of their texts. Although studies show that fundamental concepts continue to influence the motives and behaviors of those who support or engage in violence, other elements that underlie terrorists' behaviour continue intolerance, moral absolute broad conclusions, and a new language that supports a particular belief system. Debates on the nature and definition of terrorism continue. And depending on one's perspective or contexts, different definitions on terrorism or violence may even be derived.[18] Inter-disciplinary and multi-disciplinary studies may therefore enlighten the re-reading of the contexts of violence and terrorism to widen our interpretation and our understanding of their texts, too.[19]

Reading Contexts as Texts

Rooted upon specific assumptions, sociology of religion must look into the contexts, among others, shape the texts of violence and terrorism. Thus to understand better the texts and the social theories implied by these texts, one may need to read their contexts as texts. For instance, the reading of the texts on terrorism by the state, by dissidents, by religious terrorists, and by international terrorists could help distinguish secular, sectarian, ethno-national and international terrorism. It can also provide a critical assessment of ideological, religious, practical, tactical and historical frameworks on terrorisrn.[20] This can help better understand the very texts on terrorism as an economic issue, a political issue, a potential maximum publicity method, an anti-colonial stance, an armed propaganda, or an ideological or religious stance.[21]

Contexts, Paradigms, Interpretation and Methods

Re-reading the different contexts on violence and terrorism is equally important. These may necessitate different attitudes, models and sources to measure research. In fact, recent researches show that contexts should not be overlooked but be read accordingly. Misheva, Kankaras and Moors, maintain that theories cannot be properly understood outside their sociological climate and their social and psychological contexts. Cressuwell even identifies the contexts of paradigms or world views that have corresponding implications to the interpretation of research problems and to the methods to be used. Hence, because of different contexts, Davie warns that European theories should not be appropriated or should not be wrongly applied to Asian and other countries.[22]

We have seen in the preceeding discussions how Vertical Intertextuality may enlighten the proper understanding not only of the texts but also of the contexts of violence and terrorism, their frameworks, their limitations and their proper applications. It has also made us aware that the contexts and texts on violence and terrorism are being transformed as new texts.[23] All these perhaps may even suggest different models, approaches and methods in the sociology of religion.

Proper reading and understanding of new/different contexts of violence and terrorism are important. For instance, the traditional study of violence; and terrorism of popular religion may need a different approach or method because of the new contexts of what is popular: to the masses, to what people simply do, or in contrast to dominant cultures.[24] The historical, geographical, doctrinal, denominational and the liturgical contexts of religions are generally good starting points for horizontal intertextuality.

Among the new emerging contexts that a study on violence and terrorism may have to consider are:

1. The globalisation phenomena,
2. New political and economic contexts,
3. The impact of the new communications and travel, and
4. The growing and deepening relationship of sociology with other disciplines, interdisciplinary and multi-disciplinary approaches.[25]

The Globalisation Phenomenon

Until recently, except for a few, sociological work in the field of globalisation did not pay attention to religion at all. Working within the global perspective, however, Robertson observes the transformation of new contexts for the sociology of religion: the; centrality of religion...that "globalisation is not a uni-dimensional, but multi-dimensional and multi-centered historical development within which religion has a central place". Hence, globalisation, specially its heterogenising or homogenising tendencies, is transforming the texts and contexts of violence and terrorism.[26] Thus researchers may have to distinguish International Terrorism from domestic terrorism and the Leftist- Rightist terrorism.[27]

Globalisation has been evolving and has been developing its own socio-political categories, communication language patterns, and its own value systems. Recognising such complexities and multi-disciplinary realities, the sociology of religion and the study of violence and terrorism may also have to consider these: either as new contexts or texts.[28]

The interplay of globalisation with culture, religion and ethnicity is also transforming a new context. As globalisation comes in contact with religion and identity and challenges the deeply held beliefs and identities traditions and religions become blurred. Religion and/or ethnicity may become the elementary core to which people could withstand assaults on their beliefs. These new contexts of revolution, ethno-nationalism, neo-Nazi, or racial violence and terrorism may demand new paradigms, new approaches, and new methods for research.[29]

New Political and Economic Contexts

Formed by post colonialism, multi-culturalism, globalisation, nationalism, ethnicity and trans-nationalism, contemporary religions do not only provide; a worldview. Their contemporary religious contexts also shape the economics and politics of their respective communities. Sociology of religion may have to see these new economic and political contexts. Violence and terrorism may have to be seen also from these contexts.

For instance, while economics may be intrinsically linked to violence and terrorism, cultural approaches to violence and terrorism may also imply social, psychological, moral entities and values.[30] Hence, intertextuality may have to consider these different, and new contexts of 'capitalism', their political and economic implications based on their geographical and cultural roots. Sociology of religion, therefore cannot but read these particularities and consider the religious implications to their cultural, economic and political contexts. These are becoming new texts for the sociology of religion and for the study on violence and terrorism, too.[31]

The Impact of New Communications and Travel

The vast and instantaneous information technology also invites the sociology of religion, and the study of violence and terrorism as well, to think globally and to think differently about, religion itself. This 'new' power and influence of Information Technology to religion, culture and identities are transforming the sociology of religion and its cognate disciplines and are becoming new texts, too.[32] And media has not been spared from this problem. Media information as power, as weapon, and as freedom are only some of the new texts born from the contexts of media.[33]

Similarly, trans-nationalism or the movement of people across the globe for permanent or temporary settlement or travel is also shaping the contexts of violence and terrorism. As transnational individuals and communities with different cultures and religions in 'diasporas' experience complex situations, the study of violence and terrorism may require sociology to explore varieties of methodologies, too hybridity, multiculturalism, integration, fundamentalism, pluralism and traditionalisation are only some of the new contexts. The study of violence and terrorism may have to consider the contexts of Law Enforcement and Counter-terrorism, International Law and Legalistic Responses, and International Cooperation, too.[34]

Relationship of Study of Religions with Other Disciplines

Recent development, in the sciences has led to a relativistic, holistic, transformative and dynamic revolution and has also affected the sociology of religion. Theories of complimentarity, uncertainty, catastrophe, chaos, and dissipative structures, require multi/inter-disciplinary approaches not only for the sociology of religion but even for the study of violence and terrorism.[35] For instance, violence and terrorism need not be exclusively a religious issue or problem. These may almost always mix with politics, economics, social injustice. And it may not even be clear which has primary determining factor.[36] Sociological materials may thus demand collaborative work. Contemporary inter-cultural and inter-religious contexts are therefore emerging texts even for the sociology of religion particularly in the study of violence and terrorism.[37]

Indeed, Horizontal Intertextuality challenges the sociology of religion to the possibilities of doing new areas of inquiry, of generating new ways of thinking, and even of formulating radically different canons. Intertextuality thus transforms the sociology of religion to become truly meaningful and relevant in the study of violence and terrorism.

Moving beyond the possibilities on how intertextuality can help us study violence and terrorism, let us now take a look at some of the ambivalences of terrorism and violence.

Vertical Intertextuality: Re-reading the Context(s) of Fundamentalism and Religious Radicalism

A re-reading of the human and the socio-economic aspects of violence and the different contexts of fundamentalism and religious radicalism may help us understand the culprit better. But first let us clarify our definitions or descriptions on fundamentalism and radicalism.

Describing Fundamentalism and Radicalism

One way of describing fundamentalism is its emphasis on the literal and verbal inspiration of the bible, beliefs and other traditional creeds. It is a social phenomenon that tries to overcome a crisis that occurs during rapid social change. By revitalising religion and the search for authenticity, fundamentalism offers resistance to secularisation.[38] Radicalism, on the other hand, is the alternative to the 'mainstream' and to the 'moderate'. The radical is a person with extreme political view, fundamental, violent, or fanatical.[39] Let us first try to ascertain their similarity.

Fundamentalism espouses its own interpretation of tenets and dogmas as it also espouses violence. Radicalism, on the other hand, also espouses violence. It desires a sudden and immediate action to bring about change, which more often than not, leads to violence. And what could possibly be the common grounds of fundamentalism and radicalism for such inclination to violence?

Faith and Human Socio-psychological Contexts

A closer look at fundamentalism and radicalism would show that, like a coin, it has two faces: the faith aspect and the human socio-psychological aspect. Naturally, almost any religion would take the faith side of realities. Hence, when religions describe fundamentalists they would almost always emphasise that they impose their own interpretations against the dogmas, teachings, tenets, or even traditions of their community. But equally, and perhaps more importantly, are the human and social aspects, in particular, the psychological facet: the experience and the problem of trust or the lack of it of fundamentalists.[40]

Observations indicate that, sometime, somewhere, the fundamentalist experience(s) of social or economic rejection has led them to react. At times these experiences had pushed them to reject and had led them even to impose their convictions, and to take a violent approach or position against people, norms and even against institutions and society. Hence, the violence of fundamentalists need not necessarily stem from their religious outlook or convictions. The fundamentalists feel that something more basic and more human has been lost: trust and failure to recognise this human need of trust causes more disturbance and leads to more fatalistic diseases of fundamentalism.[42] This, perhaps, is also the reason why fundamentalists refuse to engage in dialogue and deliberation.[43] This violent stance therefore of fundamentalists truly stems from that human experience of rejection and the overwhelming attitude of their lack of trust in people and even in society and its structures.

For the radicals, the real issue for their violence is human freedom. For them, it is this freedom that truly makes a human society. That people in society be really and truly free is their real goal. In their experience(s), however, it is this very freedom of society that at times has even caused the very subjection of individuals. The radicals, therefore, are not truly and really interested in a free society. Rather, what they are really after is that the people in society are indeed free. Hence, in their desire to preserve this freedom, radicals want immediate change. And they are also ready to take radical steps outside the established order and system to achieve that change. Desiring sudden and immediate action to bring about change, radicalism is lead to espouse violence.[44] It is for this that radicals consider themselves as the liberators desiring change for the benefit, of the human person. Although, they may even take refuge in the framework of their religion, their violent stance need not necessarily stem from their religion.[45] Similar to fundamentalism, therefore, radicals also begin to doubt and lose their trust in society and institutions that should have nourished the freedom of humanity, but, instead, have subjected this very freedom among peoples. This violent stance of radicals, therefore, may also stem from that experience of deprivation of basic human freedom and the creeping attitude of that lack of trust in people and even in society and its structures.

Our descriptions of fundamentalism and radicalism show that both tend to confront their considered inhuman realities with violence. Religion, as their reason for their insistence to the use of violence or terrorism, however, remains unclear. For, in spite of the human and religious communities and institutions they are in and live with, and the institutionalised machinery that could treat them human; the question persists: how come they still opt for a violent response?

Re-reading the Human Contexts

Although faith or the religious dimension of terrorism may not be denied, studies should also consider the human contexts or realities that lead people to get involved into violence.

Studies, in general, show that there are indeed complex human and social forces that shape people and contribute to the potential of espousing violence. It may be useful to mention some:

1. Family violence that affects those who witness this violence or who become victims themselves. These; later tend to become violent, too.[46]
2. Economic inhuman conditions like poverty, starvation, unemployment, and disenfranchisement may drive; people to seek solutions to their lots in life. On account of these inhuman conditions, they may resort to or may turn to anger and violence.'[47]
3. Insecure environment like unhealthy relationships resulting from divorce and separation. And this feeling of lack of belongingness may, at times, find its compensation in violent groups and/or violent activities.[48]
4. Low self-esteem characterised by feelings of powerlessness and worthlessness. Often, violent activities may also compensate for these feelings.[49]
5. Media portrayal of violence that leaves out effects on people. Over exposure to the constant barrage of violence desensitises viewers. Eventually, it may lead people to violence too.[50]
6. Alienation resulting from the feeling of lack of belonging and lack of connection to the community. Violence can provide the excitement, lacking in their lives. Violent groups may also provide that sense of belonging.[51]
7. Racism, classism, ethnocentricism leads to discrimination. This may later result into aggression and violence, too.[52]
8. Parasitic institutions, at times may have taken on a life of their own. Just like people, these institutions fight to survive and try to control our lives. As a reaction to this, some people may not for violence, too.[53]
9. Religious psychology implicated in religious violence has its moral ambiguity. Critical thinking may foster certitude that may forcefully take the violent option transcending human discussion and argumentation. On the other hand, critical

thinking may also foster uncertainty, thus allowing people not to agree or share the violence.[54]

Violence and terrorism are not as simple as we thought of. It may be true that some radicals use their religion and even take refuge in the framework of their religion.[55] There are no easy analyses and answers or solutions to this phenomenon. Hence, one cannot also simply say that religion is the root cause of terrorism. The truth is, there is nothing Islamic in Terrorism. Even Catholics and Christians have expressed their grievances detonating bombs in Northern Ireland, Spain, El Salvador, etc.[56] Like life, terrorism is not only complex but essentially multi-faceted.

The Ambivalence of the Contexts of the Root Causes

Let us take a look at some possible root causes of violence and terrorism.

Ferdinand Dagmang, for instance, sees violence more in the context of the poor. In his socio-political analysis of the engagement of the poor, he observed that in the whole structured relations of a generally democratic society, roles and transactions had been determined. More often than not, in this unequal distribution of power the victim is the powerless or the poor. And it is this powerless generating structured relations of society that tend to push people to become violent even in the context of any religion. In this kind of autonomous processes of relations of a democratic society, he says, violence is unfortunately inflicted and in turn pushes people to unconsciously become violent or react violently, too. While dependence and oppressions are valid issues for social-political analysis, Dagmang readily points out that the real issues and concerns of the poor and the powerless, and therefore of violence, are more basic: freedom, self-determination, and communal well-being.[57]

Khor, in his own analysis of the new radicalism happening throughout the world, cautions us of the new contexts of the threats to freedom viewed by this new radicalism. For him the true essence of today's radicalism persists to be a liberator and to bring that freedom to the individual. In his studies, Khor, presents the contexts of these new threats to freedom perceived by these modern radicals and which they would want to confront and if not to eliminate:

1. The iniquities of capitalist distribution brought by the power of the-state;
2. The excessive governmental power that is both impossible and unnecessary, especially, when, for the people, the state would cost more than the benefits it yields;

3. The state with its excessive power that may even swallow the nations' religious, social and economic communities;
4. The failure of the state to fulfill its proper function when its communities are weakened instead of being strengthened by it.

It is in these contexts and conditions that the new radicalism empowers the individual person to the use of violence to withstand even the state when it over reaches. After all, for them, the nation should have been a community of communities. In their view, the state, therefore, should not weaken nor annihilate communities.

There are times, however, that radicals hide themselves under the cloak of their religion, too. Thus, for Khor, the real issues behind the contexts of the violence of the new radicalism and of religious radicalism are far more important and basic: promoting and defending basic human freedom of individuals and groups in our society.[58]

It is also interesting to note that in the studies related to terrorism and violence conducted by Robert Wirsing *et al.,* they observed that religion, as such, has little to do with the radicalism in India, Pakistan, and Bangladesh. Rather, their study demonstrates that the contexts of Religious Identity is more often the vehicle rather than the inspiration of religious radicalism. Furthermore, their research also discloses that religious radicalism is more associated with the contexts of something more basic and human: the deterioration of democratic governance and the increased threats both to minority groups and individual human rights. Similarly, for Robert Wirsing *et al.*, the real issues behind the contexts of terrorism and violence of religious radicalism are also more human and basic: threats to individual human rights and minority groups and promoting and defending basic human freedom of individuals and groups in our society.[59]

In his study on Terrorism in the Philippines, Rafael Alunan III also readily points out that the terror threat from radical Islamists must be seen in the contexts of insurgency. According to him, Filipino Muslims, like many neglected Christians, have legitimate historical grievances and quality of life aspirations, too. Hence, in his view, armed responses are never the solution. Good government and enlightened citizens are the real solutions. Again, not religion as such but the contexts of the more basic and human issues and concerns related to violence were emphasised: freedom, self-determination, and communal well-being.[60]

For Astrid Tuminex, religion, too, is not the real problem of the Muslims in the Philippines. Rather, he identifies two major issues: autonomous self-government and ancestral domain. In his view, the contexts of ancestral domain is even a more basic issue: the search for territorial, political, cultural and economic arrangements to redress the long-term Moro Marginalisation.[61]

Silvestre A fable, too, in his observation as Head of the Government Panel engaged in the Peace Process with the Moro Islamic Liberation Front, particularly points out that, for the Muslims in the Philippines, the issue is not really religion but the context of ancestral domain. Afable looks into the issue of ancestral domain not as political but more in the contexts of basic human concerns: security of one's beliefs, community, history, and traditions plus righ:s over resources.[62]

Although it is a fact that some radicals are being labeled as religious fanatics because some of them really do take refuge in their religions,[63] it is becoming clear in our discussion that terrorism need not necessarily come from religion. Terrorism may also transpire in equally important and critical conditions within the contexts and outside the contexts of religion: the inhuman conditions, structures and situations that push people to violence and therefore: to terrorism.

In a recent research by Paris-based sociologist Scott Artan and Jessica Stern from Harvard University, they found out that although 80 per cent of known *jihadis* were Muslim emigrants, their study show that these *jihadis* were living in diaspora communities trying to seek, "a sense of community" who were often marginalised from their host society. In this study, it was also observed that in the *jihadis* search for belonging, they bond as small groups trying to find direction and purpose by surfing the *jihadi* websites. Their study illustrate that the problem with this kind of religious *jihadis* is not really religion but more human. And that this can be resolved with a more human approach like understanding small-group dynamics and psychological motivations (including isolation and brooding resentment). To them, a more human approach to religious radicalism will be a good step to combat home grown *jihadis*.[64]

In the violent riots that took place in the suburbs of France in November 7-9, 2005 where 2,581 cars were burned, President Jacques Chirac admitted that France has not integrated immigrant youths. He deplored the: 'ghettoisation'of the immigrants and recognised how the French society could not fully accept them, had not done everything possible so that that feel understood, heard and respected. He also emphasised the human factors contributing to violencc and noted the high unemployment in these recent areas, too.[65]

John Teehan saw the possible role of religion in violenee by presenting an evolutionary origin of religious ethics and violenee. While he may have distinguished the meanings of religion, the different contexts of violence of religions and explained the religious psychology involved, what remains clear for him is the ambivalence of the role of religion in relation to violence: it could be for the better or for the worse.[66]

Meanwhile, Gus Martin saw the complexities of the emerging trends on violence and terrorism: regional conflicts, new technologies, attacks on symbolic targets.[67]

The Catholic Church, too, recognizes that oppressions that try to stifle rights may eventually lead to violence and to the escalation of terrorism. Today, these have taken on new contexts and forms: like hunger, inhuman housing, illiteracy, deprivation of political power, and lack of suitable means of acquiring responsibility and moral dignity.[68] And it perceives that these threats to the quality of human life do contribute to the rise of violence and terrorism.[69]

The relationship of religion and terrorism is indeed ambivalent. Thus, religion alone should not be seen as the culprit to the religious radicalism, violence and terrorism our world is suffering from. Studying and understanding the different contexts of violence and terrorism should rather help us clarify these ambivalences and see these as new texts for the sociology of religion.

Horizontal Intertextuality: Reading New Contexts of Terrorism as Texts

New Forms of Terrorism

One of the possible responses of the marginalised and those trying to be heard to defend a more humane life could be violence and terrorism. While we may find these different forms: repression, action of dominating powers to pursue their interests and/or the suppression and subjugation of people especially the marginalised as reprehensible,[70] the violence of those trying to silence the marginalised is as real and equally reprehensible, too. These contexts of the violence and terrorism of states are becoming new texts for the sociology of religion, too.[71]

The ambivalence of terrorism continues and thus takes another slant: revolt and political struggle, opposition to oppression, terrorism from below (the violence arising from struggles against, a colonial power) and terrorism from above (actions of states against those challenging their power). Today, therefore, we have to recognise the further complexity and ambivalence of terrorism as it transforms into new contexts: becoming part of a transnational model of political engagement, an ideology and an instrument of struggle. These are but some of the contexts that can be read as new texts for the sociology of religion, too.[72]

Terrorism and the New Socio-political Contexts

After the 9/11 incident, many may readily identify and call certain violent acts as 'terrorism'. A closer look, however of the literature and discussions on the different contexts of terrorism reveal that the term is also one of the most confusing and contested words especially in the socio-political world.[73] Because of new/different contexts even Louis Rene Beres, a Professor of International Law, points out certain ambiguities in understanding terrorism itself, he observes that:

1. In the contexts of the legal law itself, there is no clear demarcation between lawful and unlawful uses of force; it is left to the individual to determine which particular criteria of legality should be applied.
2. In the context of the application of the legal laws, the definitions make no explicit and omit the essential elements of a "just cause" and "just means" and the
3. Problem of sufficient threat not clear. When is the threat sufficient to argue convincingly for the presence of terrorism?
4. The question of Permissible Anticipatory self-defense to pre-empt terrorism.
5. In the contexts of International Law, the problem and question of State Responsibility for terrorism cannot be committed by states.
6. The Ambiguity of political violence from ordinary criminality as contained in legal definitions.
7. Who is the Terrorist Enemy?[74]

All these contexts truly add to the ambiguity and ambivalence of Terrorism itself. No wonder, even the lawyers and legislators are complaining.

Radicalism and Terrorism in Media

Because of the social means of communications, our world today poses more challenges because we tend to live in a world of impressions *vis-a-vis* our realities. More often than not, impressions and not realities are given more attention. And terrorism and religious radicalism have not been spared from this. Global news would not fail to present, to feature or to discuss their daily impressions on the realities of terrorism side by side with religious fundamentalism and or religious radicalism. Unfortunately, consciously or unconsciously, media has created its own contexts: its own impressions on violence or terrorism as stemming or resulting from religious fundamentalism or radicalism. As a result, people tend to associate terrorism with religious radicalism and fundamentalism. For instance, violent and terrorisng presentations by the mass media on Islam have unconsciously created impressions upon people. And the message conveyed to viewers is that Islam is a violent religion and a dangerous threat to all who cherish modern values.[75] "Islamaphobia", the generally growing distrust with Muslims has grown and continuous to grow.[76] And this danger is truer in the Philippines because of the contexts of association by media on the Muslims with the terrorist groups like Jemaat Islamiyah and the Abu Sayaf.

With all these detrimental multi-media contexts and impressions created by the social means of communications to our Muslim brothers and sisters, the Muslims' fear and their anger must not and cannot be underestimated. We have to do away with ourselves the simplifications and distortions when confronting the terrorism presented by the media.[77] The complaints voiced by many Muslims, who often see themselves as victims are often based on serious facts.[78] There is truly, then, the need to see the contexts of terrorism in its totality and its complexity. Indeed, there is the urgent and most important need to become more critical and force ourselves to see also its human facets and go beyond the multi-media contexts and impressions.

Summary and Conclusion

A serious study and analysis of terrorism today demands intertextuality. There is need for critical dialogue, more reflection, assessment, further discussions and research not only of the different texts on violence and terrorism. The contexts of religious radicalism and fundamentalism are equally important. Our discussions on the vertical and horizontal intertextuality of the texts and contexts on terrorism showed that assessing terrorism would not be that easy. Our study also made us realise that attributing terrorism simply to religious fundamentalism is not only inappropriate but also extremely dangerous. Further analysis of texts on terrorism and their contexts made us distinguish the conditions from the real causes of terrorism; the circumstances from their root causes. Finally, we realise that terrorism and violence is truly an ambivalent situation.

The Role of Religion in the Face of International Terrorism

Religion is usually not the only reason for a conflict. Sometimes however, it is misused and abused. How then can we make religion not part of the problem but part of the solution, especially on International Terrorism?

Allow me to mention some of the recent ideas coming from different groups on how religion can take a positive role to combat or counter act international terrorism.

1. Establish a framework for religious tolerance. We have to start recognising that our world is pluralist. Everyone has freedom and responsibility for his own beliefs. Tolerance and exchange of ideas are key factors for development, peace and change. Religions should therefore prepare people to live in a multi-religious society by helping them develop religious tolerance.[79]
2. Develop a culture of conflict prevention" rather than a culture of "conflict resolution". By reflecting together on terrorism as a destructive and violent reality, religions can prevent perversion and misuse of religious beliefs to spread hatred, suspicion, harassment conflict and war. In particular they can point out the universal obligations of religions to love and help our neighbor and combat in words and deeds the poison spread by extremists in the name of religion. Thus, they can form an avenue condemning terrorist attacks and declaring that peace loving people of all religions are against a way of thinking that justifies violence against innocent persons as an instrument to further avenge one's cause.[80]
3. Engage media as partners. We have seen the power of media in changing the image, opinion and attitudes of people. Surely, asking the cooperation of media will give a big boost to religious tolerance and religious co-operation.[81]
4. Establish a framework for inter-religious dialogue.

Though it may need another study to expound the Catholic viewpoint on inter-religious dialogue, allow me just to mention the summary presented by Cardinal Cacciavillan taken from various documents of the Catholic church. The highlights include the following:

1. Meetings.
2. Contacts.
3. Relationship of openness.
4. Working together to eliminate the social and cultural causes of terrorism.
5. Reciprocal and mutual respect.
6. Fostering peaceful co-existence.

7. Scholarly exchange between experts in the various religious traditions.
8. Common action for integral human development and the defense of human religious values.
9. Public condemnation on terrorism and denying terrorists any form of religious or moral legitimacy.
10. Recognition of common values rooted in every person in humanity.
11. Recognition of common religious values and understanding their differences.
12. Bearing clear witness to love while engaging in dialogue.[82]

Now-a-days, we cannot deny the importance of inter-faith and inter-religious dialogue as a more effective means to understand and resolve the issues on international terrorism. As we emphasise the faith or religious dimension of terrorism, we should equally reiterate, too, the importance of the basic human dimension of violence and terrorism. Understanding terrorism today, therefore, needs a more holistic and total approach. Like a coin, there is the real need to see; not only its religious face or its faith dimension; but we should also see its human face. After all, the human face of terrorism is not only real but it may even be more basic and essential to encounter and resolve terrorism more humanely.

Notes

1. The headline describes the rescue of the Swiss-born resident of Mindanao who was kidnapped for almost two months by allegedly members of Abu Sayaf a terrorist group who are mostly Muslims. See *Philippine Star,* June 17, 2010. 1.
2. Azyumardi Azra. *Bomb Terror and the Religious Community*: How To respond Appropriately. August 15, 2003. Available From The World Wide Web: http://www.indopacific.net/MC Speech Trans Azyumardi Aug 1503 per cent28 Eng 29.htm.
3. Available from the World Wide Web: http: www.christiananswers. net/q-eden/islamterrorism.html.
4. T.L. Hubert. *Were The Terrorists Good Muslims?* Available from the World Wide Web: http//www.members.aol.com/kjvisbest/terr isl.htm.
5. Open quite on Bin Ladin by Rafael Aluan III. "Terrorism is the Ugly Face of Insurgency." *Kilosbayan Vol. XII, No.* 8, p. 6, March 2005. Kilosbayan Inc. Mandaluyong City, Philippines.
6. John Tir man National Catholic Reporter. Available from the World Wide Web: http://nconline.org/NCR Online/archives2/2005a/1014050/011405/011405; Charles Krauthammer. "Why That's Ridiculous" *Time Magazine,*

July 18, 2005, p. 33; Max V. Soliven. "By The Way", *The Philippine Star.* Ocotber 30, 2005, pp. 12-13.

7. Harun Yahya. *Uniting Against Radicalism.* Available From the World Wide Web: http//wwv monitor.upeace.org/archive.cfm?id_article.
8. Thomas Scheffler. *The Radicalism of Powerlessness: Imaginations of Violence in Three Religious Traditions,* Available From The World Wide Web: http/'/www.fuberlin.de/pdmideasl schetller.
9. A.H. Krieg, *Comparative Religion and Redicalism.* Available from the World Wide Web: http//www.kriegbooks.com/coinparative religion. html.
10. Robert G. Wirsing. Satu Limaye and Mohan Malik, *Executive Summary: Religion and Security in South Asia.* (August 19-22, 2002). Available From the World Wide Web: http//www.apcss.org/conference/CR ES /020819-22ES.html.
11. John Teehan. *In the Name of God: The Evolutionary Origins of Religions Ethics and Violence.* Black well Publishing: UK, 2010144-177.
12. Malory Nye Religion. *The Busies.* New York: Routtledge. 2008. See also John Teehan. In the name of God. Oxford: Blackwell Publishing. 2010. Although Teehan's focus was on texts related religious violence, these may very well be applied to the sociologies of religion.
13. Although Stephen Bevans' focus was on contexts of theology, the author saw them apt to the study of sociology of religion, too. See Models of Contextual Theology. Manila: Logos Publications. Inc., 2003 14-17. Meanwhile Max Stackhouse cites some social scientists who fail to acknowledge the impact of Christianity in shaping the dynamics and structures of society. See *Globalisation and Grace,* USA: The Continuum International Publishing Group. Inc. 2007, 37-38.
14. Text here does not only refer to words or written texts. It can also refer to contexts being used as texts. See *Mary Orr., Intertextually: Debates and Contexts.* USA: Polity Press, 2008, 11-15.
15. Mary Orr. *Intertexluality: Debates and Contexts,* USA: Polity Press. 2008. pp. 11-15.
16. Although John Paul Lederach specifically discusses religions, the writer saw its applicability to sociology of religion, too., *The Moral Imagination.* New York: Oxford Uiniversity Press. 2005. pp. vii-xi.
17. Aylward Shorter. *Towards a Theology of Inculturation.* Maryknoll: Orbis Books, 1988, pp. 3-13.
18. Gus Marting, *Essential of Terrorism.* Sage Publication: USA, 2011. 7-19;. see also Gerald Arbuckle, Violence Society and the Church. Claretian Publication: Quezon city, 2007, XI-XVII.
19. See James Adair. *Introducing Christianity,* Routledge 2008, 45-55 where the author provides historical and intellectual context of Christianity and John Lagerway, "Religion and Chinese Society, A Review", International Sociology Vol. 24 (Number 2, March 2009), 191-193.
20. *Ibid.,* pp. 164-179.

21. *Ibid.* See also Abhoud Syed Lingga, "Rethinking Govenmental Policies to get the Peace Process Moving", *Notre Dame Journal Vol. XXXIV,* No. 1 June 2008, 53-59.
22. Michael Kankaras and Moors Keenan. "Freedom in Chains: Religion as Enabler and Constraint in the Lives of Gay Male Anglican Clergy". ed. Abby Day. *Religion and the Individual,* Burlington: Ashgate Publishing Company. 2008. 165: John Cressuwell. *Qualitative Inquiry and Research Design.* California: Sage Publications. Inc., 2007. 15-30; Grace Davie, *The Sociology of Religion.* Singapore: Sage Publications, 2007, 3: Vessela Misheva, "Mead: Sources in Sociology". *International Sociology.* Vol. 24 (Number 2, March 2009). 159-168; Milos Kankaras and Guy Moors. "Measurement Equivalence in Solidarity Attitudes in Europe". *International Sociology,* Vol. 24 (Number 4, July 2009). 557-561.
23. See also John Teehan. In the Name of God: *The Exclutionary Origins of Religious Ethics and Violence.* Blackwell Publishing; UK, 2010, 193-202.
24. Malory Nye. Religion, *The Basics.* USA: Kouiledge. 2008, 208-209.
25. Geoffrey Redmond. *Science and Asian Spiritual Traditions.* USA: Greenwood Press. 2008, 14-17
26. Gus Martin. *Essentials of Terrorism,* Sage Publications: USA, 2011. 7-19
27. *Ibid.,* 158-178.
28. Gerald Arbuckle. *Violence, Society and the Church.* Claretian Publications: Quezon city. 2007, 152-170.
29. Gerald Arbuckle. *Violence, Society and the Church,* Claretian Publications: Quezon city. 2007, 173-179.
30. John Teehan. *In the Name of God; The Evolutionary Origins of Religious Ethics and Violence.* Blackwell Publishing: UK, 2010, 193-202.
31. Gerald Arbuckle, *Violence, Society and the Church,* Claretian Publications: Quezon City, 2007, 170-173; see also Malory Nye. 192-197, 209.
32. Jimmy Belita, *God was not in the Wind,* Manila: Adamson University Press, Inc. Manila, 2006, 197-199.
33. Gus Martin, *Essential of Terrorism,* Sage Publications, USA, 213-227.
34. Gus Martin, *Essential of Terrorism,* Sage Publications, USA, 2011, 237.
35. John Teehan, *In the Name of God: The Evolutionary Origins of Religious Ethics and Violence.* Blackwell Publishing: UK, 2010, 193-202.
36. John Teehan. *In the Name of God: The Evolutionary Origins of Religious Ethics and Violence.* Blackwell Publishing: UK, 2010, 198.
37. Keenan 2008. 169-175; see also John Teehan. *In the Name of God: The Evolutionary Origins of Religious Ethics and Violence.* Blackwell Publishing: UK, and Gus Marting,. Essentials of Terrorism. Sage Publications: USA, 2011.
38. Georges De Schrijiver, SJ. "Fundamentalism: A Refusal to Recognise a Religious Dimension in Secular Existence," *Fundamentalism and Pluralism in the Church,* Manila: DAKATEO De La Salle University Press, 2004, 9-20.

39. Leopold Kohr. *The New Radicalism.* Available from the World Wide Web: http://john.papworth@btinternet.com.
40. Georges De Schrijver, SJ. "Fundamentalism : A Refusal to Recognise a Religious Dimension in Secular Existence." *Fundamentalism and Pluralism in the Church.* Manila: DAKATEO De La Salle University Press, 2004. 9-20.
41. Agnes Brazal, "Re-inventing Pakikipagkapwa: An Exploration of its Potential for Promoting Respect for Plurality and Difference," *Fundamentalism and Pluralism in the Church,* Manila: DAKATEO De La Salle University Press. 2004. 50-53.
42. Georg Ziselsberger. "Taming the Beast, Trusting Beauty: Faith as a true Foundation of Dialogue with Fundamentalist Mentalitv." *Fundamentalism and Pluralism in the Church.* Manila: DAKATEO De La Salle University Press, 2004. 74-78.
43. Agnes Brazel. See also John Teehan, *In the Name of God: The Evolutionary Origins of Religios Ethics and Violence.* Blackwell Publishing: UK, 2010, 193-202.
44. Leopold Kohr. "The New Radicalism." John Papworth (ed.). *Resurgence.* 1967: Available From the World Wide Web: John.papworth@btinternet.com
45. Rhys H. Williams. *Radicalism.* Available from the World Wide Web: http//www.hartsem.deu/ency/radicalism.htm.
46. *Task Force on violence in Schools,* Available From the world wide web: http://www.bctf.be.ca/education/health ViolenceInSchools/canses.html.
47. William Christison. *Globalisation and The Root Causes of Terrorism.* Available from the world wide web: http://foi.missorui.edu/rootcauses.html.
48. *Task Force on Violence in Schools.* Available from the World Wide Web: http://www.bctf.bc.ca/education/health/ViolenceInSchools/causes/html.
49. Ferdinand D. Dagmang, Ph.D. *Engagement In the World of the Poor.* Unpublished article 2005, 1-24.
50. *Task Force on Violence in Schools.* Available from the World Wide Web: http://www.bctf.bc.ca, education/health/ViolenceInSchools/causes.html
51. *Task Force on Violence in Schools.* Available from the World Wide Web: hltp: www.bctf.bc.ca/education/health/ViolenceInSchools/causes.html.
52. Dr. Leonard Sebastian, *Getting the Root of Islamic Radiailism In Indonesia.* Available from the World Wide Web: http://www.ntu.edu.sq//idss Perspective research 0502 2.
53. Steven Barrie-Anthony. *Terrorism and Religious Extrenism: A Mindful Approach,* Available from the World Wide Web: http://www.causes-of-terrorism.net/entiresite text.htm.
54. John Teehan. *In the name of God: The Evolutionary Origins of Religious Ethics and violence.* Blackwell Publishing: UK, 2010, 202-205.
55. A H. Krieg. *Comparative Religion and Radicalism.* Available from the World Wide Web: http:// www.kriegbooks.com/comparative-religion.html.
56. *Christian-Muslim Relations After the Terrorist Attack.* Available from the World Wide Web: htttp://www.sjweb.info/dialogo/show.cfm?Number =14.

57. Ferdinand D. Dagmang. Ph.D. *Engagement in the World of the Poor*. Unpublished article 20054. 1-24.
58. Leopold Kohr, *"The New Radicalism"*. John Papworth (ed.) Resurgence, 1967. Available from the World Wide Web: John.papworth@btinernel.com.
59. Robert G. Wirsing, Satu Limaye, and Mohan Malik. *Executive Summary: Religion and Security in South Asia* (August 19-22, 2002). Available From the World Wide Web: http//www.apcss.org/conference/CR_ES/020819-22ES.htm.
60. Rafael Alunan III. "Terrorism is the Ugly Face of Insurgency" *Kilosbayan* Vol. XII, No. 08, pp. 5-7. March 2005. Kilosbayan Inc., Mandaluyoung City. Phillippines.
61. Astrid Tuminez "*Kilosbayan,* Vol. XII, No. 8, pp. 28-29. March 2005. Kilosbayan Inc., Mandaluyoung City. Philippines.
62. Silvestre Afable, "With Best Efforts We can Reach Agreement this year," Kilosbayan Vol. XII no. 08, p. 30. March 2005. Kilosbayan Inc., Mandaluyong City, Philippines.
63. A.H. Krieg, *Comparative Religion and Radicalism.* Available From The World Wide Web: http//www.kriegbooks.com/comparative_religion.html
64. Lawrence Gureco, ed. "Destructive Mind-Set." *Philipine Daily Inquirer,* p. A10, Thursday, September 29, 2005.
65. Binky Yatco, ed. World: "Riots Persist," *The Phillippine Star.* November 9, 2005. pp. A25-A26.
66. John Teehan. *In the Name of God: The Evolutionary Origins of Religious Ethics and Violence.* Blackwell Publishing: UK, 2010,197-201.
67. Gus Martin. *Essentials of Terrorism.* Sage Publications,: USA, 2011,312-317.
68. Synod of Bishops. *Justice in the World.* Nov. 30. 1971. Austin Flannery. ed. Vatican Council II Vol. 2. Paulines Publishing House. Pasay City. Philippines.2000. pp. 696-700.
69. Donal Dorr. *The Social Justice Agenda.* Claretian Publications, Quezon City, Philippines: 1993. pp. 151-152.
70. Synod of Bishops. *Justice in the World.* Nov. 30, 1971. Austin Flannery. Ed. Vatican Council II Vol. 2. Paulines Publishing House. Pasay City, Philippines. 2000. pp. 696-700.
71. Fred Halliday. *Terrorism in Historical Perspective.* Unpublished article. Delivered at Goodenough House in November 2003.
72. Fred Halliday. *Terrorism in Historical Perspective.* Unpublished article. Delivered Goodenough House in November 2003.
73. *Ibid.*
74. Fred Halliday. Terrorism in Historical Perspective. Available From the World Wide Web: http://opendemocracy.net/debates/article-2-103-1865.jsp. March 11, 2004.
75. *Christian-Muslim Relations: Are we missing the real story?* Available from the World Wide Web: http://www.sjweb.info/dialogo/documents/doc show. clm? Number-15.

76. Islamaphobia was a recent study and coined by sociologist Heitmeyer mentioned by Karimah Stauch. *The Contribution of Religious Communities Religious Communities to Current Socio-Polilical Challenges.* Available trom the World Wide Web: http://members.aol.com/dmlbonn/archiv/stauch.html.
77. Courtney Goto enumerates the increased false stereotypes of Arabs by American filmmakers even before 9/11. This exists in more than 900 features including blockbusters. *Current Dialogue: The Future of Interreligious Youth Education in the US.* Available from the World Wide Web: http://www.wcc-coe.org/wcc/what/interreligious/cd41-02.html.
78. Karimah Stanch mentions attacks against Muslims in Bosnia, Afghanistan, Chechnya. Tibet, Xinkiang which are hardly ever reported in European Media. *The Contribution of Religions Communities to current Socio-Political Challenges.* Available from the World Wide Web: http://inembers.aol.com/dmlbonn/archiv stanch.html.
79. *Routes Faith.* International Conference on Interreligious Dialogue. Final Report. September 14-16. 2000.
80. Prime Minister Kjell Magne Bondevik. *Interreligious Dialogue and International Relations.* Available from the World Wide Web: http://www.odin.dep.no/smk/norsk/aktuelt/taler_statsmin/later/001001-090555/dok-bn.html.
81. *Rites of faith.* International Conference on Interreligious Dialogue, Final Report. September 14-16. 2000.
82. Cardinal Agosto Cacciavillan. *Dialogue Between Cultures and Between Religions.* Available from the World Wide Web: http://www.ewtn.com/library/CURIA/PATDIAL_HTM.

References

- Adair, James. 2008. *Introducing Christianity.* Routtledge: New York.
- Afable, Silvestre. "With Best Efforts We Can Reach Agreement this Year." *Kilosbayan,* Vol. XII, No. 8, p. 30. Mandaluyong City, Philippines: Kilosbayan Inc., March 2005..
- Alunan, Rafael III. "Terrorism is the Ugly Face of Insurgency." *Kilosbayan Vol. XII, No. 8,* p. 6. Mandaluyong City, Philippines: Kilosbayan Inc., March 2005.
- Arbuckle, Gerald. 2007. *Violence, Society and the Church.* Claretian Publications: Quezon city.
- Azra, Azyumardi. "Bomb Terror and the Religious Community: How To respond Appropriately." August 15, 2003. Available From The World Wide Web: http// www.indopacific.net/MCSpeechTransAzyumardiAugl503%28Eng29.htm.

- Barrie-Anthony, Steven. *Terrorism and Religious Extremism: A Mindful Approach.* Available from the World Wide Web: http://www.causes of terrorism.net/entiresitc_text.htm.
- Belita, Jimmy. 2006. *God was not in the Wind.* Adamson University Press, Inc.: Manila.
- Bevans, Stephen. 2003. *Models of Contextual Theology.* Logos Publications, Inc.: Manila.
- Bondevik, Prime Minister Kjell Magne. *Interreligious Dialogue and International Relations.* Available from the World Wide Web: http://www.odin.dep.no/smk/norsk/aktuelt/taler_statsmin/taler/001001-090555/dok-bn.html.
- Brazal, Agnes "Re-inventing Pakikipagkapwa: An Exploration of its Potential for Promoting Respect for Plurality and Difference." 2004. *Fundamentalism and Pluralism in the Church.* DAKATEO De La Salle University Press: Manila.
- Cacciavillan, Cardinal Agosto. *Dialogue Between Cultures and Between Religions.* Available from the World Wide Web: http://www.ewtn.com/library/CURIA/PATDIAL_HTM.
- *Christian-Muslim Relations After the Terrorist Attacks.* Available from the World Wide Web: http://www.sjweb.info/dialogo/show.cfm?Number-14.
- Christison, William. *Globalisation and The Root Causes of Terrorism.* Available from the world wide web: http:// foi.missouri.edu/ rootcauscs.html.
- Cresswell, John. 2007. *Qualitative Inquiry and Research Design.* Sage Publications, Inc.: California.
- Dagmang, Ferdinand D., Ph.D. *Engagement In the World of the Poor.* Unpublished article 2005. 1-24.
- Davie, Grace. 2007 *The Sociology of Religion.* Sage Publications: Singapore.
- De Schrijver, Georges. S.J. "Fundamentalism: A Refusal to Recognise a Religious Dimension in Secular Existence." 2004. *Fundamentalism and Pluralism in the Church.* DAKATKO De La Salic University Press: Manila.
- Dorr, Donal. 1993. *The Social Justice Agenda.* Claretian Publications: Quezon City, Philippines.
- Goto, Courtney. *Current Dialogue: The Future of Interreligious Youth Education in the US.* Available from the World Wide Web: http:// www.wcc-coe.org/wcc/what/intcrrcligious/cd4 1 -02.html.
- Gueco, Lawrence, ed. "Destructive Mind-Set." *Philippine Daily Inquirer,* p. A 10, Thursday, September 29, 2005.
- Halliday, Fred. *Terrorism in Historical Perspective.* Unpublished article. Delivered at Goodenough House in November 2003. Available from the

World Wide Web: http://www.opcndcmocracy.net/debatcsarfick-2-103-1865.jsp.

- Hubert, T.L. *Were The Terrorists Good Muslims?*. Available from the World Wide Web: http//www.members.aol.com/kjvisbest/terr_isl.htm.
- International Conference on Interreligious Dialogue. *Routes of Faith.* Tashkent, Uzbekistan. Final Report. September 14-16, 2000. Available from the World Wide Web: http://www.unesco.org/culturc/dialoguc/religion/html_eng/uzbekistan/.shtml.
- Kankaras, Michael and Moors Keenan. "Freedom in Chains: Religion as Enabler and Constraint in the Lives of Gay Male Anglican Clergy", ed. Abby Day. *Religion and the Individual.* 2008. Ashgatc Publishing Company: Burlington.
- Kohr, Leopold. "The New Radicalism." Available from the World Wide Web: http://John.papworlh@btinlernet.com.
- Krauthammer, Charles. "Why That's Ridiculous" *Time Magazine.* July 18, 2005. p. 33.
- Krieg, A.H. "Comparative Religion and Radicalism." Available From The World Wide; Web: http//www.kriegbooks.com/comparative religion.html
- Lederach, John Paul. 2005. *The Moral Imagination. Oxford* University Press: New York.
- Lingga, Abhoud. "Rethinking Government Policies to get the Peace Process Moving", *Notre Dame Journal Vol. XXXIV No.* 1, June 2008.
- Martin, Gus. 2011. *Essentials of Terrorism.* Sage Publications: USA.
- Misheva, Vessela. "Mead: Sources in Sociology". *International Sociology Vol. 24* (Number 2, March 2009).
- Nye, Malory. 2008. *Religion, The Basics.* Routledge: New York.
- Orr, Mary, Intertextuality: Debates and Contexts. USA: Polity Press, 2008.
- Redmond, Geoffrey. 2008. *Science and Asian Spiritual Traditions.* Greenwood Press: USA.
- Scheffler, Thomas. "The Radicalism of Powerlessness: Imaginations of Violence in Three Religious Traditions." Available From The World Wide Web: http//www.fuberlin.de/pdmideast/schefrier.
- Sebastian, Dr. Leonard *Getting the Root of Islamic Radicalism In Indonesia.* Available from the World Wide Web: http://www.ntu.edu.sq//idss/Perspective/research 0502/2.
- Shorter, Aylward. 1988. *Toward a Theology of Inculturation.* Orbis Books: Maryknoll.
- Soliven, Max V. "By The Way". *The Philippine Star.* October 30, 2005. p. 12-13.
- Stackhousc, Max. 2007. *Globalisation and Grace.* The Continuum International Publishing Group, Inc.: USA.

- Stauch, Karimah. *The Contribution of Religious Communities to Current Socio-Political Challenges.* Available from the World Wide Web: http:// members.aol.com/dmlbonn/archiv/stauch.html.
- Synod of Bishops. 2000. *Justice in the World. Nov. 30, 1971.* Austin Flarinery. ed. Vatican Council II Vol. 2. Paulines Publishing House: Pasay City, Philippines.
- *Task Force on Violence in Schools.* Available from the Work Wide Web: http://www.bctf. bc.ca/education /health/ Violeneeln Schools/causes, htm
- Teehan, John. 2010. *In the name of God,* Blackwell Publishing: Oxford.
- Tirman, John. *National Catholic Reporter.* Available from the World Wide Web: http://nconline.org/NCR Online/archives2/2005a/101405/011405/ 011405.
- Tuminez, Astrid. "The Key to Permanent Peace in Mindanao." *Kilosbayan* Vol. XII, No. 08, pp. 28-29. March 2005. Kilosbayan Inc., Mandaluyong City, Philippines.
- Williams, Rhys H. *Radicalism.* Availabe from the World Wide Web: http// www.hartsem.deu/ency/ radicalism.htm.
- Wirsing, Robert G., Satu Limaye, and Mohan Malik. "Executive Summary: Religion and Security in South Asia" (August 19-22, 2002). Available From The World Wide Web: http//www.apess.org/conference/CR FS/020819-22ES.htm.
- Yahya, Harun. "Uniting Against Radicalism." Available From The World Wide Web: http///www.monitor.upeacc.org/archive.efm?id article
- Yateo, Binky. ed. World: "Riots Persist." The Philippine Star. November 9, 2005.
- Ziselsberger, Georg. "Taming the Beast, Trusting Beauty: Faith as a True Foundation of Dialogue with Fundamentalist Mentality." *Fundamentalism and Pluralism in the Church,* Manila: DAKATEO De La Salle University Press , 2004. 74-78.

13

Javanese Muslims' Tolerance and Flexibility Through Syncretic Ornamentation

Hee Sook Lee-Niinioja

Java, located on the southern Indonesian archipelago, has a tropical climate, rich rainfall, and fertile soils, supplying abundant natural resource. Although Islam became the dominant religion in the 16th century, the basic patterns of ancestral, mythical belief and Hindu-Buddhism were integrated within Sufi Islam which had lost much of its orthodoxy in its spread from the Arab world. As Sufi believed mosques to be sacred, the holy pre-Islamic architecture and ornaments became a means for Islamisation, creating a combination of indigenous and Islamic ideas and forms as a distinct regionalism.

As a result, roofs of old mosques resemble the Cosmos Mountain, Meru, where gods reside, while *tumpals* (a triangular prehistoric motif) decorate mosque *mihrabs*. The political and Islamic movement in Java is divided into three periods according to the political and religious movements: (i) continuation of pre-Islamic influence in the transitory period (15C-1619), (ii) European and Islamic influences during Dutch colonisation of Java (1619-1945), and (iii) a pure Islamic movement in the contemporary period (1945-to the present).

Based on these facts, (1) the study discusses the syncretic ornamentation whether their ideas and forms were inherited from pre-Islamic or Islamic tradition by a broad view of mystical ideas in animism, Hindu-Buddhism, and Islam in Java, (2) It identifies how three stages of Islamisation developed their mosque ornamentation in parallel with incoming Chinese, European, and Islamic motifs, (3) It suggests how tolerant Javanese Muslims who adore their tradition could teach to the world, in order to enhance understanding and dialogues between different faiths and religions beyond time and space.

Regional Flavour

Islamic culture and art have been influenced and remodelled by local traditions with countries which they came into contact, in order to comply with its religious and philosophical ideas. This interaction has enriched both the material culture of the Muslim world and those pre-existing ones (Rogers 2005).

Today, Southeast Asia (the Malay) including Java represents almost one-quarter of Islam's global community. Islamic civilisation is inextricably linked to the message of the Prophet since its arrival to Java in the early 15th Century. Islam not only altered local cultural landscapes, but also created a unique regional heritage. It could be asked why a characteristic regionalism had to take place greatly in this archipelago. Was it due to the awareness of continuing Javanese cultural heritage?

This can be claimed that the geographical long distance between the Arab world and Southeast Asia prevented the direct influence of Islamic center into this region at the beginning.

Consequently, the expression of faith in art and architecture articulated the creed of Islam and produced complexity of regional variations. Two factors can be argued to create the regionalism. Firstly, living in a spirit of tolerance, flexibility, and openness, the Malay people were able to accept changes through careful selection, reflection, and modification without discarding their wealthy cultural traditions. They witnessed Hindu-Buddhist, Chinese, Islamic, and western cultures, which had a great impact on the lifestyle.

Secondly, the arrival of Islam to the archipelago coincided with an era of zealous spiritualism in the Islamic world. Sufi mysticism had first appeared in Persia, and following the Mongol seizure of Baghdad in 1258, it rapidly spread through international trade routes. As the Sufi precept of 'universal toleration' could negotiate with pre-Islamic culture, a new Malay identity was quickly expressed in Malay art to affirm 'oneness of God'. Artists drew inspiration from diverse heritage and chose to transform existing symbolism in accordance with Islam.

Until the late 19th Century, mosques were constructed in a vernacular style with Hindu-Buddhist multi-tiered roof, using mostly wood to accommodate local conditions. The persistence of indigenous buildings had to take into account the local profusion of natural resources and variable climates, resulting in exuberant and diverse architectural styles. As pre-Islamic traditions underline the form and setting of sacred places, mystical Sufis borrowed them, based on their belief of mosques to be sacred, creating a combination of indigenous and Islamic ideas and forms in mosque architecture.

Three-tiered roof symbolises the mystical paths to God. Soko *guru* signifies the spiritual context of the vertical unity between God and his believers, continued from the Hindu belief in the identity of self and the universal soul. Although the avoidance of figurative representation separates Islamic art from Hindu-Buddhist aesthetic style, Islamic art needed reconciliation of the ambivalent relationship between the two religions, caused by the ruler's indigenous belief of the magic in art. Accordingly, the depiction of non-Islamic images, such as Hindu deity Ganesha or zoomorphic and anthropomorphic symbols combined by Koranic calligraphy was to be understood in the context of the earlier animism. This method was intended to represent non-Islamic images fitting into an aesthetic attitude tolerable to Islamic orthodoxy.

Among many types of pre-Islamic motifs which appeared in Javanese mosques, kalamakara (fish and elephant trunk) and floral motifs seemed to continue the most, particularly lotus flower. Islamic poets describe flower as a book, where one can study the knowledge about God. And its combination with birds can be considered as the characteristic of Islamic Javanese decorative art, despite a ban by the hadith.

Van Leur in his book, *Indonesian Trade and Society* (1960) argues that Indonesian history must be understood in its own terms, not in those borrowed from other cultures. This view seems to be shared by others: 'We are Javanese, then, our religion is Islam'. Tjandrasasmita (1984) attempted to prove that Islam took over local conditions and, to a certain extent, contributed to the preservation of indigenous cultural values and traditions. This could be due to the fact that the Islamic propagators and the Indonesian themselves have always known tolerance, which is not only obvious in architecture and decorative art, but is also in other aspects of their culture.

For instance, Astana Mantingan (1559) in Central Java and Sendang Duwur (1561) in East Java exhibit a blend of Hindu-Javanese and Islamic cultural elements, indicating a close relationship between Hindu Majapahit and Islamic cities on the coast. The importance of ornaments in integrating Islam into Javanese culture encouraged artists to adjust gradually to new realities, instead of putting any imposition on them.

Prijotomo (2004) underlines a combination of pre-Islamic and Islamic ideas and forms in floral decoration at Sendang Duwur: 'It is not a real floral, but a modified one, seen as floral. This ambiguity is a Javanese characteristic. Javanese mosques use Hindu-Buddhist motifs in an Islamic way. The form is Hindu, but the idea is Islamic, or vice versa. As Islam allows liberty, everybody can make their own style, but keeping continuity'. Islam penetrated slowly into Indonesian minds without force, due to its principal concept. Sendang Duwur reflects the process of acculturation with tolerance, syncretism, local genius, friendship of the Javanese in the transitory period. It is the earliest product of the Islamic Indonesian art.

Islamic art became an extension, rather than a radical change from earlier aesthetic traditions. These comments raise a question on unique Javanese attitude to Islamic culture. Broadly speaking, it was inspiration of the Malay people which has played the most significant force in creating a regional Islamic culture and Malay identity in this archipelago.

Three Islamic Periods

There were three Islamic periods in Java. Each period created syncretism between regional tradition and incoming Islamic culture, based on mutual tolerance and flexibility. These steps are (i) parallelism between old and new culture, (ii) adaptation between the two, and (iii) creation of a new syncretic culture.

The First Syncretism: Transitory Period (15C-1619)

The Islamic transitory period starts from the foundation of the earliest Islamic kingdom of Demak around 1479 after the conquest over Hindu Majapahit kingdom, and ends with the beginning of Dutch colonisation of Java in 1619. During this time, remnants of Hindu-Buddhist influence were very visible in Javanese mosques. The tradition says that the oldest mosques were likely re-used buildings within palaces or small prayer halls in villages. They modelled on existing building types used for a similar sacral purpose. The four main columns (soko *guru*) support the uppermost roof, separating it from the double-layered outer roof, in order to admit light and to allow ventilation of the prayer hall. The earliest large mosques are venerated as the oldest of their kind in Southeast Asia, and the first mosque is said to be Agung Demak (1479), becoming a standard for the mosque building in the 20th Century.

Why so? Geographical isolation from the Arab world allowed Malay local culture to be the only source for mosque architecture and ornamentation. Syncretism occurred between Sufism and Javanese faiths, thus *walis* said that the direction of the *qibla* was the 'west'. Strong continuity of pre-Islamic tradition was shown, but Javanese Muslims designated new functions and meanings to their mosques. Syncretic Islamic motifs were created by local genius, as a result of modifying local motifs within an Islamic context, learned from missionaries who brought orthodox Islamic ornaments to Java. New regional ornaments, termed 'local Islamic or Malay Islamic', differ from orthodox ones. Chinese motifs contributed partially to this process.

The Second Syncretism: Dutch Colonisation Era (1619-1945)

During the last decades of the 16th Century, a European administration was set in place to regulate production in response to the demands of their home markets. The Dutch had already influenced the courts of Central Java. Traders from any part of the Muslim world settled down harbours in Java, forming communities with mosques as their life focus. Rather small in scale, the previous traditional Hindu-Buddhist style was still echoed in mosque. From 1818, once controlling Java, the Dutch government built the first Mogul dome of Baiturrachman (1881) in Aceh, combined with the local *serambi*. In the end of this century, European liberal movements against injustices in the colonies brought mosque renovations and large new mosques in the next century. A departure from local tradition was seen in the addition of a freestanding tower, and a wide range of ornaments of Middle Eastern and Indian, sometimes of European, such as the *palmette*, and Chinese or even regional inspiration, were applied.

It means, sources for inspiration during this phase became Mecca and Madina, because *ulamas* (religious leaders) were able to visit Mecca and bring orthodox Islamic architecture and ornaments back home, which were later adjusted to the local ones. Ulamas said that *qibla* directs 'around the west'. However, the lack of skills also played a role in the postponement of replication until the Dutch colonisers' engagement in teaching techniques. In architecture, a combination of dome and local *serambi* took place. Constant but a lesser use of pre-Islamic ornaments as an outcome of the new contacts between Java and the Arab world prompted calligraphy to become popular.

The Third Syncretism: Contemporary Period (1945-to the Present Day)

From the end of the 19th century, new directions in theological education and social reform throughout the Islamic Arab world introduced alternative architectural styles which emanated from Cairo and Arabia. They were somehow accepted in Java, but were resisted by other nationalistic sections of the *ummat*. After Independence in 1945, this trend was reversed in a movement towards solidarity among Muslim nations and the development of a combination of Javanese and international styles in variety, in the context of modern technology and characteristic design.

An extensive 'Islamic' building program was initiated by President Sukarno and continued by President Soeharto of Indonesia during the early 1980s. A standard design and symbols of mosques, inspired by Demak (1479), was set up. The expansion of population has brought about the need for many larger mosque complexes, and designs from the Middle East, India, and North Africa have taken over local traditions. However, details such as material or structural method on mosques still reflect their predecessors. During this time, every Muslim could travel and get sources from the whole world. Pan-Islamic ornaments were blended with local tradition, bringing plurality.

Muslims could interpret Islamic architecture and ornament to their own tastes, since the modern science and technology and Islamic environment in daily life are closely related. Ulamas established the true location of the *qibla* as being the 'northwest'. Orthodox Islamic motifs of arabesque, geometry, and calligraphy gradually replaced pre-Islamic ornaments. Flat roofs, the absence of *mihrabs* or columns, geometry and arabesque became a trend. In the midst of this, a new consciousness to formulate a style which reflects regional flavour and diversity became stronger towards globalization, either traditional or pan-Islamic or combined, in order to keep Javanese cultural heritage.

Conclusion

A Javanese term, *'Bhinneka Tunggal Ika'* (unity in diversity), was created by the Javanese people to emphasise their own identity and culture. Java has been a centre where mystical animism, Hindu-Buddhism, and Islam co-existed together, moving toward a syncretic religion. In an interview, Tjandrasasmita (2005), a distinguished Indonesian scholar and specialist in syncretic Islamic archaeology, argued that Javanese Islam has a few distinct characteristics. Javanese Muslims are greatly concerned with continuity of their cultural heritage, which was created by local genius (Wale's theory) across centuries, beyond religions and faiths. Furthermore, Javanese Muslims emphasise the importance of holy ornaments that were derived from Hindu-Buddhism, and try to link them with Islam.

Javanese Muslims are very familiar with their cultural heritage. Through existing media, Islam was effectively penetrated into their hearts, because of the love for heritage and the similarity to Islamic concept (Sedyawati 2006).

Java is a peaceful melting pot; Javanese Islam is syncretic; Javanese descendants adore their cultural heritage; and Javanese Muslims are tolerant, inventing a beautiful amalgamation from many sources, beyond faiths and religions, in order to pay tribute to Allah. Orthodox Islam has to encourage this, in order to coexist in the tropical and multi cultural Java.

I hope, we can learn tolerance and flexibility from Javanese Muslim's syncretic approach to their existing and incoming cultures, thus more communication can take place between faiths and religions in current violent places.

14

Terrorism Cause and Concern

P.K. Choudhary, S.N. Yadav

Almost all magazines, newspapers are flooded with information about terrorists, government action and its impact on different sections of the society. In recent two decades, literature on terrorism has grown enormously. Terrorism is an interdisciplinary area of study. It can be seen and understood from different perspectives: political, science, psychology, sociology, history and law. In the present work the psychological aspect of terrorism has been taken, however isolating terrorism from politics is difficult as present day terrorism has political implications.

Defining Terrorism

The word Terrorism is defined as "the covert or secret resort to violence, or threat of violence, on the part of a group seeking to accomplish a purpose against some recognised authority." (Kaplan, 1981)

According to the official FBI definition, terrorism is "the unlawful use of force or violence against persons or property to intimidate or coerce a government, the civilian population, or any segment thereof, in furtherance of political or social objectives."

The objective of terrorism may be to gain publicity for some cause, or the desire to obtain concessions or bring about social change. However, there is no universally accepted definition of terrorism. (Long, 1990).

Terrorism may be classified in different ways, based on there geographical area. and motive (Kaplan, 1981).

1. *Domestic*—In own country against own people.
2. *International*—An act of terrorism involving more than one state. The most common form of international terrorism is events in which terrorists belonging to one nation attack the citizen or

property of another. Less frequent are incidents in which terrorists attack their own country men on the territory of another country.

3. *State sponsored*—Terrorism by groups, which are logistically or operationally aided by states. When a ruling regime provides funds intelligence or material resources to terror groups, usually operating outside their borders (Iran, Iraq, Libya. Afghanistan).

Motives

1. *Political* - For ideological and political purposes - Groups that focus on gaining power and supremacy, removing Government intrusion or changing beliefs (Aryan Nation, Posselomitatus, Freemen).
2. *Non-political* - For private purposes and gain.
3. *Quasi-terrorism* - Skyjacking and hostage taking.
4. *Limited Political* - Ideological but not revolutionary.
5. *Official or State* - Used by nation against nation or people.
6. *Revolutionary* - Aims to overthrow or replace an existing government (Red Army faction, PLO, Hizbollah).
7. *Nationalist* - Promotes interests of an ethnic or religious group that is seen as being persecuted by another.
8. *Caused based*- Groups devoted to social or religious case using violence to address their grievances (Islamic holy war, Anti-abortion campaigns).
9. *Environmental:* Groups dedicated to slowing down development that is harming animals, (Animal Liberation Front, Earth 1st).
10. *Genocide* - When a government seek to wipe out a minority group in its territory. (Cambodia, Rwanda, Bosnia, Iraq, Turkey). None of these typologies are satisfactory however, characterised as they are by overlapping categories and subjective definitions.

Historical Backround

The word terrorism traces its roots in the English language to the French revolution (1789-1794). The German philosopher, Immanuel Kant used the word in 1798 to describe a pessimistic view of the destiny of mankind. Russian anarchist Peter Krapat Kin (1842-1921) called it- "Propagnada by Deed". Carlos Marighelta wrote the Latin American handbook on terrorism, claiming it required adherence to a "higher morality" and that one man's terrorist is another man's liberator. Countries like Ireland, Cyprus, Algeria and Israel might not have become independent republics without "terrorism". (Merari. 1994).

Despite the historical regency of the term, terrorism is probably as old as human society. Two of the better-known old groups which used terrorism systematically to promote their political interests were the Jewish Sicarii (1st Century A.D.) and the Ismail Shiite Assassins (Hashishin; 11-13th centuries) In 19th Century terrorism gained notoriety with the rise of the anarchist movement. Terrorism was regarded as the recommended mode of struggle which combined destructive goals with a destructive method. Other types of social ideological movements also used terrorism as their main mode of struggle in the second half of the 19th century and the beginning of the 20th Century. These included the Russian Narodnaya Volya (people's will) and later the Social Revolution areas which fought against the oppressive Tsarist regime and even influenced by Marxist more than by anarchist ideology. Much of the terrorist violence in the US was linked to labour struggle between unions and employers and focussed on concrete demands related to labour conditions. (Merari, 1994)

In 20th Century terrorism was increasingly used as the principal strategy or as an auxiliary instrument by groups, which fought for national liberation, as well as by groups. which espoused social-ideological issues.

The late 1960s and the early 1970s were marked by the establishment of main terrorist groups. Since that time terrorism attracted more attention than ever before. It has become a frequent item on the agenda of international organisations, become a subject of international accords and generated much publicity and was a major issue in the SAARC summit held in Kathmandu, Nepal.

Is there a Terrorist Personality ?

Thirty years of terrorism research has found psychopathology and personality disorder no more likely among terrorists than among non-terrorists from the same background. Individuals suffering from serious psychopathology are unlikely to be able to plan and implement a successful attack. (Mccauley, 2001).

Though it is believed that certain personality types are attracted to terrorist groups. The first groups are extremely self-centered individuals with little regard for the feelings of others. They seek stimulation, are easily bored and are attracted to the exciting life of the revolutionary as a path to recognition and involvement. The second group resembles paranoid personalities. These individuals are suspicious and aggressive sensitive and always ready to defend themselves. The motivation for joining the group is that it provides a setting which provides sanction for projecting the person's own hostility upon the social environment. (Post 1983).

According to psychologist B.J. Berkowitz there are certain psychological types who would be most likely to threaten or try to use weapons of mass destruction (WMD) paranoids, paranoid schizophrenics, borderline, and anti-social personalities. He considers sociopath the most likely actually to use WMD. Though some believes that schizophrenics and sociopaths, for example, may want to commit acts of mass destruction, but they are less likely than others to succeed. "As large-scale dissemination of chemical, biological, or radiological agents requires a group effort, but that "Schizophrenics, in particular, often have difficulty functioning in groups. A case study of Ahmed Ramzi Yousef, mastermind of the World Trade Center (WTC) bombing on February 26, 1993, concluded that he appeared to be a well-educated, highly intelligent Islamic terrorist. (Hudson, 2002)

According to some, rather than analysing terrorism in terms of psychopathology, it should be seen in the context of culture, politics and religion. Terrorism is the product of its own time and place, there are no specific personality traits predicting one person more likely to become a terrorist than another.

Terrorism as Normal Psychology

No one wakes up one morning and decides that today is the day to become a terrorist. The trajectory by which normal people become capable of doing terrible things is usually gradual, perhaps imperceptible to the individuals. They kill for cause and comrades, i.e., with a combination of ideology and intense small group dynamics.

The psychology of the cause: Every normal person believes in something's more important in life, something that makes sense of our life and our death. The closer and more immediate death is, the more we need the group values that give meaning to life and death. [Glorifying death]. These values include the values of family, religion, ethnicity and nationality—the values of our culture. (Mccauley, 2001). Though there are no special-socialist groups with no religious roots (the Red Brigade in Italy, the Baadei-Meinhof gang and the Red Army faction in Germany).

The psychology of the comrades: The groups values represented in the cause are focussed to a personal intensity in the small group of like- minded people who perpetrate terrorist violence. The members of these groups drop themselves from other groups. The group gets enormous power. This power can make violence against the enemy not just acceptable but necessary. Every army aims to do what there terrorist group does: to link a larger group with small group dynamics that can deliver individuals to sacrifice. Every army cuts trainees off from their previous lives so that the combat unit can become their family; their fellow-soldiers become their brothers and their fear of letting down their comrades greater than their fear of dying. (Maccaule. 2001).

Group Dynamics

A group consists of two or more interacting persons who share common goals; have a stable relationship, are somehow interdependent and perceive that they are in fact part of group (Paulus, 1989).

Individuals come together and form groups as it satisfies important psychological and social needs such as belonging and receiving attention and affection, helps to achieve goals difficult for individuals alone, membership of a group provides knowledge and information otherwise inaccessible, satisfies need for security, gives identity that becomes part of the self-concept.

The same group dynamics are involved in terrorist groups. Individuals who are alone, alienated, on the margins of society, seeking to belong, to find acceptance, to find others who feel the same way, that it's the establishment's fault, that it's not me, for them it is a wonderful feeling to find one is not alone and that there are other like-minded individuals.

Identification with the group and its collective beliefs, the need for solidarity, and pressure toward conformity contribute significantly to individual commitment. Goup cohesiveness is obviously important for practical reasons as well as psychological needs, since an underground group needs to maintain strict secrecy for security purposes.

According to Bion there are three states of emotional group (Post. 1983)

1. ***The dependency group*** - turns to the omnipotent leader for security. The members blindly seek and follow directions.
2. ***The pairing group*** - Acts as if the goal of the group is to bring-forth the messiah. Someone who will save them, that there is a new world around the corner.
3. ***Flight*** - Fight group acts appositionally in relationship to the outside world which both threatens and justifies it existence - which the only way for the group to preserve itself is by fighting against or fleeing from the enemy.

Perceptual distortions and lack of objectivity are likely. Reliance on the group also facilitates the abandonment of responsibility for one's actions and the claim that one is acting merely as an agent and not an actor.

Terrorism's Strategic Concepts

Terrorism has often been described as the weapon of the weak. Indeed, there is manifest disparity between terrorist groups' capabilities and their ambitious goals. The strategy used by these groups is varied to bridge the gap between their meager means and extreme objectives. Terrorism is a strategy based on psychological impact. All forms of warfare have a significant psychological ingredient, both in trying to hamper the enemy's morale by sowing fear in its ranks and in strengthening its own forces' self-confidence and will to fight. Although terrorists have been rarely clear enough as to lay down a complete, coherent strategic plan, it is possible to discern several strategic ideas that terrorists have held as the cardinal practical concept of their struggle. These as described below as district notions although they are not necessarily mutually exclusive and terrorist have often espoused them concurrently. (Merari, 1994)

1. Propaganda by the Deed

The original concept of propaganda by the deed as explained and exercised by the 19th century revolutionaries was more refined than its modern usage in the post WW-II era. Whereas the earlier users of this idea were careful to choose symbolic targets, such as heads of state and infamous oppressive governors and ministers, in order to draw attention to the justification of their cause, the more recent brand has turned to multi-casually indiscriminate attacks. In doing so, the terrorists have exchanged the propaganda value of justification for a greater shock value, which guaranteed them massive media coverage.

However, it is not a complete strategy, the idea is only meant for the first stage of struggle.

2. Intimidation

Another salient psychological element is the intention to spread fear among the enemy's ranks. For a regime and its key functionaries, whose very existence is challenged by the insurgents, the struggle is a matter of life or death and they are generally unlikely to give up because of the terrorists threat.

Nevertheless, terrorists have sometimes succeeded, through a systematic campaign of assassination, kidnapping, to intimidate select categories of people, such as judges, jurors or journalists. An extension of this idea of coercive terrorism applies to the general population when they refuse to cooperate the insurgents.

3. Provocation

The psychological motive behind this strategy is that the anticipated terrorist attacks would provoke the government to resort to harsh measures, which would alienate it from the populace. Terrorist attacks tend to draw repressive responses by any regime. These measures in turn, make the government unpopular, thus increasing public support of the terrorists and their cause. When government's counter terrorist actions proved to be ineffective, anti-government sentiment is bound to prevail.

4. Strategy of Chaos

In this the terrorists attempts to create an atmosphere of chaos so as to demonstrate the government's inability to impose law and order. The insurgents hope that the public will under such circumstances demand that the "weak" liberal government be replaced by a strong regime. In order to create an atmosphere of disorder and insecurity, terrorists have resorted to random bombings of public places to create panic in the population.

Like other strategy it is not a comprehensive plan for seizing power. It is merely a way to create public mood, which, as the insurgents hope, will give them a better chance to continue their struggle in an unspecified way.

5. Strategy of Attrition

This is the only strategy viewed as a complete way of achieving victory, rather than part of a bigger strategy. This perception has been typical of modern anti-colonial terrorist groups. The insurgents are fully aware of their inferiority as a lighting force compared to the strength of the government and do not think that they have a greater stamina than the government and if they persist, the government would eventually yield. As they believe in perseverance rather than building stronger force.

6. Expressive Terrorism

In severe cases terrorism has seen emotional response with no clear strategic aim although the acts of violence have been perpetrated by a group, in a tactical organised manner.

Terrorism, here is an expression of an emotional state, rather a rationally selected instrument in the framework of a strategy of insurgence.

Increasingly, terrorist groups are recruiting members with the framework of a strategy of insurgence with expertise in fields such as communications, computer programming, engineering, finance, and the sciences. Ramzi Yousef graduated from Britain's Swansea University with a degree in engineering. Aum Shinrikyo's Shoko Asahara recruited a scientific team with all the expertise needed to develop WMD. Osama bin Laden also recruits highly skilled professionals in the fields of engineering medicine, chemistry, physics, computer programming, communications and so forth. Whereas the skills of the elite terrorist commandos of the 1960s and 1970s were often limited to what they learned in training camps, the terrorists of the 1990s who have carried out major operations have included biologists, chemists, computer specialists, engineers, and physicists.

The Making of a Terrorist

Why is mankind so wrought with hatred and violence that some would take the lives of the innocent as readily as take a breath? What pushes children from the cradle of innocence to the den of brutality? What creates a terrorist.

Terrorism is not typically the result by psychopathology nor is there single "terrorist personality" instead the individuals attracted to terrorism are diverse linked to commitment to a shared ideology and membership in the group. Each individual terrorist has a different combination of determinants that makes him a terrorist. There are different psychological models explaining the developments of a terrorist.

Social Learning Model

It is not a coincidence that many terrorists come from places like the Middle East or Northern Ireland, where what is the present generations of young people have known is regular extreme, well-publicised violence, violence could be the norm for such young people, whether it is on a wide scale or a smaller community or family. It may come to be considered the normal response to achieve objectives. Silke (2000) describes the process of becoming a terrorist as being primarily an issue of socialisation. He further states that the move from being disaffected to becoming an active terrorist is usually precipitated by a catalyst.

In certain societies, child-rearing practices inculcate aggression in children, which later on makes them prone to terrorist acts.

For example, Arab parenting practices tend to be highly authoritarian, fostering a profound degree of blind obedience to authority. In Middle

Eastern cultures, it is believed that a child is born without 'age or reason. It is then the goal of the parent to instill and develop the reason that child needs as an adult in Arab society. A "good" child, by Arab standards, is polite, obedient, disciplined and conforms to the values of the group. Male children are generally socialised to be aggressive. Children often view violence and power as acceptable means of resolving conflicts and setting differences. Their ability to reason is so under developed that they must rely on others to guide them, even if those guides are immoral and exploitive (Medus, 2001).

Some terrorists are following family tradition, as in the case of both Protestant and Catholic fighters in Northern Ireland and some groups of Palestinians in the Middle East and the social learning model with its emphasis on imitation and role models can easily accommodate this.

This approach emphasises education and the provision of peaceful role models as a major part of the solution to terrorism particularly aimed at children in their formative years.

Psychodynamic Model

Studies on German terrorism indicate a pattern of incomplete family structure especially during adolescence loss of father was pronounced. There major conflicts with the family and society, leading to conviction in juvenile courts. There was a disproportionate pattern of educational and work failure, so that the terrorist career was seen as "the terminal point of a series of abortive adaptation attempts." (Post. 1983).

Ballinger in his in-depth interview of a small group of terrorist found that there was presence of histories of childhood deprivation, of narcissistic wounds and vividly describes individuals who came to young adult hood deficient sense of self-esteem and inadequately integrated personalities. (Post, 1983)

Alienated individuals, who did not fit, projected to society the blame for their own inadequacies. For these alienated individuals, joining a test group represented the first real sense of belonging after a lifetime family they never had.

Terrorist make a complete break from their previous social surroundings, values and norms while they develop strong feelings for their own group, they develop hatred for society. It is the need to sustain membership in such a group into the twenties which represents a prolongation of adolescent conflicts, insufficient socialisation and incomplete families.

The need to belong the need to have a stable identity to resolve a split and be at one with oneself and with society is an important concept present in most of widely different espoused motivations and composition (Post, 1983).

The early developmental difficulties lead to a primary narcissistic disorder, characterised by a failure to integrate within the self the good and the bad object. In this all or nothing, good or evil, psychological world, what is good, the idealised, and what is bad, the source of pain, the reason for the lack of success recognition and acceptance is externalised and projected on to society. And, having protectively identified society as the source of problems, it follows that the way to cure the problems is to destroy their source or destroy the government.

This approach, which generally assumes a psychopathology model of terrorists, would emphasise better upbringing, including the resolution of childhood conflicts at least part of the solution.

Behaviourist Model

Most terrorists are heroes to someone and according to this model; such reinforcement increases the likelihood of terrorist behaviour (Kaplan, 2001).

"If Osama is becoming a hero, it is because the media has given him a larger than life image, and if some Muslims are glorifying him, it is because they have no other heroes and feel alienated from a system where they are repeatedly asked to prove their nationalistic credentials". (Bhaumik, 2001).

This approach emphasises in breaking the connection between terrorist behaviour and the rewards received by the terrorists for carrying it out, as part of the solution. As with the social learning model, most of those who support this model do not assume psychopathology on the part of terrorists.

Economic Model

Some groups choose the terror option because it is relatively inexpensive and yet can have huge effects. It doesn't require large amounts of money (although some terrorists such as Bin Laden are very wealthy). It does not require large numbers of people or equipment. It is the warfare of the poor and disaffected. This approach emphasises the importance of cutting off the funding of terror groups as part of solutions (Kaplan, 2001).

However, no model is complete and terrorism has to be understood in its cultural, political, social, ideological psychological perspectives.

Impact of Terrorism

For surviving victims themselves and their friend and families, the reaction to their experiences may be post-traumatic stress (Loughrey *et al.*, 1988). To summarise, post-traumatic stress involves disturbances of behaviour that occur after a major stressful event. The common symptoms are intrusive thoughts, nightmares, sleeping difficulties, anxiety or fear, alienation from people "jumpiness" emotional numbness and problems with social relationships. They vary in type and scope enormously from person to person. Some people will need professional help others will get by with the support of the families and friends.

In children who witness chronic community violence some behavioural problems were noticed, it was found that these children have difficulty in concentrating because of both lack of sleep and intrusive thoughts, memory impairment, anxious attachment to mothers and aggressive play behaviour (Osofsky, 1988).

Media and its Influence

Many terrorists do what they do, at least in part for the huge amounts of free publicity they gets from the media. Some have described publicity in the media as the "oxygen of terrorism" without it some (but not all) terror groups relay their demands through media organisations, or make the publicising of their cause a condition of releasing hostages, for e.g., However, the relationship between terror groups and the media can become risky, if the group does not like the way it is being portrayed.

This climate of fear is what terrorists strive to create and media is responsible for this unto a large extent. It is executed by preying upon the public's justified paranoia of terrorism and by exacerbating a crisis environment with inflammatory speculation, false leads and conspiracy spinning.

In the words of Ted Kappel, ABC anchor "Television and terrorism need one another, that they have what it fundamentally a symbiotic relationship without television terrorism becomes rather like the philosopher's hypothetical tree falling in the forest, no one hears it fall and therefore it has no reason for being. And television without terrorism, while not deprived of all interesting things in the world, is nonetheless deprived of one of the most interesting. (Houghton, 2001)

The media's influence is majorly on the most sensitive and vulnerable population, either by portraying the terrorists as hero and opening terrorism as a career option or in justifying their ideology and actions the terror among the people.

A study conducted after seventh weeks of 1995 Oklahoma city bombing concluded that bomb related television viewing in the aftermath of the disaster was extensive and therefore both emotional and television exposure were associated with post-traumatic stress at seventh weeks. Among children with no physical or emotional exposure, the degree of television exposure was directly related to post-traumatic stress symptomatalogy. [pfefferbaum., *et al.*, 2001].

Some have called this second hand terrorism. In a pilot study on the PTSD and grief among the children of Kuwait following the Gulf' crisis (Nader, *et al.,* 1993) found that children witnessing death or injury and the viewing of explicit graph images of mutilation on television has measurable influence on severity of post-traumatic streets reaction.

Both the above studies suggested the need of supervised viewing for the children and need for public policy to minimise children's exposure to graphic depictions of unrelated injury, death and mutilation.

Stockholm Syndrome

The effect of terrorist acts is not always devastating for the victims, in the form of PTSD and other psychological reactions, there can be uncommon reactions too. The victims may start appreciating the terrorists for the cause and people start valuing life.

The term, Stockholm syndrome, was coined in the early 70's to describe the puzzling reactions of four bank employees to their captor. To the world's surprise, all of the hostages strongly resisted the government's efforts to rescue them and were quite eager to defend their captors. The Stockholm incident compelled journalists and social scientists to research whether the emotional bonding between captors and captives was a "freak" incident and common occurrence in oppressive situations. They discovered that it is such a common phenomenon that it deserves a name. Thus the label, Stockholm syndrome, was born.

The Stockholm syndrome is an emotional attachment between *captive* vs. *captor* that develops the removal of the threat of death generates intense feelings of gratitude and fear that combine to make the captive reluctant to display negative feelings toward the captor or terrorist.

In fact former hostages have visited their captors in jail recommended defense counsel and even started a defense fund. The victim comes to see the captors as a "good guy" even a saviour. This condition occurs in response to four specific conditions. (Kaplan, 2001) :

1. A person threatens to kill another and perceived as having the capability to do so.

2. The other can't escape, so life depends upon the threatening *per se*.
3. The threatened person is isolated from outsiders so that the only other perspective available to him/her is that of the threatening person.
4. The threatening person is perceived as showing some degrees of kindness to the one being threatened.

It has happened to concentration camp prisoners, cult members, civilians in Chinese's communist prisons, incest victims, physically and/or emotionally abused children, battered women, prisoners of war, victims of hijacking and of course, hostages.

Other Reactions

In New York and America, post September 11, the unpredictable nature of a gross violation like the terrorist attacks has stripped people of their sense of security and control. There is also a war on within the country with every fresh disclosure of anthrax, and with rumours of terrorist attacks in the near future (Melwani, 2001).

This has suddenly restrained people from traveling, *i.e.,* Getting on planes and into subways. People have started spending time with their loved and near ones. There is also an increase in sexual behaviour called as "terror sex".

Chemically speaking, stress leads to an increased flow of dopamine and testosterone-hormones associated with pleasure and aggression—stimulating the sex drive. A marked increase in shopping, smoking, consumption of alcohol, chocolates, valium and attendance at religious functions has also been seen. (Melwani, 2001).

Psychological Explanation

The increased sex drive is a result of psyche defense mechanism, which makes people regress to primitive forms of behaviour. The collapse of the sense of security in the US has led people to try to fulfill their most basic and primitive drives, such as the desire to hoard food, make love, be near loved ones or in the secure atmosphere of one's home.

On the other hand in Gujarat, india, there were cases reporting of decreased libido after the January 26 earthquake. Difference can be due to cultural and societal differences between the west and east. Secondly, it can probably be attributed to difference in reaction in man-made and natural disasters. (Mealwani, 2001).

However, whatever be the reason such disasters do bring people close, the realisation of inevitable and uncertainty of death make them value life and civilisation.

Impact on Government

Majorly the government reaction to the terrorism is in the form of crisis management and in taking appropriate decision. Decisions are influenced by lot of factors such as time pressure, extremely consequential outcomes, lack of information and concern for public image or reputation, these factors delay the decision-making process.

It is difficult to plan a single strategy to deal effectively with terrorism. As there are different types of terrorist groups depending upon their ideology and target. Therefore, strategies differ from government to government, countries to countries, and from time to time.

Certain terrorist action such as hijacking and hostage taking put the government in painful dilemma, between humanitarian goals and terrorist demands. The public gets emotionally charged and pressurises the government to give into the terrorist demands. This is further sensationalised and dramatised by media. In the past we have witnessed it during the Kandahar-hijacking. When the government had to give into the terrorist demands and few core terrorist leaders were left.

Conclusion

The psychological study of terrorism is important to identify those who are or may become terrorist with a view of aiding prevention. As nobody is born-terrorist therefore the approach should be in understanding the circumstances responsible and individual vulnerability and to develop strategies to deal with terrorism effectively and in reducing its impact.

References

- American Psychological Associations. Coping with terrorism. At: helping .apa.org/daily/terrorism.html January 25, 2002 accessed on 26/1/2002.
- Bhaumik S.N. Pent-up and silent. *Outlook* 2001; Nov. 5:40-49.
- Crenshaw M. Terrorism. In Kazdin A.E, ed. *Encyclopaedia of Psychology*. Vol. 8. New York: Oxford University Press, 2000.
- Ganor B. Terrorism : No Prohibition without definition. At: www. ict.org.il/ articlcs/ articledet.cfm?articleid = 393 October 7, 2001 accessed on 13/1/ 2002.
- Houghton B.K. The Media's Terrorism. Second hand terrorism. www.nyriles.org/140 terror-psych/2.html 2001; accessed on 6-1-01.

- Hudson R.A., The Sociology Psychology of Terrorism: Who becomes a terrorist and why? A Report.w w w.loc.gov/rr/frd/sociology - psychology% 20 of % 20 Terrorism, him 1999; accessed on 16-1-01.
- Jenkins B.M. Terrorism. In: Borgatta M. L. ed. *Encyclopedia of Sociology,* Vol. 4 New York: Macmillan Publishing Company, 1992.
- Kaplan A. The mind of a terrorist.www.blueoceans.com/education/ terror.psyche.html 2001; accessed on 25-12-01.
- Long D. The Anatomy of terrorism. New York: Free Press 1990. As given in Kaplan A. The mind of a terrorist.www.blue-oceans.com/education/ terror.psychc.hlml 2001; accessed on 25-12-01.
- McCauley C. The Psychology of terrorism: An interview.www.ssrc.org/ sepl l/essa\s/ McCualey. Htmn 2001; accessed on 6-1-02.
- Medhus E. The Making of a Terrorist.www.drmedhus.com/making of a terrorist, htm 2001; accessed on 25-12-01.
- Melwari L. Love in the time of war. *The Week* 2001: Nov. 25-12-19.
- Merari A. Terrorism as a strategy of insurgency. At: www.st-and.ac.uk/ academic intrrcl research/ cstpv/publications 3.htm accessed on 13/1/2002.
- Merari A. Terrorism. In: Ramachandran V.S. ed. *Encyclopaedia of Human Behaviour*, Vol. 4. New York: Academic Press. 1994:4:399-409.
- Nader K.O., Pynoos R.S., Fairbanks L.K. Al - ajecl M. Al - Asfour A. A preliminary study of PTSD and grief among the children of Kuwait followed by Gulf crisis. Br. J. *Clin Psychol* 1993; 32:407-416.
- Osofky J.D., Evers SW, Hann DM, Pick AC. Chronic community violence:what is happening to our children?, Psychiatry 1993; 56:36-45.
- Paulus P.B. Psychology of Group Influence. Hillsdale, N.J.: Erlbaum;1989. As given in Baron RA, Byrne D. *Social psychology: Understanding Human Interaction.* Prentice Hall of India. New Delhi. Ed. 7:1995.
- Pfefferbaum B. Nixon S.J. Tivis R.D. Doughty D.I.: Pynoos R.S. Gurwitch R.H. Foy D.W. Television exposure in children after a terrorist incident 2001:64(3): 202-211.
- Post J.M. Individual and group dynamics of terrorist behaviour. In Pichot P. Berncv P. Wolf R, Thau K(Ed.). *Psychiatry:the State of Art.* New York: Plenum Press. 1985:6.
- Riley T. Psychology of terror. At: www.ticket.com/errtravel/2001/ errterror.htm October 31, 2001 accessed on 13/1/2002.
- Schmid A.P., Jongman A.J. Political terrorism. Amsterdam: North Holland Publishing Company, 1998. Cited in: Merari A. Terrorism as a strategy of insurgency. At: www.st and.ac.uk/academic/intrrel/research/cstpv/ publications3.htm accessed on 1 3/1, 2002.
- Silke A. Terrorism. The Psychologist 2001:14:580-581. As given in Kaplan A. The Mind of terrorist, www.blue-oceans.com/education/terror. psych.html 2001. Accessed on 25/12/2001.
- Tassey. 1. Coping with the aftermath of a disaster. At: helping.apa.org/ daily/tessey.html January 25, 2002 accessed on 26/1/2002.
- Wilkinson P. The strategic implications of terrorism. At: www.st-and.ac.uk/ academic/ intrrel/reseaech/cstpv/publications Id.htm accessed on 13/1/2002.

15

Peace with other Species

Jacquie Lewis

Making Peace with others Species

Peace studies encompass a wide range of topics. One can find articles on recent war torn areas of the world including Bosnia (Caspersen, 2004), Afghanistan (Benini and Moulton, 2004), Iraq (Bellamy, 2004), and Israel and Palestine (Sylvan, 2004), to name a few. The myriad of topics that are discussed include, but are not limited to: globalisation (Powers, 2005), international law (Balestrieri, 2004), world trade (Steinberg and Josling, 2003), politics (Jacobson, 2004), human rights (Cummings, 2004), religion (Fox, 2004), poverty (Kampfner, 2003), gender equality (Leidenfrost, 2000), the role of media (Auerbach, 2005), economics (Koubi, 2005), and violent crime (Neumayer, 2005).

What is missing from this peace literature is a broader perspective. Creation of a peaceful world needs to also include peace toward non-human animals. True peace is not possible unless it encompasses other species. Albert Schweitzer, in his Nobel Peace prize address, "The Problem of Peace in the World Today" stated:

> The human spirit is not dead. It lives on in secret...It has come to believe that compassion, in which all ethics must take root, can only attain its full breath and depth if it embraces all living creatures and does not limit itself to mankind [sic] (Wynne-Tyson, 1989, p. 315).

In order to come to an understanding of why the peace movement has failed to address the subject of peace with other species we should look at its beginnings. Peace Studies, which is derived from the field of Peace Research, evolved in the late 1950s, mainly in Western Europe. It blossomed in an atmosphere of nuclear tensions during the Cold War, the creation of NATO, and the Warsaw Pact. At that time peace studies focussed on an inter- or multi-disciplinary inquiry into human conflict, aggression, and violence as it attempted to offer alternatives to aggressive conflict and war. Since the advent of the nuclear age, advocates for peace have also called attention to such issues as human rights, economic and social justice, and environmental well-being (Barash and Webel, 2002).

In the West the peace movement has its roots in religion where peace advocates and pacifists have led the effort to avoid nuclear destruction. However, traditional mainstream religious movements, even the most liberal ones, have avoided embracing animal issues as a component of peace studies. This is, in part, because animals have been viewed as without emotions or intellect and as lacking souls. These prevailing attitudes have justified their abuse even though studies have demonstrated that animals are similar intellectually and socially to humans (Barber, 1993; Beckoff, 2000; Cavalieri and Singer, 1993; Griffin, 1981; Mauser, 2000; Linden, 1974; Linzey, 1987; Lopez, 1978; Masson and McCarthy, 1995; Pepperberg, 2002; Van Lawick-Goodall, 1971).

It stands to reason that if humankind is to truly create a global peace culture it must include other species. Peace with the animals can be accomplished on a personal level by individuals choosing to change their consumer behaviour patterns. Most people do not do this because they remain ignorant and apathetic to how their personal decisions perpetuate animal abuse. However, individuals can live a cruelty-free lifestyle, which means choosing not to consume products that harm animals (Mason, 1993).

In the United States most individuals are unaware how their belief systems about other species are derived from cultural biases. Hall (1976) estimates that, with most individuals, their out-of-awareness cultural assumptions outnumber explicit assumptions by a factor of 1000 or more. Because of this cultural blindness it is important for individuals to educate themselves in order to develop awareness and understanding. Most often, an awakening of cultural blindness brings a deeper understanding of other peoples and cultures which can foster peace among neighbours and countries. However, often when self-reflecting on cultural biases other species are overlooked. For example, individuals may reflect on classism, white privilege, male privilege, disability awareness, ageism, homophobia, or racism but never consider speciesism (Mason, 1993).

This study addresses two areas of cultural biases in the US. Both involve the unnecessary use of non-human animals at great suffering to them. By understanding the inherent cruelty to other species performed by institutional systems it is hoped that individuals reading this will make wiser, more peaceful, and compassionate consumer choices in their daily lives. The two areas to be discussed are the production of personal care and household products, which use animals in testing and food production that consists of animals.

Product Testing Using Animals

In the US millions of animals suffer and die annually in painful tests to determine the "safety" of household products and cosmetics. Products ranging from lipstick and eye shadow, to soap, furniture polish, weed killer, and oven cleaner are typically tested on rabbits, rats, guinea pigs, dogs, and other animals. These tests are conducted in spite of the fact that test results show that they do not help prevent human illness or injury (Sharpe, 1988). This is all the more tragic in light of the fact that there are numerous alternative products available to consumers that are not tested on animals and that have been proven to be safe and effective.

In testing laboratories there are two basic tests that are utilised. The first is the Draize Eye Irritancy Test. In this test, a flake, granule, powdered, or liquid ingredient is dropped into the anaesthetised eyes of fully conscious albino rabbits. During the tests, the rabbits' eyelids are often held open with clips and their bodies are immobilised to prevent pawing of the eyes in attempts to remove the caustic substances. Immobilisation is accomplished by holding the rabbits in stocks that allow only their heads to protrude. Many animals break their necks as they struggle to escape (Pratt, 1976).

Once the ingredient or substance being tested is placed in the rabbits' eyes, the laboratory records the extent of damage to the eye tissue. This is checked at specific intervals over an average period of 72 hours. However, some tests are conducted from as long as seven to 18 days. Reactions to the substances include swollen eyelids, inflamed irises, ulceration, bleeding, massive deterioration, and blindness. (Fadali, 1996; Weil, 1991).

Fadali (1996) states that these tests have questionable validity because they vary from lab to lab-and sometimes, from rabbit to rabbit. US law does not require that product ingredients be tested on animals. In addition, household product and cosmetic companies can use ingredients that have already been proven safe or use natural ingredients that are known to be safe. When one compares this with the number of alternative tests to using animals such as, in-vitro cultures using corneas or skin tissue, the Agrose Diffusion Method involving the use of seaweed, corneas from eye banks, cell cultures, sophisticated computer and mathematical models, and, human clinical trials, the conclusion is obvious. The Draize test is not necessary (Fadali, 1996).

Many companies continue to conduct the Draize Eye Irritancy Test for historical reasons, that is because they have been doing it this way for a number of years, sometimes since the 1940's when the test was first invented. It is also because their legal departments and insurance companies advise they conduct the tests in case they are sued. However, the fact that the Draize test is conducted does not indicate that products have been altered in order to make them less harmful to humans. Product companies merely insert a disclaimer on the product label such as "harmful if swallowed." This means that the term "safety testing" is really a misnomer (Fadali, 1996; Pratt, 1980; Rowen, 1984; Sharpe, 1988).

The second test used in product testing involving animals is the LD 50, or lethal dose 50 per cent test. The LD 50 test is an acute toxicity test which measures the amount of a toxic substance that will kill 50 per cent of the animals in a single dose. Death usually occurs within two to four weeks. Each year, in the United States, about five million dogs, rabbits, rats, monkeys, and other animals die in LD 50 testing (Greek and Greek, 2002; Pratt, 1980; Rudacille, 2001).

The LD 50 test is extremely brutal. When laboratories conduct the LD 50, a substance is forced by tube into the animals' stomachs or through holes cut into their throats. Sometimes this process causes death from a ruptured stomach due to the sheer weight of the dosage. Ingredients can also be injected subcutaneously or into a vein, or into the lining of the abdomen. Other testing methods involve mixing the substance into lab chow; or restraining the animals so they inhale through gas masks. It can also be rubbed into the eyes, rectum, or vagina. Lab technicians then observe the animals' physical reactions, which include reactions such as skin eruptions, abnormal posture, or more serious conditions such as, laboured breathing, diarrhoea, constipation, emaciation, bleeding from the eyes, nose, or mouth, or convulsions (Ruesch, 1978; Sharpe, 1988; Smyth, 1978).

Like the Draize Eye Irritancy Test the LD 50 does not accurately measure human health hazards because it is imprecise and crude (Fano, 1997). Test results can also be affected by variables such as the age or sex of the animals tested, their housing environment or nutritional conditions, room temperature, or the time of day and year. It should also be noted that one species may react differently to substances than does another species. In addition, reactions between individuals of the same species can vary greatly (Pratt, 1980).

In response to public pressure, some laboratories have begun reducing the amount of animals used in the LD 50 test, referred to as "limit" tests. However, the tests still remain cruel and imprecise (Fadali, 1996). Computer modeling, cell and tissue cultures, the Ames test, which uses salmonella bacteria, are among the non-animal testing methods available as alternatives to the LD 50.

As with the notorious Draize Eye Irritancy Tests, it will take pressure from concerned consumers to move cosmetics and household product companies into the 21st century. Although many of the larger companies still test on animals, in this day and age, it is relatively easy to buy cruelty-free products since over 550 companies (usually small and independent companies) do not, or no longer test on animals (National Anti-Vivisection Society, 2000). Fadali (1996) believes the Draize eye irritancy test and the LD 50 test will someday meet their overdue demise when enough consumers refuse to buy products tested in this manner.

If a peaceful world is to be accomplished this should include non-violent consumer choices, such as purchasing products not tested on animals. This cruelty-free lifestyle is already practiced by many animal advocates and it makes sense that it should also be adopted by those who care about peace.

Agri-business and the Use of Animals

The second area where individuals can demonstrate peace towards other species is with their food choices. In the US mass production of meat has resulted in great pain and suffering for farmed animals. Most factory farmed animals spend their entire lives indoors confined to small metal cages with artificial lighting or no lighting at all. Because of the intense confinement of these animals the air in factory farm buildings smells strongly of ammonia, which is caused by the animal urine. In chicken factory warehouses the noxious fumes damage or destroy the animals' lungs (Marcus, 2005).

In addition to the factory farm conditions, animals are also subjected to a number of mutilations, including tail docking, ear cutting, castration, and beak searing, all without aid of anesthetics (Marcus, 2005; Robbins, 1987). Animals raised on factory farms also have their genes manipulated and are fed antibiotics to prevent disease and hormones to engender high productivity. In the US, almost 50 per cent of all antibiotics are administered to farm animals (Schlosser, 2001).

Pigs, which are intelligent and highly social, suffer physically and emotionally when they are confined. Most pigs in the US today are born and raised inside buildings that have automated water, feed and waste removal. Until they are shipped for slaughter they spend their entire lives never seeing sunshine. In the US 90 per cent of all pigs raised for meat production are confined at some point in their lives. Sows are kept pregnant and confined to narrow cages where they are unable to turn around. Under these conditions many pigs suffer from boredom and develop neurotic, repetitive behaviours. Out of frustration, they often engage in mouthing, where they continuously mouth the bars of their cages. Others develop nervous ticks or show aggressive behaviour, which involves fighting or cannibalism. At about six months of age, pigs go to slaughter (Marcus, 1998; Mason and Singer, 1980; Robbins, 2001).

Much like the life of pigs, cows on dairy farms face inhumane conditions. Half of the cows in the US are raised in intensive confinement, where they are deprived of social contact with others of their own species and are also unable to engage in natural behaviour, such as grass grazing. Cows are held in buildings where they are fed, watered and have their waste removed mechanically. Twice a day they are brought to a milking parlour where automated machines milk them. In order for factory farmers to double their milk production cows are injected with Bovine Growth Hormone (BGH). To keep them pregnant and lactating, so they will produce milk flow on a continual basis, cows are impregnated ten months after giving birth (Midkiff, 2004). Female calves are kept to restock the dairy herd while male calves are usually sold off to Veal farms (Marcus, 2005; Riebel and Jacobsen, 2002). Usually when milk production decreases, at about four years of age, they are sent to slaughter (Schlosser, 2001).

Veal farms arguably have one of most cruel methods of confinement. Calves, many of them as young as two-days old, spend their entire lives chained at the neck in small wooden crates. Because veal is considered a delicacy when the flesh is tender and pale the animals are restricted from as much movement as possible and are fed an iron deficient diet. They live their lives in darkness, except at feeding time, which is twice a day. After four months they are shipped to the slaughterhouse (Marcus, 1998; Mason and Singer, 1980).

The US broiler chicken industry, which produces six billion chickens a year for consumption, fares no better than animals. Broiler chickens are raised in overcrowded, unlit broiler houses. Their beaks and toes are severed in order to prevent injury from fighting among birds. These birds are genetically altered and selectively bred in order to produce bigger breasts and thighs, the chicken parts most in demand. This manipulative breeding system makes standing extremely difficult because it creates birds so heavy that their bones often cannot support their weight. They often develop arthritis and other joint diseases because of this genetic manipulation (Marcus, 2005). Birds are bred to reach the market weight at an amazing rate, 31/2 pounds in seven weeks (Marcus, 2005; Mason and Singer, 1980).

One of the most brutal methods of agri-business production is the conditions on factory egg farms. There are about 250 million hens in egg factories which supply ninety-five per cent of the eggs to US consumers. In these facilities the animals are confined in small battery cages where anywhere from five to eight birds live in a space consisting of 14 square inches. Because they live their lives on slanted wire floors it is not uncommon for birds to experience severe discomfort from foot deformities. Since the birds have no room to act naturally, nor can they form a pecking order in a building with 100,000 birds, it is not unusual for them to become aggressive and attack each other. To prevent aggression that can result in cannibalism the birds have their beaks seared off with a debeaking device. Since this is an imprecise method many times the entire beak is removed rather than just the tip. The result is that the animal is unable to eat and dies a slow death of starvation (Mason and Singer, 1980).

On factory egg farms baby chicks are sorted, sexed, and separated by gender at birth. Since there is no use for males chicks on egg farms newborn males are either gassed, thrown in trash bags one on top of the other, where they suffocate, or more commonly, thrown into a grinder while fully conscious (Marcus, 2005). Layer hen factories manipulate lighting, subjecting hens to constant light, in order to encourage greater egg production. Another way to encourage increases in egg production is by forcing birds to molt. At the end of their laying cycle birds are deprived of food and water for seven to 14 days. This brutal procedure shocks their systems into molting and produces another laying cycle. The results tax the birds' systems. Because of excessive egg laying many birds deplete the minerals from their bodies. When they can no longer lay eggs they are shipped to the slaughterhouse (Robbins, 1987).

This brief analysis of the treatment of animals on factory farms suggest that the only way to avoid animal suffering and death is for consumers, including those in the peace movement, to adapt a plant-based diet. The horrible treatment of animals will be stopped only when there is no longer a market for them as food. In addition, there does not seem to be any rational reason for continuing to consume animals as food because studies show that a plant-based diet is healthier for the individual and the environment (Barnard, 1993; Campbell, 2004; Cook, 2004; Lappe, 1978; Ornish, 1990; Riebel, 2002; Robbins, 2001; Schlosser, 2001).

Conclusion

This study has addressed two issues that stress the relationship between consumer choices and animal welfare. The above situations illustrate just two scenarios, testing laboratories and factory farms, which show what life is like for some animals. These issues raise serious questions about the responsibility individuals have when making consumer decisions. As consumers we can decide not to buy products tested on animals and refrain from meat, egg, and dairy consumption. By making these choices individuals can make peace with the animals.

Recently, the environmental movement and the peace movement have merged to cause a historical shift. Most notably this is evident in the work of 2005 Nobel Peace Prize recipient, Wangari Maathai who planted thirty million trees throughout Kenya with the Green Belt Movement. This grassroots peace movement involved civil rights, woman's rights, social justice, and environmental concerns to reforest entire areas of her country. The movement was also instrumental in overturning a corrupt regime that had ruled Kenya for 25 years (Maathai, 2004).

There is no reason to believe that a similar blending could not occur between the peace movement and the animal advocacy movement. Without concern for other species the peace movement lacks a certain generosity. As the psychologist Eric Fromm (1962), who wrote so eloquently on the subject of love, has stated unless humankind considers the well-being of all, we fail to understand the true depth and meaning of love. Few would argue that love is the foundation of the peace movement. It is at the core, nourishing its members to push forward in their goal of peace. This underpinning of love, which drives the peace movement, should expand and embrace the many issues involving other species. Only then can true peace be realised in its fullness.

References

- Auerbach, Y. (2005). Media framing and foreign policy: The elite press *vis-a-vis* US policy in Bosnia, 1992-95. *Journal of Peace Research,* 42(1), 83-89.
- Balestrieri, E.B. (2004). Abu Ghraib prison abuse and the rule of law. *International Journal on World Peace, 21(4),* 3-21.

- Barash, D.P., and Webel, C.P. (2002). *Peace and conflict studies.* Thousand Oaks, CA: Sage.
- Barber, T.X. (1993). *The human nature of birds.* New York: St. Martin's Press.
- Barnard, N. (1993). Food *for life: How the new four food groups can save your life.* New York: Harmony Books.
- Beckoff, M. (2000). Animal emotions: Exploring passionate natures. *Bio-science,* 50(10), 861-870.
- Bellamy, A.J. (2004). Ethics and intervention: The 'humanitarian exception' and the problem of abuse in the case of Iraq. *Journal of Peace Research, 41(2),* 131-147.
- Benini, A.A., and Moulton, L. H. (2004). Civilian victims in a conflict: Operation enduring freedom, Afghanistan. *Journal of Peace Research, 41(4),* 403-422.
- Campbell, T.C. (2004). *The China study.* Dallas, TX: Benbella Books.
- Caspersen, N. (2004). Good fences make good neighbours? A comparison of conflict-regulation strategies in post-war Bosnia. *Journal of Peace Research, 41(5),* 569-588.
- Cavalieri, P., and Singer, P. (Eds.). (1993). *The great ape project.* New York: St. Martin's Press.
- Cook, C.D. (2004). *Diet for a dead planet: How the food industry is killing us.* New York: The New Press.
- Cummings, R. (2004). Human rights, international law, and peace in the Middle East. *Tikkun,* 19(1), 23.
- Fadali, M.A. (1996). *Animal experimentation: A harvest of shame.* Los Angeles: Hidden Springs Press.
- Fano, A. (1997). *Lethal laws: Animal testing, human health and environmental policy.* London: Zed Books.
- Fox, J. (2004). The rise of religious nationalism and conflict: Ethnic conflict and revolutionary wars, 1945-2001. *Journal of Peace Research,* 41 (6), 715.
- Fromm, E. (1962). *The art of loving.* New York: Harper and Row.
- Greek, C.R., and Greek, J.S. (2002). *Sacred cows and golden geese: The human cost of experiment on animals.* New York: The Continuum International Publishing Group.
- Griffin, D.R. (1981). *The question of animal awareness: Evolutionary continuity of mental experience.* New York: The Rockefeller University Press.
- Hall, E.T. (1976). *Beyond Culture.* Garden City, NY: Anchor Books.

- Hauser, M.D. (2000). *Wild minds: What animals really think.* New York: Henry Holt.
- Jacobson, M. (2004). Modern history and politics: Power, terror, peace, and war. *Middle East Journal,* 58(4), 707-708.
- Kampfner, J. (2003). Terrorism: The price we pay for poverty. *New Statesman, 16(742),* 20-22.
- Koubi, V. (2005). War and economic performance. *Journal of Peace Research, 42(1),* 67-82.
- Lappe, F.M. (1978). *Diet for a small planet.* New York: Ballantine Books.
- Leidenfrost, N.B. (2000). Report on "Women 2000: Gender equality, development, and peace for the twenty-first century." Twenty-third session of the Beijing plus five United Nations Assembly special session. *Journal of Family and Consumer Sciences, 92(4),* 80-83.
- Linden, E. (1974). *Apes, Men, and Language: Hoe teaching chimpanzees to "talk" alters man's notions of his place in nature.* New York: Saturday Review Press.
- Linzey, A. (1987). *Christianity and the rights of animals.* New York: The Crossroad. Lopez, B. H. (1978). *Of wolves and men.* New York: Charles Scribner's Sons.
- Maathai, W. (2004). *The green belt movement.* New York: Lantern.
- Marcus, E. (1998). *Vegan: The new ethics of eating.* Ithaca, NY: McBooks Press. Marcus, E. (2005). *Meat market: Animals, ethics, and money.* Ithaca, NY: Brio Press.
- Mason, J. (1993). *An unnatural order: Uncovering the roots of our domination of nature and each other.* New York: Simon and Schuster.
- Mason, J., *and* Singer, P. (1980). *Animal Factories.* New York: Crown.
- Masson, J. M., and McCarthy, S. (1995). *When elephants weep: The emotional lives of animals.* New York: Delacorte Press.
- Midkiff, K. (2004). *The meat you eat: How corporate farming has endangered America's food supply.* New York: St. Martin's Press.
- National Anti-Vivisection Society. (2000). *Personal care for people who care.* Chicago: The National Anti-Vivisection Society.
- Neumayer, E. (2005). Inequality and violent crime: Evidence from data on robbery and violent theft. *Journal of Peace Research,* 42(1), 101-112.
- Ornish, D. (1990). *Dr. Dean Ornish's program for reversing heart disease.* New York: Random House.
- Pepperberg, I.M. (2002). *The Alex studies: Cognitive and communicative abilities of grey parrots.* Cambridge, MA: Harvard University Press.

- Powers, K.L. (2005). Globalisation and armed conflict. *Journal of Peace Research, 42(3),* 363-364.
- Pratt, D. (1976). *Painful experiments on animals.* New York: Argus Archives.
- Pratt, D. (1980). *Alternatives to pain in experiments on animals.* New York: Argus Archives.
- Riebel, L., and Jscobsen, K. (2002). *Eating to save the earth: Food choices fora healthy planet.* Berkeley, CA: Celestial Arts.
- Robbins, J. (1987). *Diet for a new America.* Walpole, NH: Stillpoint.
- Robbins, J. (2001). *The food revolution: How your diet can help save your life and the world.* Berkeley, CA: Conari Press.
- Rowen, A.N. (1984). *Of mice, models, and men: A critical evaluation of animal research.* Albany: State University of New York Press.
- Rudacille, D. (2001). *The Scalpel and the Butterfly: The conflict between animal research and animal protection.* Berkeley: University of California Press.
- Ruesch, H. (1978). *Slaughter of the innocent.* New York: Bantam Books.
- Schlosser, E. (2001). *Fast Food Nation.* New York: Houghton Mifflin.
- Sharpe, R. (1988). *The cruel deception: The use of animals in medical research.* Northamptonshire, England: Thorsons.
- Smyth, D.H. (1978). *Alternatives to animal experiments.* London: Whitstable Litho.
- Steinberg, R. H., and Josling, T. E. (2003). When the peace ends: The vulnerability of EC and US agricultural subsidies to WTO legal challenge. *Journal of International Economic Law,* 6(2), 369.
- Sylvan, D.S. (2004). Forecasting Israeli-Palestinian relations. *Journal of Peace Research, 41(4),* 445-463.
- Van Lawick-Goodall, J. (1971). *In the shadow of man.* New York: Dell.
- Weil, Z. (1991). *Animals in society: Facts and perspectives on our treatment of animals.* Jenkintown, PA: Animalearn.
- Wynne-Tyson, J. (Ed.). (1989). *The extended circle.* New York: Paragon House.

16

Globalisation- An Underpinnings of Terrorism: A Study of Kashmir Conflict

Mohmad Saleem Jahangir

Abstract

In the world today, there is a growing trend in violence, both domestically and internationally, in the form of terrorism. It is present in our everyday lives and in every part of the world—some more than others. After the September 11, terrorist attacks against the US, the very discourse of international relations and global politics has been transformed. Prior to September 11, the dominant issues were geo-economic in nature. Globalisation and humanitarian issues occupied the agendas of international summits and international organisations. But now geo-politics and security concerns have once again become the central issue and the "old language and institutions" of the Cold War are shaping our thinking about global politics. Globalisation of the world has become the ultimate celebration of the political, economic and social homogenisation of the global populations. After the advent of globalisation, the third world countries proved to be very helpful in strengthening the process particularly after September 11, that strengthened the process more in the form of economic imperialism as is evident from the attacks on Afghanistan and Iraq. The study on the parallel lines seeks to assess the sustainability of the Kashmir Conflict on the basis of Globalisation which provided a good market of ammunition to international scene in form of India and Pakistan and thereby strengthened the conflict in this part of South Asia.

The term globalisation is one of the most commonly employed phrases in contemporary society. It propounds a wide range of connotations in diverse disciplines, and to different individuals, making it a rather vague concept. It is mainly used to portray the augmentation in international trade and financial flows that have taken place since 1960, but especially in the post-1980 era. Yet this phenomenon has historical precedents. Globalisation has made it increasingly necessary to break with nation-state centered analysis in macro-sociologies. Social structure is becoming transnationalised, and an epistemological shift is required in concurrence with this ontological change. New interdisciplinary transnational studies have been predicated on a paradogmatic shift in the focus of social inquiry from the nation-state as the basic unit of analysis to the global system as the appropriate unit.[1]

Ascendance of globalisation has opened up new dimensions of development and exploitation in developing societies. Globalisation focusses on the emergence of supranational institutions in order to decide to shape up and constrain the policy options for any particular developing society. Although its wide connotation stands for the overwhelming impact of global economic processes, including processes of production, consumption, trade, capital flow, and monetary interdependence. It also signifies the rise of neo-liberalism as a hegemonic policy discourse; the emergence of new global cultural forms, media, and technologies of communication, which shape the relations of affiliation, identity, and interaction within and across local cultural settings.

Globalisation is a polyvalent, promiscuous, controversial word that often obscures more than it reveals about recent economic, political, social, and cultural changes. It is best used to denote a multi-centric, multi-scalar, multi-temporal, multi-form, and multi-causal process.[2] Globalisation is controversial because it is a multi-sided process, a major tendency in the movement of contemporary world history, every day, every hour affecting all spheres of life, activities, and relations among national states and the lives ofhuman beings everywhere on the planet. Furthermore, at the turn of the twenty-first century, the world is facing global issues that no country can solve alone without multi-lateral co-operation.[3]

Globalisation has many definitions, but at its root it is about the planet getting smaller and the free-flow of people, goods, capital, and ideas across borders. It has been sped up by technology (computers, jets, etc.) and it makes traditional notions of sovereign nation-state powers more and more irrelevant.[4] All theses definitions of the term agree on the economic aspect of globalisation. The process began as one of increasing international business dealings. A good definition for it is an economically driven process of business which also makes ideas, cultural behaviours, technologies, and politics global concepts and lead to greater interaction among previously separated groups and nations. But has September 11 changed all that? Globalisation as a process was facilitated by the liberalisation of trans-border transactions by the dilution of sovereignty. Globalisation is essentially a measure of the ease with which, labour, ideas, capital, technology and profits can move across borders with minimal governmental interference. This measure of liberalisation is also a surrogate measure for security.

It is ironic that global terrorism, the phenomenon of terrorists operating in and against several nations simultaneously, was facilitated by globalisation and now it has become the biggest challenge to globalisation. Global terrorism depends on the success of globalisation. In fact one may always conceive of global terrorism as a facet of the global culture resulting from globalisation.[5] In the nineteen eighties as international theorists realised the growing power of economic interdependence they began to theorise what would happen to the anarchic nature of global politics with the increased economic co-operation between nations. Liberals argued that international institutions created to facilitate global co-operation and manage interdependence would eliminate anarchy. The realists however maintained that economic co-operation was not a guarantor of security and therefore we would live in a world that was economically orderly but politically anarchic. Neo-liberals and neorealists agreed to describe this condition as a state of co-operation under anarchy.[6]

The Kashmir dispute has a long history, dating before the vagaries of partition in 1947. As one of the princely states, Kashmir - a border state with a Muslim-majority - had the choice to accede to either India or Pakistan when the British withdrew from the sub-continent. When Maharaja Hari Singh did not chose either India or Pakistan, tribesmen from Pakistan, with the support of Pakistani Army, invaded Kashmir in order to occupy it by force.[7] Pushed to the corner, Hari Singh signed a treaty of accession with India in exchange of Indian military assistance to push back the invaders. At the time, India's first Prime Minister, Jawaharlal Nehru, promised that the accession would only be confirmed after the Kashmiris had their say. The accession took place as a conflict erupted between the Indian and Pakistani troops over Kashmir and the legacy of what became the first Kashmir War locked both countries into historical positions that they find too difficult to grow out of today.[8]

At the core, the Kashmir dispute between India and Pakistan is not a contest over strategic territory or resources, say experts. Instead, they contend, it is the result of competing visions of nationalism and state-building: secular nationalism in the case of India, religious nationalism in the case of Pakistan.[9] Between the Indian and Pakistani nationalism lies the Kashmiri nationalist claim to independence which is based not on religion but on *Kashmiriyat* - a separate Kashmiri ethnicity.[10] An ethnic notion of independent Kashmir, however, is difficult to realise given the three ethnically separable geographical regions in J&K: Dogra Hindu-dominated Jammu region, Muslim-majority Kashmir Valley, and the Ladakh region which has a significant Tibetan Buddhist population. As several academic and independent surveys indicate, the first-preference of the Dogra Hindus (in Jammu) and Tibetan Buddhists (in Ladakh) is to stay with India rather than be a part of Pakistan or an independent Kashmir. Similarly, a sizable number of Gujjar and Punjabi Muslims in Jammu, who are not ethnically Kashmiris, prefer to stay with India as opposed to their co-religionists from the Valley who favour an independent Kashmir.[11] In sum, these "three compromised nationalisms" drive the conflict in Kashmir, reinforcing each other in a manner that makes the problem particularly intractable. The change of stance from Muslim-based ideology to the secular and that time Leader Sheikh Abdullah by renaming Political Party from Muslim Conference to National Conference also fuelled the conflict.

The history of the dispute is intrinsically linked to the various UN resolutions on the Kashmir dispute. From the UN resolutions passed, which upheld plebiscite for the Kashmiri people as a means to resolve the conflict, to the most recent UN Security Council Resolution 1172 of 14 May 1998, urging upon India and Pakistan to resume dialogue to address all issues and find mutually acceptable solutions to address the root causes of tensions, including Kashmir, signify that the Kashmir issue remains the core issue between India and Pakistan even on the UN agenda and as a threat to regional security.

The Indian media's position on the UN resolutions is in line with the official stance that nothing agreed by India in the UN resolutions alters the status or in any way modifies Indian sovereignty over the State. Hence, the approach is that of non-compliance to the various resolutions. Since 1989, there have also been some sort of official moves to declare the UN Resolutions as redundant, in view of the signing of Simla agreement of 1972, even though that agreement also acknowledges the UN resolutions as the basis of the dispute.

Pakistan maintains that the final solution will be a durable one if the UN resolutions are implemented in letter and spirit. The international media's approach in recent times is to see the resolution on the conflict as possible only through bilateral talks. The dispute is portrayed as a case of domestic militancy, where India is unlikely to yield to these international resolutions. Or Indian sources are cited when these refer to cross-border terrorism. The international media tends to bypass the reference to these resolutions. While human rights violations are reported, the freedom fighters are portrayed as Islamic militants, and speculations are given regarding their linkages with similar organisations in other countries, such as the Taliban of Afghanistan. This diverts attention from the actual issue which has given rise to these 'militants' in the first instance.

Like all princely states, Kashmir had acceded to the Indian Union only with regards to defense, foreign affairs, and communications portfolios and its special status was recognised within the Indian Constitution. The Centre's undue interference in Kashmir's internal affairs planting "puppet" State Chief Ministers through patently rigged elections - slowly but surely alienated the Kashmiri public.[12] Decades of misrule, "few institutional channels for expression of political discontent and dissent,"[13] "the increased media penetration and the subsequent high political assertiveness among Kashmiris".[14]

But surprisingly in 1988-89, the conflict took the shape of 'terrorism' when the peace in Kashmir valley turned to be hell in itself killing thousands of people, destroying property worth billions and leading to migration of communities altogether. The insurgency grew quickly - partly because of the exceptionally heavy-handed Indian counter-measures, partly because of covert Pakistani support giving rise to many militant outfits in form of pro-independence Jammu and Kashmir Liberation Front (JKLF), Hizb-ul-Mujahideen - the largest and most influential outfit, Lashkar-e-Taiba (LeT), Harkat-ul-Mujahideen (HuM), Jaish-e-Mohammad (JeM) and Al-Badr, etc. which resulted in the appearance of guns in practice in Kashmir.

Besides, killing of thousands of innocent people, migrations, property destructions, etc., one unique and extraordinary process of globalisation was also witnessed. Pakistan, used to buy the ammunition from countries like US, gave it to militants for use and in-turn much has been captured by the Indian army, that too free of cost by investing a little defense force into it. As such, what actually Pakistan bought reached India free of cost thereby concluding the fact that 'if Pakistan is strategic alliance of America, India is a natural alliance'. So after 1989, a clear flow of ammunition could be witnessed across borders.

Presented by the media as a conflict regarding the status of Kashmir, the role of US foreign policy in feeding this conflict is invariably overlooked. Since the end of the Cold War, Washington has deliberately contributed —through covert intelligence operations— to fuelling the Indo-Pakistan conflict. In the wake of September 11, amidst new terrorist attacks and ethnic riots in India, conditions have developed which favour the outbreak of war between the two countries.

The Kashmir conflict must also be seen in the broader regional context of Indo-Pakistan Relations. The US is presently involved in several related war theatres extending from the Middle East to Central Asia like the war in Afghanistan is marked by the militarisation of the entire Central Asian region with US troops stationed in several of the former Soviet republics. The persistence of the Kashmir conflict between India and Pakistan, not only raises the spectre of a nuclear holocaust in a region which encompasses almost a quarter of the World's population, it also raises the possibility of a broader war which could potentially engulf a much larger region, with far-reaching implications for the future of humanity.

The economic sustenance of US on the expenses on defence budget of India and Pakistan cannot be ignored. As is evident that most of the money, the two countries spend is on developing the nuclear power and ammunition to set themselves safe from each other because of the lingering Kashmir issue and as such both the countries buy most of the things like F16 from US' companies providing them a huge profitable margin which otherwise is not possible on the successful resolution of Kashmir issue. So as to keep the market at peak, the policy of US has been to avoid the peace in Kashmir which, for them has become hub of market for ammunition.

The geographical location of Kashmir provides it with the strategic importance for the rest of the countries. For US, Kashmir could be the best geographical location to deal strategically with China for whom it is not carrying a good notion as America has a threat that China may bye-pass it from being a super power in 2050. So as to keep it at low profile by creating disturbances with the neighbours particularly with Pakistan and to deal with it whenever need arises, America is trying to keep the issue of Kashmir live.

So apart from projective goals put forth by the followers and advocates, hence there is a good scope for reinterpreting and reinventing the executing aspect of globalisation in relation to terrorism. Once these problems are studied and analysed, it comes to our mind as to "Is globalisation for terrorism or vice versa?" Sociologically speaking, if these invisible repercussions are not taken care of, there could be much adverse effect especially on the youth of developing societies, and all the projections set forth by the experts would turn to be bogus. It is not out of place here to mention that if youth of today are targeted then the development which the globalisation promises will in shortest time span collapse. Besides we need to redefine globalisation apart from the premises of economic Imperialism and militarism. It has to be used as a tool to cross borders for development and peace not to let it to intensify terrorism for interests of 'few' at stake of 'huge population'. And Pakistan and India turn to be allies rather than intensifying the conflict and terror activities, not only would India be more secure *vis-a-vis* China, but both countries would also excel the developmental processes in relation to each other that would be a step-ahead for the peace process and development for rest of the South Asia. The resulting lower defense budgets would mean more trade and more prosperity for the region as a whole. The gateway for the development in South Asia would mean to give hand to globalisation for development and not for terrorism and this would be achieved by giving a breakthrough to it by avoiding terrorism in Kashmir.

References

1. William I. Robinson. 1998. 'Beyond Nation-State Paradigams: Globalisation, Sociology, and the Challenge of Transnational Studies' *Sociological Forum*; Volume 13, Number 4 / December, 1998, p. 561.
2. Bob Jessop. 2002. *Time and Space in the Globalisation of Capital and Their Implications for State Power Time, Space*. Rethinking Marxism, Volume 14, Number 1 (Spring 2002), p. 97.
3. Cap, Van Chu. 2002. 'Marx and Engels on Economic Globalisation' *Nature, Society, and Thought*, Vol. 15, No. 2 (2002), p. 241.
4. http://www.globalenvision.Org/library/8/703.
5. Terrorism and Globalisation <http://www.glocaleye.org/ terglo.htm>
6. *Ibid.*
7. Ayesha Jalal. 1990. *The State of Marital Rule*. Cambridge: Cambridge University Press, pp. 56-60.
8. Alexander Evans, "Reducing Tension is Not Enough", *The Washington Quarterly* (Spring 2001), p. 183.
9. Sumit Ganguly and Kanti Bajpai. 1994. 'India and the Crisis in Kashmir', *Asian Survey*, Vol. 34, No. 5, p. 402.
10. Ashutosh Varshney. 1992. 'Three Compromised Nationalisms: Why Kashmir has been a Problem', in *Perspectives on Kashmir: The Roots of*

Conflict in South Asia, edited by Raju G.C. Thomas. Boulder Colo.: Westview, p. 198.

11. Sumantra Bose. 2003. *Kashmir: Roots of Conflict, Paths to Peace*, Cambridge: Harvard University Press, p. 153.
12. Meredith Weiss, "The Jammu and Kashmir Conflict: Overview", 25th June 2002, Available: http://www.yale.edu/ycias/globalisation/kashmir.pdf.
13. Sumit Ganguly and Kanti Bajpai. 1994. *op. cit.* p. 404.
14. Sumantra Bose. 2003. *op. cit.* p. 45.

17

Contemporary Conflict Resolution among the Sukuma of Tanzania

R.E.S. Tanner

Introduction

In central Tanzania to the south of Lake Victoria there are about five million Sukuma and their neighbouring two million Nyamwezi, the biggest tribal group in the country, who have a similar culture, a mutually intelligible language, living by a combination of subsistence farming and pastoralism. A culture combining the iron *hoe* with an ideology of cattle accumulation for a combination of social, economic and possible religious reasons (Malcolm 1953).

They have lived for at least two centuries in widely dispersed hamlets based rather on haphazard associations than on *affinal* and *agnatic* connections, since they segment as each son attains adulthood and getting a wife exogamously wants to set up his own household independently.

This pattern of living is well-suited to their dry Savanna environment as it prevents any concentration of people and cattle in particular areas. As their population has increased they have moved out into previously unoccupied areas repeating the same pattern of dispersed settlements except towards the east where their expansion came up against the pastoral age-graded warrior system of the Maasai.

There appear to be several types of conflict which all have the characteristic of being on-going rather than being aimed or involving solutions. There is only an on-going system of reaching a balance which leaves both sides of disputes still in acceptable social positions and not so aggrieved as to renew the quarrel immediately.

Firstly inter-tribal tensions with the Maasai to the east which swings backwards and forwards according to the irritations to the Sukuma ethnic pride building up. The young men break out in raiding for cattle which is abetted by the older men whose status depends on supporting rather than objecting to such violence.

Quarrels between neighbours over field boundaries, livestock fields, misuse of water and grazing cattle too early in dry season reserved land in which only those involved have any interest into solutions.

Quarrels over women which do not involve neighbours over issues of marriage payments, ownership of children and adultery.

Quarrels over communal issue such as the maintenance of water holes and protection from thieves. The political push for communities to provide for their own development even if not all those implicated by village boundaries will benefit.

Then quarrels involving suspicion of witchcraft which have increased enormously in the last decades and have involved the killing of 2347 suspected witches and wizards 1970-1984 of which the majority were women (Tanner, 1970; Mesaki, 1984).

Lastly quarrels over thieving. A constant anxiety over property in a society which does not have much moveable goods and who see development as an accumulation of private property. This was kept under control in the past by the young men's organisation which is supposed to have been replaced by the police. The person who has been stolen has to walk for days to a police station only to be asked 'who did it' to which this Sukuma would have replied "if I knew who did it they would already be dead".

In this society traditionally existence was based on the necessity of having to continue to live together or moving away which as subsistence farmers cannot be done. The expulsion or killing of those who are seen not so much to be up setting a reasonable and continually negotiable social existence, but as persistently flouting the rules which make such accommodations possible. How has this system changed or continued under contemporary conditions.

The Nature of Conflict among the Sukuma

Inter-relationships between people are always in the process of being modified; the ageing of those involved and changing circumstances so that socially there is no such thing as a constant. A dispute is always an on-going event so we have to accept that it comes out of or is created by a time tied set of circumstances; it can increase in social importance and it can be diminished by circumstances. Any dispute will always have a potent latency so that ancient quarrels can be refreshed by contemporary pressures.

It is always easy to think that a dispute can be cleared away but all those involved have their own agendas for making the issue diminish or to become more important. Even though main disputes have the appearance of being dyadic particularly when they enter the legal system of any modern society depending as it does on literacy, this is rarely so.

Any temporary accommodation between those involved may not be a solution but a temporary truce in which what has been agreed is no more than a move in a prolonged Chinese chess game between those involved in which several levels of adjustments are involved.

A divorce is a legal fact which does not terminate a relationship but merely puts it into a new social frame in which arguments over property may continue for years. A death has not terminated anything since there are issues of inheritance, descendants are in a new relationship with each other and the influence of the dead on the living is an objective fact.

All conflicts are ongoing in the minds of those involved as well as socially so that memories of dubious substance can be reactivated into social realities by a range of accidental or induced stimuli.

The Weakness of Law in the Resolution Conflict

Most states pride themselves on the abstract virtues of their legal system-based on written codes. Disputes between individuals or between individuals and the state are planned to be resolved by resorting to pre-existing written codes in which the whole dispute is processed according to a code of procedure before professional people who have no connection with those involved or the issues. The whole process is tied to arguments presented by professionals which have to be recorded in writing on the basis of which decisions are made.

Its most distinguishing feature is that it is dichotomous; it is an either or process in which a single solution is provided and the matter is regarded as closed in law, whatever may be the feelings of those involved. The court as a referee has not only ruled that a player has broken a rule but that now the whole game is over.

Reduction of Conflict among the Sukuma

Since the millions of Sukuma are social beings we can assume that they have proportionately just as many quarrels over women, parenthood, land, property and drunken behaviour as any other society and yet they make very little use of the courts much as the Japanese. Whereas North

Americans and East Indians could be said almost to 'love' litigation. The latter appear to use their legal system to prolong disputes through legal stratagems so that any solution has to be in terms of financial exhaustion or social indifference to any possibility of finite solutions. The Japanese use the issue of 'face' where to go to court displays the litigants' lack of social power to negotiate a solution. So-called finite solutions to disputes can only work where there is a third party which sets up a system of adjudication and enforces solutions through the system which it created for its own purposes.

The customary law of the Sukuma was recorded (Cory, 1953) after lengthy discussions with knowledgeable elders and published in Swahili and a copy was placed in every local court it seems doubtful whether this code was ever referred to by magistrates. This did not encourage the Sukuma to use these courts as they tended to say that these are the principles with which we conduct our affairs when there are no people actually involved but when there is an actual dispute then what is decided depends on the social circumstances of each case which cannot be settled according to any book solution which knows nothing of the particular social environment of each case.

The Sukuma are a rural people who avoid living in villages and the central government, does not have the police or the incentive to involve itself in rural quarrels or to enforce judgements which they do not consider to be politically disturbing. If the Sukuma do not want to bring their disputes to the local courts, then the government is not over concerned.

There are a number of customary ascriptions which relate to the ways in which the Sukuma keep their differences under what they consider to be reasonable control. Firstly, those who quarrel are usually related by blood or marriage or are neighbours so that there have to be solutions rather than judgements within these circles of people known to each other and socially interdependent.

If one party to a dispute is a stranger with no circle of local associates and the other a locally connected person, then the solution is likely to be against the stranger who is an outsider with whom future relations need not be considered.

The increase in rural crime can be correlated to the transfer of local power to branches of the one-party and to geographically and socially distant branches of the central government combined with the dismantling of traditional local authority susceptible to local public opinion. Thus, crime came only under control by the reintroduction of traditional young men vigilantes - the "basumba batale" - who effectively controlled the intrusions of outsiders into each small community (Abrahams, 1987).

The boycott has always been an effective means of isolating serious offenders and causing them to move away since even in their dispersed pattern of living others are always necessary for emergencies such as the digging of graves, carrying the sick to hospital and communal work parties doing field work and house-building.

The reintroduction of the traditional sanction of lynching against those who were considered to be threats. As thieves to the owners of property, thought and well-being generally of any community as witches and wizards. There is always the possibility of burning the house of the unpopular somewhat reduced now by the growing popularity of corrugated iron roofs (Tanner, 1955).

Throughout their lives there is the difference between the nature of the difficulty. Urinating or being sick in the water supply is of public concern to all who use that spring or well, while killing someone when drunk is a private delict of concern to the families involved and not a matter of public anxiety. Contemporary governments' revise this important distinction.

The Aim of Communal Dispute Solutions

No one or no small group have the physical power to impose solutions on any party to a dispute, but those in publicly accepted traditional authority are listening and talking about a dispute with one part of their brains, while the other part is thinking in communal terms. There is no suggestion of impartiality because all involved know the background to the dispute and thus would see suggestions of oaths to speak the truth as just ridiculous.

The assessors come from the community and thus know the background to the dispute before it came out into the open as beer drinking sessions insure that gossip keeps the community aware of tensions between their members; they are seeking agreed solutions in which the disputants are to some extent both found half guilty and half innocent.

Each party to a dispute has to leave the arbitration which is not a judgement with their personal prestige in some way intact or at least recognised. The complexity of the dispute is paralleled by the complexity of solutions which leave the disputants still able to live in close proximity. Solutions which take an enormous amount of time to be talked about, both as a form of public entertainment but also as a recognition that leaving disputants in public animosity does not benefit anyone.

The Aim of Disputation and Social Relationships—A Digression

The aim and nature of disputation depends on the nature of the disputants connection prior to the dispute. In the village near to Kipumbwi on the Pangani coast of Tanzania, thirty-five households out of the thirty-six houses were on one genealogical diagram. In such a situation all disputes would the resolved in terms of the longer term relationships of blood or marriage in which there could not possibly be any solution which was not acceptable to all the other households (Tanner, 1962). Amongst the Afro-Arabs of Mombasa in Kenya in which a very high proportion of marriages were between both single and double cousins from a total community coverage (Tanner, 1964) so that in-laws were also matrilineal and patrilineal uncles and aunts, disputes would be resolved within these kin groups; the disputes might well be binary but not necessarily dyadic.

So, we can see that all disputes are only theoretically dyadic as between opposing persons within social groups in which those involved cannot afford to think in terms of someone winning or indeed losing. The reality parallels games in which there are no time limits and in which any move by one party means a repositioning of the others; everyone is always still in the game in which there are no finite gains and losses only proportionate temporary ones.

Much the same would apply to boundary disputes between village domains between which there are permanently fluid relationships and the lines on the maps are bureaucratic creations and in which solutions to such disputes are inevitably temporary according to multi-lateral changing pressures. A boundary dispute in northern Myanmar on which a temporary solution was imposed in 1946 probably started around 1746 and is almost certainly still an active issue in 2005 on the combined issues of ethnicity, religion, land and population pressures.

Put a line on a map which few of those involved can read and a third party is automatically involved in the results and who use it for innumerable purposes of little advantage to those who are thus separated whereas before the boundary united. Borders divide whereas previously the physical features chosen may have united communities.

Bureaucratic systems are never geared to loose ends and they want finite solutions to every issue confronting them. Social relations are rarely if ever finite since whatever is decided, there are always loose ends if only because it is usually out of date by the time it has been recorded.

Western legal systems deal with creating solutions according to a balance of proof as presented in court and reach clear-cut decisions which masks itself as a finite solution-based on the philosophical point that it is not possible to be both this and that at the same time.

The Means of Conflict Resolution among the Sukuma

Societies which are not overly influenced by societies greater than themselves usually evolve their own systems for social stability. The armistices which they realise are no more than temporary solutions to over quarrelling since they do not have the means to impose anything which is not already agreed to by those involved.

The invention of writing creates the growing impersonality of societies which are always undergoing massive internal migrations and in which the major amount of disputes take place between those who do not know each other at all or are in no more than touch and go relationships. Legal systems based on literacy largely take inter-personal negotiations out of the solution as a negotiated process by restricting complex situations to written words and the key words have inorganic meanings, subject to interpretations by impersonal outsiders; the fan of meanings come to be outside the control of those involved.

By conducting their dispute settlements without putting anything into writing and in relying on what those involved thought they remembered, means for the Sukuma that changes in the social environments of disputes cannot be made more difficult by reference to written records which are stuck in the time when they were written.

Sukuma custom regards disputes as being similar to moving staircases onto which new issues can get on and others get off as the situation fluctuates over time. By avoiding commitment to writing and the restriction of a human dispute to a single dimension of three dimensional situations which are never static and indeed cannot be so, negotiations are possible and impersonality is avoided. It is their basic assumption that disputes can only be ameliorated within the changing social context of those involved and this is done by the use of arbitrators who are accepted because of their personal reputations.

The Basis of Conflict Resolution is Binary

The first objective is to keep the community intact by accepting the plain fact that every community is split by real and potential conflicts; a dialectic for the continuation of a viable community. No community can survive by making membership untenable by one-sided solutions. It is a binary framework of thinking in that there are rarely if ever quarrels for which one-sided solutions are possible.

The second objective is keeping the community intact by systematic institutionalised oppositions. The viability of any community large or small is in part the hostility of its neighbours; quarrels within and without over boundaries and feuding as an ongoing balancing act.

The Discontinuation of the Traditional Approach of Balance

No community which has a sense of cultural and religious identity likes to have its internal affairs and personal disputes dealt with by outsiders; this applies as much to contemporary Chinese and Bangladeshi in London as it does to the Sukuma in Tanzania. The limited recourse to outside institutions is because of several intermingled factors.

The Sukuma now more than in the past is a population on the move either in changing the sites of their houses or in where they choose to live. Population pressure and land shortages insures that this will always be happening; a core area with a relatively stable older population and new previous uninhabited areas with younger newly arrived populations.

Within this situation of instability, potential assessors do not want to be involved as there is no status gain for them when compromises are virtually impossible to organise. An unstable population has participants who want binary solutions tied to paper which can be potentially taken elsewhere for supportive action.

Communities may no longer be stable enough to provide enough positive benefits and inducements to make participants accept internal compromises which no longer have satisfactions equal to binary solutions. At one time most communities were composed of cultivators and small minorities of traditional healers and chiefly families. Now there are numerous occupations apart from commuters to the provincial towns who are tailors, bicycle mechanics, small traders and the part-time and seasonal unemployed who are landless.

The Continuation of the Traditional Approach of Balance

The traditional system worked because the participants to disputes had nowhere else to go should they wish to reject local compromise offers. So, we can expect this still to work in the core areas where the ownership of land insures that their owners are not likely to move. This is the system which works well among the Amish and Hutterite communities in north America and the small urban slum communities in the slums of Lima and Mexico city. There is a necessary close relationships of these people-based on mutually appreciated interdependence. So-called traditional methods of conflict resolution can only be effective within small circles of social distance within which the suggestions of arbitrators have a social return comparable to the loss of what may have originally triggered off the dispute.

We have to accept that the vast majority of contemporary human relationships whether in Bombay, Birmingham or Banaras, are controlled by folklore which is largely outside the boundaries of literacy and written records; we quarrel with our tongues rather than with our pens. There is no reason to suppose that 'custom is king' or indeed in any way substantially modified except insofar as electronic communication and written documentation has created new developments for inclusion.

So we can expect the Sukuma folklore of disputes and their solutions to adjust itself to new situations and that this would possibly develop in response to two different social and environmental stimuli. Firstly, in the old core areas attached to the main roads and the one railway line with the possibilities of working in the townships while retaining a holding of cash valued land (Tanner, 1956) kept under cultivation by women and their absentee men.

In this area much of the purely traditional ways of folklore will have been substantially modified by the compulsory villagisation campaign which made people abandon their centuries old dispersed pattern of living correlating to irregular rain and variable soil fertilities and its subsequent official abandonment (Hyden, 1980).

Then in the previously uninhabited areas to the south and west into which the younger Sukuma have moved with a more sexually balanced and younger demographic profile there may be a repetition of more traditional folklore. Here each group of households will have an extended family or affinal basis or indeed a client-patron foundation as newcomers will have to find food until their new holdings can be cleared, planted up and their first crops harvested.

It is probably wrong to call any system of conflict resolution traditional as there are processes of settling differences by word of mouth in every society today as was the case in history. All these processes are constantly updating themselves in terms of the social and economic convenience they offer to participants. It is moreover a process which is almost existential in the ways by which its methods of problem solving come to fit into the needs of those involved without much recourse to the benefits of literacy.

References

- Abrahams, R. (1987). 'Sungu Sungu village vigilante groups in Tanzania' *African Affairs,* 86: 17-96.
- Cory, H. (1953), *Sukuma Customary Law.* Oxford University Press, London.
- Hyden, G. (1980). Beyond Ujamaa in Tanzania. *Underdevelopment and an uncaptured peasantry,* Heinemann, London.
- Jekshus, H. (1977). 'The Tanzanian Villagisation policy Implementation and ecological dimensions'. *Canadian J. African Studies* 11(2).
- Malcolm, D.W. (1953). *Sukumaland. An African people and their country.* Oxford University Press, London.
- McCall, M. (1985). 'Environmental and agricultural impact of Tanzania's Villagisation Programme' in J.I., Clarke *et al.* (eds). *Population and Development Projects in Africa.* Cambridge University Press, Cambridge.
- Mesaki, S. (1994). "Witch killing in Sukumaland". In R. Abrahams, (ed). *Witchcraft in contemporary Tanzania.* African Studies Centre, Cambridge.
- Tanner, R.E.S. (1955a). 'Law enforcement by communal action' *J African Administration.* 7(4). 159-165.
- ________, (1955b). "Land tenure in northern Sukumaland". *East African Agricultural J.* 21(2)120-129.
- ________, (1962). "The relationship between the sexes in a coastal Islamic society". *African Studies.* 21 (2).
- ________, (1964). 'Cousin marriage in the Afro-Arab community in Mombasa, Kenya.' *Africa,* 34(2). 127-138.
- ________, (1970). *The witch murders in Sukumaland. A sociological commentary.* Scandinavian Institute of African Studies, Uppsala.

18

Reasons and Suggestion of World Terrorism

Purabi Nandi, Ravi Prakash Pandey

The terrorism was the spontaneous outburst of intense feeling of nationalism. One important cause of the growth of terrorism in India is the well advertised impotency of the government in dealing with any group, which could show its capacity for mischief and make the government simultaneously feel that enforcement of the law of the land will be bad for its electoral interests. The general image of the government is made up by the manner in which the lawless elements are dealt with everyday. The government officials, the nationalist leaders, the revolutionaries and others differed with regard to the reasons of the rise of the revolutionary movement.

As conceived by the *Times of India* October 2007, page No. 8, Pakistan is the most dangerous country in the world and has become a safe haven for terrorists, a media report says.

"Unlike countries such as Afghanistan and Iraq, Pakistan has everything Al-Qaida chief Osama Bin Laden could ask for Political instability, a trusted network of radical Islamists, an abundance of angry anti-western recruits, secluded training areas and security series that don't always do what they're supposed to do." Says Newsweek in an investigative report.

Then there's the country's large nuclear programme, the report adds ominously. "What is new, and mere frightening, is the extent to which Taliban and Al Qaida elements have now turned much of the country, including some cities, in to a base that gives militants more room to manoeuvre, both in Pakistan and beyond."

Taliban militants, the magazine reports, "now 'Pretty much come and go' as they please inside Pakistan".

There are several featurs of world terrorism such as:

(*a*) ***Blatant Corruption*:** There is widespread corruption in all fields of administration and at all levels from the ministers down to peons. The situation is still not so bad as it was in declining years of the Turhigh empire of Tsarist Russia or Chiang Kai-Shekh's Kuomintang in the years 1940-1948; in the higher rungs of the administration there are still honest and dedicated officers but their influence is just little because since 1970 or so they can not always pass the test of 'loyalty'- not to the country or the constitution - but to their political boss. The demands of 'loyalty' became sharper after 1977. Even quite a few honest bureaucrats at the top are unaware of the realities. When the intelligence agencies report that a number of well-trained and well-armed extremists have crossed from Pakistan into India an alert is sounded along the Indo-Pak border. The top thinks that it has done its duty by sending a wireless message. The top has never bothered to find out how dishonesty makes most of government instructions almost futile. It is a long story of how lakhs of Bangladeshi nationals, with either fake travel documents or no documents at all, have effectively used bribery to get into India. Similarly, the Punjab-Pak border has been a haven for smugglers. There is no doubt that the lower-ranking police officers, posted at the border, get their small amounts for each illegal entry but this colossal evil could not continue in its big dimension without political support. In Assam, the foreigners formed the vote bank of the Congress Party and in Punjab the smugglers gave money generously to both the Congress and the Akalis. It was not at all honest to blame only Bhindranwale and his going for being in league with smugglers. Dishonesty cannot operate under set of rules, which permit corruption in all fields except in terrorism. It has been estimated that the profits from smuggling on the Indo-Pak border in Punjab amount to about rupees two thousand crores per year. While the religions fundamentalism of Bhindranwale is highlighted this aspect is quietly ignored.

In this atmosphere of all pervading corruption the terrorists in the Punjab have been able to purchase sophisticated arms and ammunition from Army stores. They got whatever intelligence they needed and they could cross the international border almost at will. Anti-terrorist strategy requires a high degree of secrecy in many offices - both which issue policy directives and those which carry on the operational job. The latest spy scandal is proof of the fact the government's top most secrets were freely available for sale.

(*b*) ***Political Motivation in Dealing with Terrorism***: Even when the Government of India became serious in dealing with terrorism it failed because the civilian bureaucracy and police, meant to crush it, had become pretty useless instrument for this job. However, the reason why a tiny creative of terrorism became a big monster has to be found in political motivation in dealing with all law and order problems. The principal reason for failure in both Assam and Punjab was political motivation. Widespread police mutinies in 1979 testified to the incompetence of the Ministry of Home Affairs. Their incompetence and lack of basic knowledge, however, paled into insignificance when the higher bureaucratic echelons were reconstituted by Mrs. Gandhi in 1980. Mrs. Gandhi's choice was much narrower that of Janata because the following categories were excluded.

(i) Those loyal to Janata;

(ii) Those loyal to Mrs. Gandhi in Pre-March 1977 period, but whose loyalty became doubtful in 1977-79.

On the other hand, it included many who were incompetent but whose loyalty was taken as proved because the Janata regime harassed them. This poor bureaucratic set-up went about undetected because many competent Congress ministers, like Mr Y. B. Chavan, no longer enjoyed Mrs. Gandhi's confidence. The sum-total of all this was that deterioration in the law and order situation became rapid and Assam and Punjab situations were handled with a degree of incompetence which was truly amazing. It was obvious that even basic principles were not understood since early 1960s several factors were operating to make all the agencies responsible for maintaining law and order weaker and weaker.

(*c*) ***Serious weakening of the law and order machinery***: Since early 1970s, the common man has been taking of increasing lawlessness. This has made no impact on the authorities. When the average citizen talks of lawlessness he or she certainly does not even think of official crime statistics. Several State Police Commissions and National Police Commission of 1978-81 have commented on these false statistics. It should not be necessary to waste valuable space in disproving the apparently false nature of crime statistics except of the fact that non-registration and non-investigation of crime is the single most important cause of drift to lawlessness.

(d) ***Sighs of lawlessness*** - The rate of murder per lakh of the population is continuously rising in India even according to official crime statistics. The reason is that very few murder cases can be concealed by showing them accidents or suicides. Though crime statistics are not available for the whole world, it will not be two wide off the mark to accept that the world murder rate is near about three per lakh. The United State is one of the worst countries in this respect. There the murder rate has climbed from 4.7 per lakh in 1933-37 to more than ninety-five at present. The countries where the Kuranic laws are in force—Saudi Arabia is - at the other end of the scale. The rate there is unusually low. In London murder rate was quite low even twenty years ago about 0.4 per lakh - but if has gone up sharply in recent years to more than 1.6 per lakh.

India was a low murder - incidence country about thirty years ago when the rate was about 2.2 per lakh. Even in 1966, it had not risen to over 2.5. From 1967 onwards it has been slowly climbing up and has now reached nearly 3.3 per lakh. India is now having over 24,000 murders a year. Indeed, allowing for ten per cent concealment on account of sheer callousness or corruption or pressure or the desire for a good statistical record, our real rate should be deemed to be about 3.6 per lakh.

Signs of lawlessness is the increase in gang wars. There are generally only two reasons for gang warfare: first is the dispute over sharing of illicit gains. In areas where large-scale gambling or illicit distillation or illegal sale of liquor or smuggling is rife the leaders of gangs divide territories among themselves. Encroachment by one gang over the territory of other leads to gang wars. The second reason is revenge for the murder of members of one gang. Both reasons imply a poor state of police control and failure of the police to bring the culprits to book.

Organised gangs of criminals are now a phenomenon of practically all big cities as well as in several rural areas of Bihar, UP, Madhya Pradash, Rajasthan etc. It is much more difficult for law enforcing agencies to deal with syndicates of crime than with individual criminals. Syndicates are organised on business lines and crime flourishes as long as it pays. The earnings are mainly from smuggling, Illicit distillation, sale of liquor, gambling, black mailing, financing from politicians in return for help in election etc. Expenditure is incurred on bribing politicians, police, magistrates, doctors, jail staff etc, looking after the families of members in jail, purchasing arms and ammunition.

(e) ***Rise in Political Murders*** - No separate statistics have been complied on politically motivated murders. But there can be no doubt that the rate of detection and prosecution in such murders, as compared to other murder cases, is very low. The rate of conviction is even lower and in the majority of these cases, sentences have been commuted or remitted altogether.

(f) ***Killing in Hundreds*** - In West Bengal after 1967, first the Marxists and later the Congress (I) killed their opponents not in terms but in hundreds. Similarity in Kerala the murder of political opponents began during the first Marxist government in 1957-59. Both the Marxist governments in West Bengal and Kerala released political activists convicted of murder and dacoity. In 1980-81, Marxist and RSS cadres in Kerala almost treated natural killings as a sporting event in which each party kept count of the scores.

Terrorism as an instrument of politics cannot be eliminated merely by expressing a sense of shock when someone big is killed. Proper investigation careful prosecution and non-interference with punishment inflicted by courts are the only methods of dealing with the problem.

(g) ***Increase of Private Armies*** - Every group, political, linguistic, religious, caste-based, class-based. etc. has somehow acquired the freedom to raise private armies, which are trained, financed and equipped with weapons — legal or illegal to achieve the objectives of the group. If finances are sound there is no shortage of instructors retired personnel from the army or para - military forces and fire arms. To avoid objections it is usually stated that they are being raised for self-defence.

(h) ***Peoples Perception*** - Having noticed a few of the apparent signs of lawlessness increase in murder cases, gang wars, the boldness with which gang leaders behave, phenomenal increase in political murders, increase in private armies we have to notice as to what is the perception of the common man. A few noticeable

changes even during last ten years are significant.

(i) In vast areas of U.P., Bihar and West Bengal etc., villagers do not move out at night. In summer months travelling at night has always been more convenient.

(ii) The respectable middle classes are afraid of sending unescorted ladies by night trains except in compartments where large numbers give a security.

(iii) Even 10-12 years back well to do people with their families often made long distance journey by road in their private cars in the cool nights of summer. They no longer do so.

(iv) Though employment opportunities and other factors are mainly responsible for the continuous shift of population from rival areas to cities yet the increase in insecurity in rural areas as compared to cities is also one of the causes.

(v) Tens of millions have acquired illegal firearms, only a small minority has done so for evil motives, the rest majority have done so on account of a sense of insecurity.

Causes of Rising Lawlessness

There are socio-economic causes on which there is hardly much agreement. Moreover, this is a plea often taken by a lazy or motivated administration to divert the attention from its own failures. Many of the agencies have a vital role to play. There are :

(i) *The Government of India* — Under the Constitution, law and order is the responsibility of the states but the government of India has the overall responsibility of ensuring that the constitutional machinery does not breakdown. If there are such widespread disturbances in which lawful government is not possible. The government of India has a duty to help the State Government.

As conceived by the *Times of India,* 5th December 2007, Page No. 6 : Finance Minister P. Chidambaram said on Tuesday, "the Government was tracking at least one case of suspected terror-stained money on the bourses confirming intelligence inputs that terror funds were following into them." Speaking in Rajya Sabha, Chidambaram said, "Recently, one case has come to our notice, it is suspected that it may be linked to a person under watch. I cannot divulge further details." The Finance Minister's assertion sparked intense speculation and questioning. But what

Chidambaram said tallied with national security advisor M.K. Narayanan's assessment that terrorists could target the bourses. This is the first time the government has admitted to the presence of terror investments in the financial market. Till recently, finance ministry officials had sought to dismiss reports of terror funds on Dalal Street as "good topic for dinner table discussion."

In September, TOI had reported that Research and Analysis Wing (RAW), the country's external intelligence agency, had alerted the government and Securities and Exchanges Board of India (SEBI) about investments made by a prominent Saudi businessman alleged to have links with Osama Bin Laden.

Sources said intelligence agencies are currently investigating the Saudi billionaire's links in India as well as his networks and investments abroad. However, the agencies have not met with much success so far in nailing the tycoon, who has interests in a leading satellite phone company.

"A lot of money is coming into the country from the Gulf and West Asia. It is difficult to say which is good and which is bad money," A senior spokesperson said. The government is, however, keeping a close watch on all investments coming into the country, particularly from that region the official added.

Earlier this year, though, the government and SEBI had scoffed at Narayanan's warnings about the possible use of terror funds in stock markets. Narayanan had in fact, said that tainted money had found its way into the bourses through markets like the one in Chennai. A note prepared by the national security council secretariat has also suggested the use of participatory notes a derivative instrument used unregistered foreign entities to invest in India - as a possible instrument being exploited by terror financiers.

The Governments flip-flop on the issue came in for criticism in Rajya Sabha with BJP's Ravishankar Prasad saying that Chidambaram had earlier denied any such investment in the markets. He wondered aloud what one could make of the FM's statement of "Suspected" involvement of terrorists. But with Chidambaram in no mood to speak in detail, Prasad's concerns weren't entirely addressed.

(ii) **State Governments** — The state Government went to the extent of issuing illegal instructions and otherwise undermining the rule of law. Most democratic Governments are reluctant to do anything which may undermine their political support in the electorate. There is a serious erosion of faith not merely in the police but in the entire machinery of law and order which includes the magistracy, the police and the courts.

The main instrument for combating terrorism is the police. The Government of India, the State Governments, the District Magistrate and even leadership of the police have to depend mainly on the rank and file of the police to maintain law and order.

Intelligence plays a vital part in combating terrorism. Its role in other law and order situations is also important. However, intelligence is not the remedy for all serious ills of the administration. Owing to financial constraints it cannot be made a mammoth organisation, prying into all aspects of a nations life, in a democratic country it is also undesirable because the liberty and privacy of the citizen must not be tampered with except for fighting serious risk to national security.

Often a scapegoat - whenever a big failure in law and order occurs often those very people, who failed to size up, anticipate and act, unofficially brief the press and there one big headlines indicating that there was total failure of intelligence. This is done with impurity because an intelligence chief, by the very nature of his assignment, cannot meet the press.

Diversion of resources to election work, evaluation of intelligence and executive action, intelligence about rural areas, the courts, order according to law, faulty judgements can lead to agitations, attitude of courts, detention cover for inefficiency and exhaustive criminal records must for combating terrorism.

As conceived by the *Statesman* 22nd October, 2007 page No. 5 while India has equipped itself with documentary evidences to suggest the hands of Pak terror groups behind blasts in Hyderabad, Samjhauta and also in Ajmer during the Indo-Pak Anti Terror Mechanism (ATM) meeting starting 23rd October 2007, it has little hope that Pakistan would extend help in weeding out Pak terror groups involved in planning subversive activities in India.

In the ATM meeting held after a long gap. India would seeked details of the action taken by the Pakistan Government on the evidences and the photographs provided by the Indian Government.

> Though the picture in the Ajmer and Ludhiana blasts is not yet clear as to who were involved in the blasts, the investigating agencies have some specific leads that indicate the hands of Pak terror groups behind almost all the blasts that took place during the past one year - including that of Ludhiana and Ajmer Dargah blasts.

The second ATM meeting is quite crucial particularly after the recent blasts in Ludhiana and Ajmer and the blast that hit former Pakistan Prime Minister Ms Benazir Butto's caravan.

Home Minister officials are hopeful that in the present political scenario Pakistan government has little option but to come forward and accept certain 'truths' and take actions against terrorists hiding in Pakistan.

The Indian side will be led by the additional secretary (International organisations) in the Ministry of External Affairs, Mr. K.C. Singh, whereas the Pakistan delegation would be headed by the additional secretary (UN) in the Pakistan Foreign Minister, Mr. Khalid Aziz Babar.

The meeting also included a generalised discussion where India based its concerns about the continued influx of terror elements from Pakistan, including many that maintain their command and control operations involvement in the Baluchistan problem.

Both sides denied the changes against each other, which has now become standard operating procedure.

There was little action forthcoming from the Pakistani side but sources said they agreed to take back the intelligence given. Nobody seriously expected anything concrete to come out of this meeting. So far, the effort, at least on the Indian side, has been to keep this mechanism different from the secretary-level dialogue.

Therefore only "actionable leads" are presented to the Pakistan side. Indian sources said they would only count a success when terrorists demanded by India are delivered.

References

Nath, Shaieswen, 1980: Terrorism in India.

Saxena, N.S., 1985 : *Terrorism History and Facts.*

Indian Intelligence Bureau, 19-7-1936, 1974 : Terrorism in India.

The Hindustan Times, 14th Dec 1979 : The Growing Roots of Terrorism.

Indian Express, 19th July 1984.

Times of India, 23rd October 2007.

The Statesman, 22nd October 2007.

Times of India, 5th December 2007.

19

Challenges that Terrorism Poses to Public Health

Syad Iqbal Imam Rizvi and Y. Nath Pandey

Terrorism can cause injury, illness and death; create fear, anxiety and other psychological reactions; destroy the physical infrastructure and social fabric of communities and cause profound adverse economic and political impacts on individuals, communities, nations and our global society.

Terrorism can be defined as prolifically motivated violence on the threat of violence, especially against civilians, with the intent to instil fear.

Terrorism is a problem we have been facing in India for more than three decades. Terrorism is perceived as a problem capable of destabilising not only national but also international politics. In recent times, terrorism has affected both the developed and the developing countries terrorism is an organised system of intimidation. Broadly defined as 'violent behaviour designed to generate fear in the community, or a substantial segment of it, for political purposes'. It is also defined as 'a method whereby an organised group or party seeks to achieve its avowed aims chiefly through the systematic use of violence' *(Encyclopaedia of Social Sciences).* The US Central Intelligence Agency's 1980 definition of it, duly accepted by the State Department is: "The threat or use of violence for political purposes by individuals or groups, whether acting for or in opposition, when such actions are intended to shock, stun, or intimidate a target group wider than the immediate victims" *(The Hindustan Times,* January 15, 1996).

Terrorism appears in many forms—from planting a crude, homemade bomb, hand-grenade or other explosive in a shopping centre, a railway station, a bus-stand and a bus, a train or an aeroplane to kidnapping and assassination of important personalities. The main aim of terrorists is to wreak havoc upon those whom they regard as obstacles or enemies or oppressors.

Characteristics

Terrorism is characterised by a technique of perpetrating random and brutal intimidation, coercion, or destruction of human lives and property, and used intentionally by sub-national groups operating under varying degrees of stress, to obtain realistic or illusory goals. The main characteristics of terrorism are:

- It is against the state or community.
- It has a political purpose.
- It is illegal and unlawful.
- It aims at intimidating and creating impact of fear and panic not only for the victim but also for the people at large, caused for the purpose of coercing or subduing.
- It is accompanied by a feeling of impotence and helplessness on the part of the masses.
- It stops rational thinking.
- It leads to reaction of fight or flight, and
- It contains arbitrariness in violence as victims' selection is random or indiscriminate.

Objectives of Terrorism

The goals of terrorists may vary from movement to movement but the main objectives of terrorism are the same in all terrorist movements. These are:

(1) Cause the regime to react and also to overreact. Reaction is required to compel the government/community to concede the demand of the terrorists. Overreaction or indiscriminate reaction is required to demonstrate the repression by the regime so that the people are alienated and their sympathy is achieved. The security forces used by the government (because of overreaction) to protect the VIPs and the public installations will reduce the amount of security forces

available to protect the general public, which will enhance their feeling of insecurity and helplessness and also increase the sense of terror amongst them;

(2) Mobilise mass support and urge potential sympathisers to greater militancy, or increase the involvement of more people. In a foreign territory, the objective of terrorist activity is to influence people rather than win friends. The chief objective in these places is a show of strength and to demonstrate the incapacity of the regime to protect people and maintain order;

(3) Eliminate opponents and informers and remove threat to the movement and also ensure obedience of the followers; and

(4) Give publicity or magnify their cause and strength.

Prevention of Terrorism and its Consequences

Public health professionals distinguish among primary, secondary, and tertiary levels of prevention, and use this framework in developing and implementing policies and programs.

Primary prevention attempts to prevent disease or injury from occurring. Examples of primary prevention of terrorism include national laws and regulations to control the purchase and possession of small arms; international treaties to control the production, distribution, storage, and use of chemical weapons; and strategies to control, and ultimately eliminate, nuclear weapons.

Secondary prevention attempts to identify and control disease at an early, treatable stage. With regard to terrorism, examples of secondary prevention include physicians' and other health care providers' recognising and treating the signs and symptoms of diseases that might be caused by terrorist use of biological or chemical agents, and screening asymptomatic individuals for evidence of exposure or sub-clinical infection with anthrax or other potential infection with anthrax or other potential bio-terrorist diseases, as deemed appropriate in specific bio-terrorist events. Immunisation against small-pox, anthrax, or other potential bio-terrorist agents may be used for either primary or secondary prevention.

Tertiary prevention attempts to prevent disabling consequences of disease or injury by helping individuals regain their optimal level of function after a disease or injury and accompanying damage has already occurred. With regard to terrorism, examples of tertiary prevention include treatment and rehabilitation of individuals who have been seriously burned or otherwise injured by a terrorist bomb, and treatment and supportive care of persons affected by chemicals during a terrorist attack.

Of these three levels of prevention, primary prevention has the greatest human appeal and is the most effective from a cost-benefit perspective.

Major Challenges of Terrorism for Public Health

- Improving Public Health System Capabilities to Respond to Health Consequence of Terrorist Acts.
- Controlling Terrorist Weapons.
- Addressing Factors That May Breed Terrorism.

Roles of Health Professionals

Responding to Health Consequences of Terrorist Acts and Threats

- Diagnosing and reporting,
- Providing primary preventive measures,
- Preventing secondary spread of disease,
- Assisting in the investigation of outbreaks of disease,
- Discouraging inappropriate responses,
- Developing improved preparedness for future terrorist acts or threats,
- Educating the public and other health professionals,
- Participating in preparedness planning,
- Evaluation preparedness policies and programmes.

Taking Actions to Help Prevent Terrorism

- Helping reduce access to biological agents that can be used as bio-terrorist weapons.
- Advocating the control, reduction, and elimination of weapons of mass destruction.
- Promoting a balance between response to terrorism and to other public health concerns.
- Maintaining support for other public health priorities.
- Promoting the protection of civil rights and Human Rights.

Psychologists have advanced theories to explain the working of the terrorist mind and the making of the terrorist personality. For example, Lawrence Zelic Freedman writing on "Perspectives on Terrorism" has offered four hypotheses in this regard (see D.S. Maini, *The Hindustan Times*): (a) *the affirmation of self-esteem,* where an ego has been deeply hurt and denied identity; (b) *deeperserialisation,* i.e., the surrender of one's personality in the service of a group; (c) *a method of establishing intimacy,* i.e., becoming a terrorist as a means to enforce recognition and thus establish a subjective relationship with one's victim; and (d) *a belief in 'the magic of violence',* where in the elements of secrecy, mystery and wonder fuse to propel the terrorist toward an unknown territory. To this list, Maini adds other factors like: (i) a big business linking-up with the underworld and the local magic, (ii) a form of revenge to redress insult (iii) as an aspect of messianic (confusing) politics, (iv) as an intolerable urge for action, (v) as a surrogate sexual activity, and (vi) as a group narcissism (mental state in which there is self-worship). All this indicates that the phenomenon of terrorism is a complex issue of inflamed sentiment, thought and passion, and of action and abstraction.

The Government of India cannot face the problem of terrorism merely by enlisting public sympathy or by blaming countries of giving support to terrorists. Helping terrorists in a hostile country is a fact of life which no organised government in modern times can ignore. Our country has to evolve its own system of dealing with terrorists.

Some methods which may prove to be helpful to our government in this regard are (Saxena, 1985: 33-34)

- Seeking cooperation of the citizens by the police to get information against the terrorists;
- Reducing the finance at the disposal of the terrorists to contain their operations;
- Refusing to accept any demands of any group of terrorists;
- Giving swift and judicial punishments to arrested terrorists. The greater the delay in prosecution and greater the detention in the jail as undertrials, the greater the possibility of their (terrorists') escape;
- Adopting more effective intelligence methods in retrieving information about the terrorists, their associates, their *modus operandi*, and their sources of finance and weapons, etc.;
- Improving security measures continuously at important places, and
- Giving more scientific training to forces dealing with terrorist.

Conclusion

Terrorism is a threat to public health and to society as a whole. Health professionals can do much to mitigate the health consequences of terrorist threats or acts, and to help prevent them. Preventing terrorism and its health consequences should be in the curricula of schools of public health, medicine, nursing, and other health fields and disciplines. Health professionals of all types need to learn more about terrorism and their roles in addressing it. At the same time, health professionals must maintain and promote a balanced perspective that gives terrorism preparedness an appropriate priority amidst the many other health problems people suffer from as well as the underlying societal factors that contribute to the development of these health problems.

20

World Terrorism:
(The Socio-economic Factors of World Terrorism)

S.M. Fahimuddin Pasha

Terrorism is a disintegrated social phenomenon that enables to deconstruct the society. It is the systematic use of terror or unpredictable violence against governments, publics, or individuals, to attain a political objective. It evolved from numerous attacks in the 20th century, to less frequent but more destructive assaults in the 21st century. It is a fact that terrorism is related with religious fundamentalism and geo-politics of a particular area but if we will go through it deeply then we will find that basically socio-economic reasons are in its roots. Terrorism has not only destroyed the socio-economic fabric of the society but also it has harmed the world peace largely. Although various hypotheses about the causes of terrorism have been proposed, a number of important factors have been largely ignored. Geo-politics, especially rich-world attempts to control oil, help incite terrorist attacks on the rich by people from developing countries. However, socio-economic factors, especially poverty, inequality and large numbers of young men facing dim economic prospects, are likely contributors to terrorism.

Now, we have the question that do socio-economic factors really breed terrorism. Some of them say yes and few of them say no.

Nemat Shafik identified Third World countries with legacies of economic stagnation, high levels of unemployment, and uneven economic development as a fertile ground on which terrorist seeds can flourish. Alesina *et. al.,* suggest that poor economic conditions increase the probability of political coups.

Blomberg, Hess and Weerapana assert that economic recessions increase the probability of terrorist activities in democratic high-income countries because they find that terrorists tend the lower end of the socio-economic distribution. In a same manner, Li and Schaub find that economic development decreases the number of international terrorist incidents.

Piazza (2006) has given a statistical data and tries to explore that there is no significant relationship between terrorism and income equity, per capita GDP growth, unemployment, and so forth.

Krueger and Laitin (2003) suggest that poor countries do not generate more terrorism than rich countries with similar levels of civil liberties. Krueger and Maleckova (2003) find no statistical relationship between involvement in terrorism events and economic activity. They investigate the relationship between a country's GDP per capita and the frequency of terrorist attacks coming from that country. They collect the data from the US State Department's record of international terrorist events from 1997 to 2002. The dependent variable is the number of international terrorist events originating from each country. Here they find a negative binomial regression with independent variables for three GDP quartiles, religion, illiteracy, and level of civil liberties. Krueger and Maleckova have given their conclusion that there is a little evidence that poorer countries have more terrorists than richer. However, their study does indicate that countries with greater civil liberties are more susceptible to originate terrorism. The study concludes that there is little reason to believe reduced poverty or improved schooling could decrease international terrorism. They argue that terrorism is not a response to low market opportunities, but rather a manifestation of political turmoil and frustration. Furthermore, they emphasise that terrorist ambitions arise not from a desire for personal economic gain but rather from passionate support for the political movement. Therefore, policies that work to eliminate poverty and strengthen education are not likely to influence the terrorists' motives.

Causes of Terrorism

Socio-economic conditions are possibly conducive to creating terrorists, especially because of its severely unequal distribution among nations, is obviously one of the most important. Friedman asserted that it has been claimed that Islamic rage against the United States is caused in part by the relative failure of Islamic nations to achieve economic success.

There are several socio-economic factors that provide a fertile ground where the seed of terrorism can fluorish easily and hampers the social harmony of the society by destructing the fabrics of society.

Economic Inequality

Economic inequality plays a vital role in the distribution of scarce resources that causes terrorism. It is a fact that when a group is absolutely or relatively deprived they rebel. If we look at the unequal exchange of resources in world scenario then we find that only fifteen per cent of the world population consumes 85 per cent of the resources. UN statistics show that citizens in the third world are worse off now than thirty years ago, while a small faction in those countries enriched themselves. Lichbach (1989) emphasised on the hypothesis of Economic Inequality and Political Conflict (EI-PC) and came to the conclusion that "EI-PC studies have produced a vague answer about the EI-PC nexus".

Globalisation

Globalisation, an important aspect of economic inequality is responsible for the unrest of third world countries. Guelke (1995) explores globalisation, inequality and the Third World from another direction and explores the possible links between economic prosperity and a stable liberal democracy, thereby assuming that it would reduce incidence of terrorism. However, at the same time he asserts that a liberal democracy "has proved little more successful than other forms of political systems in overcoming the relative weakness of the state in many Third World societies" and that economic development is a more important factor to maintain law and order.

Social, Cultural and Historical Facilitation

Social, cultural, and historical facilitation consists of shared attitudes, beliefs, opinions, habits, myths and traditions that permit the development of nationalism, fanaticism, violence and terrorism in a sub-group of population.

Terrorist leaders, theoreticians and members, the cultural and intellectual elite can use four major channels to communicate with others in order to exchange their ideological beliefs. The alternative and mass media, higher education, international travel and broadcasting of intellectual knowledge are four of them. If the organisation or group has apolitical ideology, advocating violence then should be higher motivation to act upon this dictate.

It shows that the longer an identifiable sub-group exists within a dominant majority, the greater its tendency to develop grievances. It also indicates that the higher the social, cultural, and historical facilitation, the greater the support of terrorism.

Religion

All religions emphasise that one should treat others as we wish to be treated, and that one should not kill another human being (the latter with a few exceptions, e.g. Just War Theory). So how can we say that religion plays an important role for providing a fertile ground where seeds of terrorism flourish. In fact it's not religion itself. But it is religious fundamentalism and fanaticism which causes terrorism to a large extent. So, we can say that Islam as a religion is not responsible for the terrorism but the fanaticism that emerges from this particular religion is liable for terrorism. Michael Radu (2001), senior fellow at the Foreign Policy Research Institute in the US, provides a simplification: democracy is declared un-Islamic by all ideologues of Islamic terrorism, Islamists hate capitalism and believe in a new Caliphate (who will lead the community of Muslims worldwide) and oppose individualism.

Yahya argued on above assertion that, "From an Islamic perspective, there are scholars who consider Western society, which is based on Christian theology, as the main cause of terrorism, and Darwinism and materialism in particular".

Dehumanisation

Rathbone and Rowley (2002) proclaimed that dehumanisation is one of the vital factors for terrorism. They, and others, are essentially trying to dehumanise terrorists. According to them terrorists are fighting for: being heard, recognised and treated as equal human beings.

Level of Modernisation

Crenshaw asserted that there are several factors in modern society that encourage terrorism. He pointed out many reasons of the so-called modernity that increase the probability of terrorism. These factors include; a variety, better, more sophisticated, vulnerable targets, destructive weapons and technology, mass media, populations with increased literacy, conflicts with traditional way of life, and networks of transformation. Modern societies encompass urban environments and lead to pressure that frequently encourage the establishment of democratic political systems. In general, modern societies are causally prior to democracy because they press for democratic changes.

Geographical Reason

Cities are more likely than rural environments to facilitate terrorism. Urban environments allow terrorists several advantages over country sides (Creashaw, 1981). Logistic advantages include better fields of fire, closer proximity to and more soft targets, more resources, larger availability of weapons, explosives, a greater immediate audience, higher and quicker access to media, case of surprise and speed, greater number of people to be affected, and case of kidnappings. Another urban advantage is various supports from sympathisers who may aid terrorist organisations. A city offers various potential sources from which to recruit new members, including the slums, shanty towns and universities. Various research in this regard shows that the higher the percentage of country's population is urbanised, the greater the amount of terrorism that the country should experience. In the same way, where the large population is living together there is higher probability of unrest among the different groups.

Ethnicity or Separatist Movement

Radical ethnicity believes in the existences of separate territory-based on cultural differentiation that consist of language, religion and region to a great extent. Probably the most contested cause of terrorism is a distressed group resorting to violence for nationalist or separatist reasons; depending on one's point of view, this can be considered as resistance of oppressed (internal) against oppressor (external). According to Drewemann (2001) "Thus far only Mahatma Gandhi and his followers of the freedom movement managed to liberate themselves from foreign occupation by peaceful means, whereas in most other (previously) colonised states "nationalism movements turned to terrorism". Williams (1994) provides an overview on the relation between ethnic minorities and the likelihood of conflict. He also includes factors like civil and political rights and privileges and regional-ethnic parity in the economy. He believes that when an ethnic group feels subordinated or disadvantaged in economic opportunity, social status, political voice and rights, or cultural expressions, it generates the perception of competition or rivalry among them.

While raising the issue of minorities Dworkin (1997) stated that political violence is morally justifiable in a democracy in two occasions: "Firstly, there is the case of the minority whose basic rights and liberties are denied or taken away by arbitrary action of the government or its agencies. Second, when one minority is attacked by another minority and does not receive adequate protection from the state and its forces of law and order."

Arguably, based on these claims, we can say it exactly as absence of a 'correct' implementation of democratic ideals and negligent attitudes towards minorities' issues.

South Asian Countries and Terrorism

After the incidents of 9/11 South Asia has emerged as the epicenter of the war against terrorism. It is true that South Asia has been facing the various forms of terrorism even before the 9/11 attack. At one level, there is inextricable link between unfulfilled needs of development and the emergence of violence, while on the other, the threat posed by terrorism is likely to undermine the political stability of countries.

South Asia remains extremely vulnerable on both counts. Endemic poverty, growing inter-regional disparities and increasing dependence of foreign aid shows the pathetic socio-economic conditions of South Asian countries that causes terrorism. So, here we will see the socio-economic condition of some South Asian countries and the problems they face in terms of insurgency.

Afghanistan

Afghanistan is located in south Central Asia. It is surrounded by different countries such as Iran in the south and west, Pakistan in the south and east, Turkmenistan, Uzbekistan and Tajikistan in the north and China in the far northeast.

Afghanistan is an impoverished country, one of the world's poorest and least developed. Two-thirds of the population lives on fewer than US$ 2 a day. Its economy has suffered greatly from the 1979. Soviet Union invasion and subsequent conflicts, while severe drought added to the nation's difficulties in 1998-2001. According to the World Bank, "economic growth has been strong and has generated better livelihoods" since 2001. As of 2005, the official unemployment rate is at 40 per cent.

After the incident of 9/11 in America, Afghanistan came into the world scene in a different way. Now, America considered that this is a country where seeds of terrorism can flourish easily. No doubt Taliban is responsible for all the things. So, in 2001 U.S.-led invasion toppled the Taliban government and in late 2001 the United Nations Security Council authorised the creation of an International Security Assistance Force (ISAF) composed of NATO troops.

Still Afghanistan is continuing to confront the challenges of building a stable, democratic, and tolerant government. Terrorist attacks by anti-Afghan forces on coalition forces, civilians, international NGOs, and other soft targets are increasing day by day, most notably through improvised

Explosive Devices (IEDs) and suicide bombings. Supported by the international community, the Afghan government has made suppression of such terrorist attacks and the establishment of effective law-enforcement mechanisms a high priority. The US and countries are helping in this regard.

Under the Disbandment of Illegal Armed Groups (DIAG) programme, which is one of the important measures taken by the government to follow-on to the earlier Disarmament, Demobilisation, and Reintegration (DDR) programme, authorities have disbanded 362 illegal armed groups and collected over 42,000 weapons in 84 districts since its inception in March 2005. In April 2007, in an effort to achieve greater local government support, DIAG began offering development assistance to qualifying districts. Forty-eight of the eighty-four targetted districts currently qualify for this assistance and are considered to be in compliance with DIAG disarmament regulations. DIAG operations expanded, intensifying efforts to build political will at the provincial and local levels to target the more threatening illegal armed groups.

The International Security Assistance Force (ISAF), led the coalition forces' is also playing a vital role in counter insurgency. The insurgency continued to suffer heavy combat losses, including among senior leaders, but its ability to obtain Al-Qaida (AQ) support and recruit soldiers remained undiminished. Taliban information operations were increasingly aggressive and sophisticated.

It is a major question as to from where Taliban is getting funds to lead the terrorism. Streams of Taliban financing from across the border in Pakistan, along with funds gained from narcotics trafficking and kidnapping, have allowed the insurgency to strengthen its military and technical capabilities. To address this issue, a "mini-jirga" between Pakistani and Afghan officials and tribal leaders was held in October. The participants also discussed other ways to end terrorism along their border, including the possibility of holding talks with the Taliban insurgents—a proposal the Taliban subsequently rejected.

Terrorists continued to target police, police recruits, government ministers, parliamentarians, civil servants, and civilians, including urban crowds, in numerous violent incidents. Terrorists, often supported by criminal gangs, also increasingly turned to kidnapping. Afghans and foreigners, most notably several reporters and at least one district governor were kidnapped. Most of these kidnappings were done for ransom, presumably as a means of raising money to support their operations.

According to officials of America, terrorists also targetted international non-governmental organisations (NGOs), Afghan journalists, government workers, UN workers, and recipients of NGO assistance. They attacked teachers, pupils (especially girls), and schools. They also threatened and often brutally killed those who worked for religious tolerance, including ex-insurgents, tribal leaders, and moderate imams, mullahs, and religious scholars. Insurgents coupled threats and attacks against NGOs with continued targetting of Provincial Reconstruction Teams, demining teams, and construction crews working on roads and other infrastructure projects.

Bangladesh

Bangladesh is one of the countries of South Asia. As of 2005, Bangladesh is the seventh most populous country in the world and is among the most densely populated countries in the world with a high poverty rate. However, per-capita (inflation-adjusted) GDP has more than doubled since 1975, and the poverty rate has fallen by twenty per cent since the early 1990s. The country is listed among the "Next Eleven" economies. Despite continuous domestic and international efforts to improve economic and demographic prospects, Bangladesh remains a developing nation. Its per capita income in 2006 was US$1400 (adjusted by purchasing power parity) compared to the world average of US$10,200. Most of the population is young with about sixty per cent under the age of 25, with only about three per cent over the age of 65 (life expectancy is 61 years). Twenty per cent of the population was deemed to be urban in 1998, making Bangladesh's population predominantly rural.

Bangladesh came into existence at the time of 1971 when it got independence from the Pakistan. Being a developing country its estimated population is very high. Unemployment is another major issue. So poverty, unemployment and geographical condition of the Bangladesh are giving fertile land where the seeds of terrorism can flourish easily.

Jamaatul Mujahedin Bangladesh (JMB) and Harkat ul Jihadi-Islami-Bangladesh (HUJI-B) are responsible for various terrorist attacks in Bangladesh and its neighbouring country. During the national Parliamentary election campaign in Bangladesh, authorities arrested several suspected JMB members and uncovered weapons caches that included grenades and chemicals that could be used to make explosives.

The neighbouring country India also blamed the terrorist group Harakat ul-Jihadi-Islami-Bangladesh (HUJI-B) for bomb attacks within

India. India also alleged that the United Liberation Front of Assam (ULFA) and other anti-India insurgency groups operated from Bangladesh with the knowledge of senior Bangladeshi government officials. Bangladesh strongly denied those allegations. The absence of counter-terrorism cooperation between India and Bangladesh fuelled mutual allegations that each country facilitated terrorism inside the borders of the other.

Bangladesh Government is taking initiatives in order to prevent terrorism. So, it established the Money Laundering Prevention Ordinance and the Anti-terrorism Ordinance. These laws facilitated international cooperation in recovering money illegally transferred to foreign countries and mutual legal assistance in criminal investigation, trial proceedings, and extradition matters.

In order to check terrorist activities Bangladesh is getting assistance from USA itself. USA and Bangladeshi law enforcement agencies cooperated well on several cases related to domestic and international terrorism. Bangladesh cooperated with the United States to further strengthen control of its borders and land, sea, and airports of entry.

Leading up to the national elections on December 29, Bangladesh's Care-taker Government attempted to crack down on those accused of terrorism and criminality. The Awami League won a landslide electoral victory, claiming 230 of the 299 seats in Parliament. It has pledged to focus serious attention on Bangladesh's counter-terrorism needs and has championed the creation of a South Asia counter-terrorism task force to enable countries to work together regionally to stamp out the rise of violent extremism.

India

India ranked among the world's most terrorism-afflicted countries. India is also a developing country and believes in multi-culturalism. It is considered home to all main religions of the world. However, in various cases some religious minorities are always suspicious about their security. The recent Sachchar Committee report asserted that in many cases minorities are not getting proper representation in various economic and political areas. It improves the unrest among the members of a particular religion and makes them deprived. Report of various organisations explore that the demolition of Babri Mosque (6th December, 1992) and the series of communal rights which took place after the incident inflicted the terrorist activities. In India, the terrorist activities focussed on numerous attacks from both externally-based terrorist organisations and internally-based separatist or terrorist entities. Several attacks inflicted large number of casualties. Officials of America asserted in this regard "Although clearly committed to combating violent extremism, the Indian government's counter-terrorism efforts remained hampered by its outdated and overburdened law enforcement and legal systems".

In 2008, India ranked among the world's most terrorism-afflicted countries. On November 26, on an essential moment that is now called "26/11", terrorists struck at a variety of locations in Mumbai killing at least 183 people, including 22 foreigners, six of whom were Americans and 14 members of the police and security forces. Over 300 more were injured.

United Nation High Commissioner for Refugees said, "The attacks in Mumbai targetted places frequented by foreigners and wealthy Indians" and "Local and state police proved to be poorly trained and equipped, and lacked central control to coordinate an effective response. This attack was the most recent in a long list of lethal terrorist incidents this year".

India has been experiencing a number of terrorist attacks in the recent decade. Kashmir, Assam, Mumbai, Hyderabad, Delhi, Ahmedabad and many other places in India were victimised by terrorist attacks. The Indian government assessed that South Asian Islamic extremist groups including Lashkar-e-Tayyiba, Jaish-e-Mohammad, and Harakat-ul-Jihad-i-Islami (Bangladesh) as well as indigenous groups were behind these events. The Government of India believed these attacks were aimed at creating a break-down in India-Pakistan relations, fostering Hindu-Muslim violence within India, and harming India's commercial centers to impede India's economic resurgence.

Eastern India has a long history of Maoist (left-wing extremism), and insurgent terrorist activity that has challenged state writ and control, governance structures, and the ruling political class. Report says that in 2008, there were fifty terrorist attacks in Eastern India that killed approximately 500 individuals.

Insurgent groups, often fighting for recognition, political, and economic rights, or independence, were also active in the Northeast. Failure to properly accommodate the competing interests of diverse ethnic groups, low levels of development, and the success of previous insurgent movements in creating new Indian states were cited as explanatory factors for the appeal of insurgent movements. In 1990, the Government of India banned United Liberation Front of Assam (ULFA). ULFA is alleged to have been involved in several terrorist attacks.

Naxalism is also a form of terrorism which is influenced by the Communist ideology (Marxist). The Communist Party of India (Maoists), commonly referred to as Maoist/Naxalites, were active in the states of Chhattisgarh, Andhra Pradesh, Karnataka, Orissa, Bihar, Jharkhand, and West Bengal. State governments have expressed interest in augmenting their security forces by either creating or buttressing state-level assets, or hosting central level units to address the increased terrorist threat.

Specifically, in response to the Mumbai attacks, the Indian government has proposed a new agency, the National Investigative Agency, to create national-level capability to investigate and potentially prosecute such acts.

Illegal funding sources that may have been exploited to finance terrorist operations were being closely investigated. Indian authorities believe that the Mumbai terrorists used various funding sources including credit cards, hawala, charities, and wealthy donors. In addition to the Mumbai attacks, the rise in terrorist attacks and their coordinated nature throughout India suggested the terrorists were well-funded and financially organised. Terrorists are having illegal funding sources such as credit cards, hawala, charities and wealthy donors. It is a matter of close investigation and Indian authorities are taking initiatives in this regard.

Nepal

Nepal which is officially known as Federal Democratic Republic of Nepal, is a landlocked country in South Asia and the world's youngest republic. It is bordered to the north by China and to the south, east, and west by India. With an area of 147,181 square kilometres (56,827 sq miles) and a population of approximately thirty million, Nepal is the world's 93rd largest country by land mass and the 41st most populous country. Nepal is a country of highly diverse and rich geography, culture, and religions. Nepal's gross domestic product for the year 2008 was estimated at over US$12 billion, making it the 115th - largest economy in the world. Agriculture accounts for about 40 per cent of Nepal's GDP and 76 per cent of the workforce is engaged in agriculture. The rate of unemployment and underemployment approaches half of the working-age population.

Recently, Nepal is in transitional stage of political stability. While Nepal experienced no significant acts of international terrorism, several incidents of politically-motivated violence occurred across the country. Now, Nepal is governed by the Coalition government which is headed by Communist Party of Nepal (Maoists). It is notably that CPN (Maoist) is a designated organisation on the Terrorist Exclusion List (TEL). The Maoist-affiliated Young Communist League, which included former members of the People's Liberation Army and grew increasingly prominent during 2007, carried on the Maoist militia's tactics of abuse, abduction, murder, intimidation, and extortion in cities and villages. In response to continued violence by Maoist-affiliated youth, other political parties condoned the use of violence for their youth wings. Unrest in the southern Terai plains increased with the proliferation of numerous armed groups. Nepalese government made some headway in this regard, specifically with the passage of anti-money laundering legislation and the arrest of individuals suspected of terrorist ties.

There were no indications that Nepal was a safe haven for other international terrorists; however, authorities arrested several individuals with suspected ties to Pakistani terrorist organisations using Nepal to transit between Pakistan and India. From Indian point of view, it is a major problem that insurgency is taking place from this country to a large extent.

Pakistan

Pakistan is popularly known as Islamic Republic of Pakistan. It's the sixth most populous country in the world and has the second largest Muslim population in the world after Indonesia. It also has the second largest Shia Muslim population in the world. The country is listed among the Next Eleven economies of the world.

The structure of the Pakistani economy has changed from a mainly agricultural base to a strong service base. Agriculture now only accounts for roughly Twenty per cent of the GDP, while the service sector accounts for 53 per cent of the GDP.

Pakistan's low literacy rate greatly hampers its ability to develop and expand its economic base. Literacy averages 54 per cent nationwide, and in Pakistan's remote tribal areas can be as low as 0.5 per cent for women. The dearth of good public schools results in thousands of youth attending madrassas, schools that teach mainly religious subjects, some of which promote a radical and violent ideology. Now, Government is taking measures in this regard.

Pakistan being US ally in its fight against counter-terrorism. Recently, its Army accelerated engagement in the fight against the Islamic extremist groups.

> *"We are fighting the menace and we will continue to fight. But this is the fight for the peace of the world. This is the fight for the future of generations to come. The fight against*

extremism is a fight for the hearts and minds of people. It can't be won only by guns and bombs. The fight must be multi-faceted."

Asif Ali Zardari, President of Pakistan,
UN General Assembly, New York City, September 25, 2008

This country is getting assistance not only for anti-terrorist activities but also for the various socio-economic development programmes. The following data shows that how much US is providing assistance to Pakistan for achieving the goal.

Account	*FY-2006*	*FY-2006 Supplemental*	*FY-2007*	*FY-2007 Supplemental*	*FY-2008*	*FY-2008 Supplemental*
CSH	22,800	5,300	22,400		29,800	
DA	27,000	10,500	95,300		29,800	
ESF	296,600	40,500	283,700	110,000	347,200	
FMF	297,000		297,000		297,570	
IMET	2,037		1,992		2,129	
NADR	8,600		10,000		9,700	
P.L. 480 TITLE I & II	17,700					
ERMA					5,300	
IDFA		70,000			6,500	
Total	**709,320**	**126,300**	**731,750**	**110,000**	**749,000**	

- Child Survival and Health (CSH),
- Development Assistance (DA),
- International Military Education and Training (IMET),
- International Narcotics and Law Enforcement (INCLE),
- Antiterrorism Assistance (NADR-ATA),
- Export Control and Border Security (NADR-EXBS),
- Small Arms and Light Weapons (NADR-SALW),
- Terrorism Interdiction Programs (NADR-TIP),
- Food for Peace (P.L. 480 Title I & II),
- Emergency Refugee and Migration Assistance (ERMA),
- International Disaster and Famine Assistance (IDFA).

(The chart above offers a comparison of selected types of assistance and does not include security cooperation or coalition support fund requests).

According to officials of America, "The mix of US assistance for Pakistan reflects the diverse ways the United State is cooperating with Pakistan in pursuit of critical USG policy goals. These include countering nuclear proliferation; building a stable and democratic Afghanistan; ensuring peace and stability in South Asia through the continuation of the India-Pakistan reconciliation process; supporting Pakistan's efforts to become a modern, prosperous, democratic state."

US Foreign Military Financing (FMF) is being used by Pakistan to upgrade and maintain helicopters, aircraft, weapons systems, munitions, and other equipment, which have enabled Pakistan's armed forces to operate against foreign terrorists and militants in the rugged border areas along the Pakistan-Afghanistan border. Since 2001, over 2,000 Pakistani military personnel have been killed carrying out counter-terrorism operations.

International terrorist organisations, including Al-Qaida (AQ) and its supporters, continued to operate and carry out attacks in Pakistan. Violence stemming from Sunni-Shia sectarian strife, ethnic tensions, and militant sub-nationalists claimed civilian lives. Attacks occurred with greatest frequency in the regions bordering Afghanistan: Balochistan, the North West Frontier Province (NWFP), and the adjacent Federally Administered Tribal Areas (FATA), but militant attacks continued to grow and target urban centers including Lahore, Islamabad, Peshawar, and Rawalpindi.

The coordination, sophistication, and frequency of suicide bombings that increased sharply in 2007, continued to grow in Pakistan in 2008. It is also believed that militants were responsible for the assassination of former Prime Minister Benazir Bhutto on December 27, 2007.

Despite an increased number of infiltrations across the Line of Control, Pakistan-India relations were improving, with trade opened for the first time in over sixty years, until they were significantly set-back by the terrorist attacks in Mumbai, India in November. From Indian point of view the fund which is pumped by US to promote war against terrorism in Pakistan is misused by Pakistan against India and for their political rivalry.

Conclusion

In the society where there is illiteracy, hunger and economic disparity the terrorism flourishes rapidly. All these factors lead to increase in poverty which itself is the mother of terrorism. Famous philosopher Aristotle had agreed on the assertion stating, "Poverty is mother of Terrorism and Revolution". We see for example in Muslim countries there is a huge amount of poverty and that is why, it becomes easier for the terrorist groups to find the interested persons due to their poor economic conditions. Among the multitude of causes that may lead a person to resort to terrorism are ethnicity, nationalism/separatism, globalisation, (non) democracy, dehumanisation, and religion. But apart from these factors, socio-economic reasons are key factor that promote a fertile land to flourish terrorism.

Daniel Pipes (2002) says, "As long as there is poverty, inequality, injustice and repressive political systems, militant Islamic tendencies will grow in the world."

From the above discussion we came to know that how South Asian countries are facing terrorism as a challenge. Mainly these countries are developing in nature and facing internal revolt and external insurgency. It shows that those countries which are economically not sound are having maximum chance for terrorist activities. It is true that socio-economic backwardness is hampering the social harmony but we should not consider that this is the only reason that is destroying the fabric of society. There are other factors also that cause insurgency in society. Even though, the country likes USA and Israel are economically developed but still they are facing the same problems.

It is a fact that the society in which the people are ignored and have to suffer from socio-economic and political injustice provide conducive environment to promote terrorism. When the people and their problems are neglected or kept aloof, they ultimately express their resentment in the form of violent behaviour to attract the attention of the state and the people. Therefore, we can say that socio-economic factors are responsible for terrorism to a large extent.

References

- Sridhar K. Khatri and Gert W. Kueck, (2003), *Terrorism in South Asia: Impact on Development and Democratic Process*; Shipra Publication; New Delhi. Crenshaw, Martha, (1981), *The causes of terrorism*'. *Comparative politics*. Doyle, Rodger, (2003), 'By the numbers - Fundamentalism'. *Scientific American,* March 2003.
- Dworkin, Andrea, (1997), *Life and Dead*. New York: The Free press. Guelke, Adrian, (1995), *The age of terrorism and the international political system.* London, UK. I.E. Tauris.
- Lichbach, Mark Irving, (1989), 'An evaluation of "Does economic inequality breed political conflict?" studies', *World Politics.*

- McGurn, William, (1987), *'Terrorist or freedom fighter? - The cost of confusion'*. Wilkinson, Paul, (1977), *Terrorism and the liberal state.* London: Macmillan Press. Williams, Robin M. Jr., (1994), The Sociology of Ethnic Conflicts: Comparative International Perspectives'. *Annual Review of Sociology.*
- Yahya, Harun, (2002), 'The Real Ideological Root of Terrorism: Darwinism and materialism'. Islam Denounces Terrorism, online edition. Date accessed. Institute for European Defence and Strategic Studies, Occasional Paper. http://ipr.sagepub.com/'cgi/eontent/abstraci/30/3/317 (SAGE JOURNAL) http://www.state.gOV/s/ct/rls/crt/2008/index.htm (US Department of State, Country Reports on Terrorism 2008).

21

Democracy in the Age of Terrorism: The Basic Challenges and Future Prospects

Vijay Kumar, Shailesh Anand

An action of violence is labelled "terrorist" when its psychological effects are out of all proportion to its purely physical result... The lack of discrimination helps to spread fear, for no one in particular is a target then no one can be safe.

— **Raymond Aron**[1]

Terrorism has been a dark feature of human behaviour since first recorded history. Great leaders have been assassinated, groups and individuals have committed incredible violence and entire cities and nations have been put to the sword — all in the name of defending a greater good. It is an active confrontation, evidenced by the fact that the incidence of significant terrorist attacks often spikes to several levels. 9/11, 12/13, 3/11, 7/7 and 26/11 — These are no longer just number or dates but have become turning point for countries who have suffered bloody and ghastly terror attacks. The whole world, especially, the democratic world[2] shivers constantly at its threat potential. It is a problem capable of destabilising not only national but also international politics. Today, usually all states are expending resources to combat terrorism — setting up specially trained police squads, planning policies and programs and holding operations to track terrorist groups in their own countries. America has in particular, been spending a lot of money since mid-1990s on counter-terrorist operations.

The democratic community, totals about thirty per cent of the world's population, holds about seventy per cent of its wealth and is more stable, united and prosperous. But in areas where conditions are not nearly so good and progress is less rapid have begun to threaten the democratic world.[3] This especially is the case along the so called "Southern arc of instability" that stretches from the Middle East to the Asia littoral. This huge zone is rendered chaotic by a number of problems: absence of clear-cut boundaries, security vacuums, power imbalances, poverty, ineffective governments, high unemployment and extremist religious fundamentalism. The result is a fertile ground for breeding terrorist groups engaged in supporting rogue governments, ethnic rivalries, drug-trafficking, weapon smuggling and organised crime.[4] So much so that, Walter Laqueur, with his lifetime of research is terrorism, has called this era, 'The Age of Terrorism'.[5]

Democratic societies are easy victims to terrorism. But extreme political terrorism in democratic situations carry the seeds of its own destruction. The very principles on which terrorism is based, viz., indiscriminateness, unpredictability, arbitrariness, ruthless destructiveness and its implicit amoral and anti-nomian nature, if carried to the extreme, has a tendency to fire back. The ruthless techniques of terror ultimately isolate the terrorists from the people who begin to defend themselves through self-defense units, refuse to have any truck with terrorists and pass to security forces any information available to them regarding terrorist organisations.[6]

However, in a bid to counter the threat of terrorism the people in democracy have to suffer curtailment in their political freedom, legal constitutional guarantees and human rights besides getting encumbered by heavy taxation and hindered in exercise of religion according to the dictates of conscience.

The paper aims to delineate the incompatibility of democratic and authoritarian values and to show why some states patronise terrorists and their activities. It also seeks to examine as to why initially democratic states seem to suffer badly under terrorist threats and then counter them forcefully if they stand united.

Peace, prosperity and freedom—these fundamental principles fuel the unique form of liberal governments known as democracy. Democracies maintain the long cherished human value of promoting ideals like freedom of speech, the right to vote, freedom of religion, a free press, and other such related values which allow people to live a "good life," based on the principle of "dignity and worth of human person".[7] As such democracies, in general, maintain and maximise following eight standards :

1. Liberty of thought and expression, including opportunities for dissenting minorities to make their views known to other citizens.
2. Opportunities for citizens to participate in political life.
3. When political conflicts occur, control over decisions of government by majorities of citizens.
4. Rationality in political discussions and decision-making.
5. Attempt to evolve consensus in political discussions and decision making.
6. Peaceful management of conflicts and the minimisation of political violence.
7. Resolution of urgent policy questions to the satisfaction of largest number of citizens.
8. Widespread confidence in and loyalty to a constitutional and democratic polity.[8]

As a matter of fact, democracy is an "ideal". It is a "utopian" concept. "It is a form of government, it is a kind of economy, it is an order of society, it is a way of life, it is all these things together"[9] and many things more.

Citizens in a democracy enjoy an extensive array of freedoms. Consequently the 'citizens manage to create and maintain a supportive political culture'[10] ideals and practices of equality, liberty and justice — creating a delicate balance between authority and citizens. Maintaining an exquisite balance between equality, liberty and justice is a perennial challenge before democracy. However, this balance provides the best opportunities for human development on the one hand and keeps the human beings safe from the senseless violence of war on the other. Dahl informs that of the "34 international wars between 1945 and 1989 none occurred among democratic countries". He further informs that this is true of times before 1940.[11]

On the other hand, totalitarian and authoritarian regimes are autocracies. When they call themselves democracies, qualifying it by "peoples" or 'popular', they just suggest they are good or at least praiseworthy, but they still remain autocracies. Most of the princely, military regimes of the Middle East Asia, South East Asia belong to this category. They are just an adaptation of the autocracy to the present society. The specific procedure in there political systems are generated by the desire for "total control" including control over thoughts and attitudes as well as the activities of the citizens by the ruling masters.[12] These regimes feature a syndrome or pattern of inter-related traits which may be following :[13]

1. An elaborate ideology or a promise of a chiliastic claim-based upon a radical rejection of the existing society.
2. A system of terror, whether physical or psychic, effected through secret police control, party system or other formal institutions against 'enemies' of the state - Classes, states or individuals.
3. A near complete monopoly of control of all means of effective communication the press, the radio, the motion picture - in the hands of the party and/or the government.
4. A similar control of the effective use of all weapons of armed combat and the military.
5. A central control and direction of the economy.

The citizen as an individual, and even in a group, is simply defenseless against the technological superiority of the rulers who physically coerce the mass of citizens. This phenomenon is called "state terrorism". Such states are afraid of the democratic set up of their neighbours and make attempts to destabilise them through "state sponsored terrorism" with the help of disgruntled minorities in these countries.

Such use of terror as a political instrument in varying degrees to political ends, even to consolidate and run the state machinery, has been advocated by amoral philosophers and practitioners of state craft, from Machiavelli to Robespierre, from Lenin to Hitler. No wonder, "all terrorist groups were forgiven once they had become the government; in the pursuit of power, success leaves few enemies. The horror of modern times, however, has been the scale of the use of state terror, which has managed to massacre in the last century more than 100,000,000 people."[14] Democracies, on the other hand, have been struggling between 'rule by men and rule by law' for over last 200 years.[15]

In democratic societies like India where a plurality of religions, linguistic, ethnic, and cultural minorities exist, a secular democratic framework-based on consensus and accommodation with elaborate human, civil and political rights is maintained. The founding fathers of the Indian constitution seeked for unity without sacrificing its characteristic diversity.[16]

The Constitution provides a detailed list of Human Rights and incorporates them in the form of Fundamental Rights (Part III) and the Directive Principles (Part IV). The Fundamental Rights incorporate Right to Equality, Right to Freedom, Rights against Exploitation, Right to Freedom of Religion, Cultural and Educational Rights and the Right to

Constitutional Remedies. A common running thread through most democratic constitutions is the acknowledgment of the Constitution as a predetermined rule of limitation upon governmental power. Normally, the vehicles for testing the ebb-and flow of governmental limitations are provided for in the Constitution with a judiciary headed by a Supreme Court, the most familiar constitutional referees.

These rights protect individual freedom by forbidding state interference with the individual. The resulting civil liberties which define the status of the individual are generally correlative to negative duties of the state. They are largely consistent with an optimistic view of man as a self-directing agent living in a safe environment, coupled with a pessimistic view of government seen as over-reaching and potentially tyrannous.

Apart from these rights to freedom of speech, expression, movement, personal freedom there are comprehensive legal regulations on behalf of privacy rights in democracies which can be readily observed by any visitor to countries like USA, UK, India, Mexico etc. The ancient law givers of the Hindus declared *"Sarvas sve sve Grehe Raja"* which means "every man is a king in his own house". The *Dharmashastras* of ancient India and their commentators expounded the laws of privacy. Even Kautilya in his *Arthsastra* written around 321-296 BC advocated privacy of the king in consultations with his ministers as well as citizens' privacy. So much so that while advocating the employment of spies for seeking information on "national security risks", he did not recommend to them the role of eavesdroppers.[17] Even today, the Preamble of the Indian Constitution assures the "dignity of the individual" and the Indian Evidence Act of 1872, and Code of Criminal Procedure make elaborate references regarding protecting the privacy of the individual against arbitrary search of his residence and admissibility of any confession of guilt made to a police officer. Such laws of searches and seizures, restrictions on the admissibility of evidence procured by improper means, and related rules, act as strong bastions in defense of individual privacy.[18]

Constitutionalism and Rule of Law being the guiding principles of the democratic systems, the states are under an obligation to not only respect these rights, but also to ensure availability of the means by which the right can legitimately, meaningfully and effectively enjoyed.[19] The media in these countries is recognised as the Fourth Estate because of its power to impact and mould the public opinion, which is critical in a democracy. Good governance, transparency and right to information are the essence of democratic governance.[20]

Democracy seeks to insure the security of the individual citizens both within and outside the state and therefore seeks internal security as well as safe air travel, maritime transport and secure borders which are critical to physical and economic security and its related prosperity. But the elaborate system of positive rights these states maintain, make democratic countries a target of terrorist states and a sitting duck to the terrorists. These societies reject terrorism in principle but are especially vulnerable to terrorists because of the extensive civil liberties they extend to their people. No wonder, citizens of United States, the most powerful democracy on earth have been the targets of about one in four terrorist incidents worldwide.[21]

Terrorists receive support through networks of financial backers and intermediaries. They raise money to support their operations through means such as common criminal activity, including fraud, extortion, kidnapping and corrupt trade. They also use front companies, skim profits off legitimate business, abuse charities and non-profit organisations, deal in counterfeit currency and work in *hawala* transactions. They not only transfer funds through *hawalas* and other formal and informal financial systems, they also engage in smuggling of cash, precious metals, gems and drugs. They are also known to deal in human trafficking. These activities threaten public safety and undermine the viability of legitimate institutions. When done in collaboration with state sponsors the problem becomes more challenging for democracies. Sometimes these terrorist organisations help in making and unmaking of governments in weak and failed/ or failing states. In the last few years scholars have talked about the emergence of "non-state actors" in world politics. While the nation - state remains the primary "actor" on world stage - It is no longer the only one and in certain instances, what nation-states do and don't do is heavily conditioned by what those non-state actors do and don't do.

It goes without saying that Al-Qaeda had demonstrated its ability as a non-state actor to both make and unmake a government and change the philosophy and course of action of various democratic and non-democratic states of the world.

In recent years international terrorist threat has become particularly difficult to deal with because certain nations find it useful to employ terrorists or support their activities as part of their foreign polices. Initially state sponsorship of terrorism had its benefits for both the state supporting terrorism and for the terrorists.

But 9/11 terrorist attack on US, though crystallised the vulnerability of democracies, it united them together to wipe out the terrorists. Still state sponsorship, which continues covertly, gives clear advantages to the terrorists.

For example :[22]

1. When a terrorist obtains legitimate travel and identification documents from a country, it becomes hard to identify and track him.
2. A terrorist who enjoys the patronage of a state has a ready source of weapons and a legitimate means to transport him. There are instances when diplomatic pouches, exempt from search by international convention, are used to carry weapons.
3. Countries like Libya, Syria, Iran, Pakistan and former Afghanistan make a terrorist's work easier by providing a place to train and learn to handle the latest automatic weapons.
4. Similarly, states can provide terrorists with refuge, an important support for going underground, or resting after an extraordinary strenuous task.
5. The states can provide safe houses to terrorists wherefrom they can plan future actions without fear.
6. Financial support from state sponsors allow terrorists to spend more time on operations because they do not need to raise funds from other sources.
7. Much wanted terrorists may be allowed to undergo plastic surgery, name and identity changes and allowed to retire from active life, playing only vital role in strategy and planning for the network.

There are, on the other hand, advantages for a state giving these benefits to terrorists.[23]

1. Terrorism is an inexpensive form of warfare. A small group of state supported terrorists cost less per year than a company of regular soldiers.
2. Terrorists can do much more damage and intimidate the target states than any army can do. The events of 9/11 on US and 12/13 and 26/11 attacks on India shocked them more than a war could have done. They were able to hurt these countries in the most sensitive places.
3. Using terrorist surrogates makes it easier for the sponsoring state to deny responsibility for actions on the one hand and refuse ownership of captured terrorists on the other. Pakistan does this most of the time its terrorists are caught in India.

4. Terrorists can be useful in dealing with political opponents or dissidents in their own countries or abroad. Libya has used terrorists to kill regime opponents in many countries.
5. Through terrorism, a small state or leader can attract the attention of the world. Bin Laden has become more (in) famous than any other political leader of the world.
6. Through terrorism some leaders are able to wrench authority from the legitimate rulers and then hang on to power as the Taliban government in Afghanistan did.
7. Through terrorism the sponsoring state is able to destabilise democratic governments.
8. By targeting economically prosperous areas and strategically significant points the sponsoring state inflicts economic damages on the target state, halting its development process.
9. Sponsored terrorism can target ethnic or religious groups which can lead to hate movements and civil war in the target states.

In the circumstances, terrorism poses important political and diplomatic challenges to democratic regimes. A society which abjures violence and terrorism, the weapons adopted by the terrorists is violence and more senseless violence to call attention of the government to bring about changes in policy favourable to the causes of the terrorists. One potential means for dealing with terrorism is law, which in most circumstances tend to fail. To take an example, after 13 long years of waiting, punishment for those guilty of the 1993 serial blasts in Mumbai that killed 257 and injured 750 people is under process, but the mastermind Dawood Ibrahim Kaskar and his conspiratorial team lives in relative freedom somewhere in Pakistan.[24] Law, both domestic and international has failed to control criminal conduct and bring terrorists to justice. Some terrorists are killed or captured during the course of their crime, as happened at the 13 December 2001, attack on Indian Parliament or as often keeps happening in Jammu and Kashmir, but few of those who evade these consequences are afterwards found and arrested. At times, the terrorist who is prosecuted is likely to be released far earlier than his sentence should require, often in exchange for hostages taken in subsequent terrorist episode. The Kandhar hijack drama immediately comes to mind in which a dreaded terrorist of Pakistan was released by India in Kandhar.

One reason for the law's ineffectiveness is that terrorism, in essence, is a criminal activity. In domestic law, governments seek to punish and deter crime as effectively as possible. But they recognise that law cannot eliminate crime. They can expect even less of the law in dealing with international terrorism.[25] The world has no international police force or judicial system. International crime police organisation, generally known as Interpol, and the International Criminal Court (ICC) are weak institutions with little power even in the territory of their member states.

Labelling terrorism as "domestic" or "international" complicates matter further. It is best conceived as a "transnational phenomenon, with domestic and international elements mixed idiosyncratically together. Given that no modern state can seal itself off from the international community, the domestic international distinction contributes to the fragmentation of a state's preparedness effort, as well as to the perpetuation of different zones of vulnerability and readiness."[26]

Democratic nations have tried to control international terrorism by condemning it, by treating it as piracy, by prosecuting terrorists under the laws of affected states, by creating international norms establishing as criminal certain acts wherever committed, and by cooperating through extradition and other devices in aiding nations attacked by terrorists. But when we look into these measures critically we can conclude that "the law applicable to terrorism is not merely flawed, it is perverse". There is no agreement among nations regarding who is a terrorist. In one of the UN Committees on legal affairs the Madagascar representative summed up the views of the nations :

> Acts of terrorism inspired by base motives of personal gain were to be condemned. Acts of political terrorism, on the other hand, undertaken to vindicate hallowed rights recognised by the United Nations, were praiseworthy. It was of course, regrettable that certain acts in the latter category affected innocent persons.[27]

So, it is no wonder that 'one man's terrorist is another man's hero' and people come out in favour of clemency for terrorists like Afzal Guru, convicted with a death sentence in the Indian Parliament attack case.[28]

UN Declaration of Human Rights, 1948 and various subsequent UN resolutions supporting "self determination" and wars of national liberations, in the pursuit of which oppressed people were authorised to resort to all available means, including armed struggle has further befogged the issue of terrorism especially in developing countries of the Third World. States supporting terrorism use local issues to pump in arms and provide training to men and women engaged in local militant uprisings and subsequently using them for their larger terrorist game plan as foot soldiers or arms peddlers.

The befuddled legitimacy of political violence is proving to be a notion that has not allowed international law on terrorism to develop properly. Consequently, countries having extradition treaties which obligate them to extradite persons accused of committing crimes associated with terrorism, such as murder, bombing, armed assault and robbery, refuse to do so often because the offence is characterised as "political" conduct which the law exempts from extradition.[29]

International law being weak, the domestic law is also not very helpful. A large number of rights and privacy rules prevent the police organisation of a democratic society to engage in anti-terrorist operations to counter the terror unleashed by the terrorists. There are not many politically acceptable and legally permissible methods available to them. Constrained by the rules of the legal system, by the independence of judiciary, by the accredited values and conventions of the liberal and democratic traditions, by political meddling, the democratic state finds itself beset with problems in tackling terror. Matching foreign sponsored terror with "enforcement terror" or "terrorism by ordinance" complicate matter because the victims are the general public. We can take the example of Prevention of Terrorist Activities Act (POTA) in India. It was a measure enacted to deal with growing terrorist activities of the terrorists. In due course allegations of its widespread misuse against religious minorities and political opponents were made. The POTA was amended in 2003 to modify some of its most objectionable provisions. It was repealed in September 2004. The same fate befell the Preventive Detention Act, 1950 which lapsed in 1969. MISA 1971 was repealed in 1978, TADA, 1985 expired in 1995. It is clear that there is too much of pressure in the democratic society for reclamation of space for procedural democracy, since these Acts are seen as draconian in theory and practice.[30] US maltreatment of prisoners of war of Abu Gharib and Guantanamo Bay have been criticised as "symbols which the long American tradition of justice and liberty deserve to see removed at the earliest".[31] But the CIA is seeking to be allowed to use seven grilling techniques to elicit information from terror suspects. These are :[32]

1. Induced hypothermia;
2. Forcing suspects to stand for prolonged periods;
3. Sleep deprivation;
4. A technique called "attention grab" where a suspect's shirt is forcefully seised;
5. The "attention slap" or open hand slapping that hurts but does not lead to physical damage;

6. The "belly slap" and
7. Sound and light manipulation.

The nature of the problem being complex, there seems to be no possible political solution, neither is there any purely military solution as is being proved in US "war against terror" in Afghanistan, Iraq and Iran. It is estimated that the US spends over $ 487 billion conducting a war against Iraq while the real terrorists are at large in the hills bordering Afghanistan and Pakistan.

Freedom loving people around the world have been targetted by scourge of terrorism. From the railway bombings of Bombay, Madrid, London, and Moscow to the commercial centre attacks in Istanbul and Casablanca and Bali, we have seen that terrorism does not discriminate among religion, race, and national origin. Negotiating peace with them is futile because they always go back upon their words or new organisations come up to take up their position. Terrorism has grown into a rich business.

A viable strategy for counter-terrorism, therefore, needs to have the following elements :

1. Firmness toward terrorists;
2. Pressure on states supporting terrorists;
3. Bankrupting terrorists;
4. Practical measures to deter, apprehend and punish terrorists.

The first essential element of any strategy to deal with terrorists must be of rejecting terrorist demands. It is an old adage in Indian philosophy that one must give an individual to save a village, a village to save a district and so on. We must be ready to give up a couple of lives to save the many. Hostage taking must prove a risky game for the terrorists as it happened in Soviet Russia when Chechen terrorists took school children as hostages in Beslan.

Focussing on and attacking terrorist money flow is another important strategy to fight terrorism.[33] By following the money trail through financial information sharing worldwide, we can save lives by unearthing terrorist cells and networks. The maintenance of terrorist networks and the acquisition and development of lethal weapons is expensive even if a particular attack does not prove costly in isolation. Identifying and isolating the sources of funding for terrorist groups incapacitates not only their execution of attacks, but also their ability to maintain international alliances, create infrastructures around the world for recruitment and training, and purchase or develop deadly weapons.

US gave a heavy blow to the terrorists when 383 individuals and entities were 'designated' as terrorists and well over $140 million in terrorist related assets were frozen internationally after 9/11 attacks.[34]

The democratic world must unite to fight terrorism together. A terrorist designated in one country must be made *'persona non grata'* in all democratic countries. To avoid religion and religious institutions being used in terrorist networks all overseas charities must be brought under a government controlled umbrella organisation. This would enable governments to control transactions between national and international charities and their affiliates.

However, the first line of defence that is available to the state fighting terrorism is intelligence. If a state knew "where, when and how", a terrorist is going to attack, it would easily thwart it and apprehend the criminals. All state police forces must develop anti-terrorist squads which should cooperate with all sections of police forces on intelligence gathering about terrorism, their activities, their motivations and goals.

There is a tendency today to talk of terrorism as "clash of civilisation". People tend to paint a picture of conflict between Islam and Christianity. There is not much truth in these assumptions which have been enforced because many of the leaders of terrorist organisations use the religious rhetoric to whip up emotions and gain sympathisers. Leaders of the East Turkistan Islamic Movement, Hamas, Hizbollah, Al-Qaida, Jaish-e-Mohammad, Lashkar-e-Toiba, etc., talk in terms of religious— discourses to gain *fidayeens* — the suicide bombers. Otherwise, why young men for whom the whole world is open would indulge in terrorist activities. Andrew Sullivan observes that:

> "The words of Osama bin Laden are saturated with religious arguments and theological language... Although some Muslim leaders have criticised the terrorists, and even Saudi Arabia's rulers have distanced themselves from the militants, other Muslims in the Middle East and elsewhere have not denounced these acts, have been conspicuously silent or have indeed celebrated them.[35]

This silence of the civilised people gives terrorists the strength to survive. This war of fundamentalism in an ever changing secular world against faiths of all kinds, including Islam that are at peace with freedom and modernity, needs to be examined in a different perspective from "a religious war" or "clash of civilisations".

Terrorists have been on rampage since the last six-seven years. They have been targeting buses, trains, planes, tourist places and even religious places. Pattern seems to be same everywhere — suicide bombers, car bombs, explosive devices explode in crowded public places causing immense loss of life and property. In some cases attackers own it up but enquiries later show that some of these groups are non-existent or functioning under fictitious names. In many cases there are suspected "Pakistan connections". It is an open secret that various extremist groups have been operating from Pakistan. Even today Al-Qaida remains a powerful and aggressive enemy of the liberal democratic world and continues to operate not only in the border region between Afghanistan and Pakistan but also in at least 60 countries worldwide. It has struck in Casablanca, Kuwait, Amman, Bali, Mombassa, Djakarta, Riyadh, India and various parts of Pakistan too.[36] It is only a matter of time when the collapsing state of Pakistan would become a target of attack of the democratic countries where production of Pakistan's *jehad* factories are still leaving their signature.

Indeed the ultimate success in fight against those who commit acts of terrorism requires the active support of all nations. Experience teaches us that democracies are stronger in promoting peace and security. Bombay train blasts and Malegaon blasts prove this fact that man-made crises forge stronger ties between democratic citizens. Democracies reject violence as a pragmatic political strategy and are able to protect human rights and fundamental freedoms while fighting international crime and terrorism because every citizen is a soldier of democracy. By uniting together in their fight against terrorism the democratic countries seek to build a more secure and economically prosperous world in which individuals can live freely and enjoy healthy and productive lives. Some people think, that violence is the only answer to democracy. But ask people in Kashmir who thought so. After losing eighty thousand people they have realised what repercussions use of violence has. Terrorism has no end. It leads nowhere except to death and destruction.

Notes and References

1. Raymond Aron, *Press and War,* London : Weidenfeld and Nicholson, 1966, p. 170. Aron seems to be repeating the dictum of the ancient Chinese strategist Sun Tzee, who said, "kill one and frighten ten thousand."
2. Karin Santoro, *et al.* "Italian Attitudes and Response to Terrorism," *Terrorism,* Vol. 10. No. 4 (1987), p. 306. They write, "... terrorists present a serious challenge to democratic authority."

3. Richard L. Kugler, "*A Distinctly American Internationalism For A globalised World*", *U.S. Foreign Policy Agenda, Electronic Journal,* Dec. 2002, p. 37.
4. *Ibid.*
5. Walter Laqueur, *The Age of Terrorism,* Boston : Little Brown and Co., 1987.
6. Vijay Kumar, "The Tenets of Terror and Counter-terrorism : Strategies and Programmes," *Indian Journal of Politics,* Vol. 22, No. 3+4 (1988), pp. 60-61."
7. Preamble, *Universal Declaration of Human Rights* (1948).
8. R.A. Dahl, "Political Opposition in Western Democracies," in Jean Blondel (ed.), *Comparative Government,* London : Macmillan, 1975, pp. 229-30.
9. *Education of Free Men in American Democracy,* quoted in J. L. Pandey and Vijay Kumar, "Democratic Theory : An appraisal of Indian Democracy", *Journal of the Bhagalpur University : Social Science,* Vol. 9. No. 3 (1976), p. 35.
10. R.A. Dahl, *On Democracy,* Delhi: East-West, 2001, p. 51. see for details of advantages of democracy, chapter 5 and chapter 12.
11. *Ibid., p. 57.*
12. C.J. Friedrich and Z. Brezezinski, "The General Characteristics of Totalitarian Dictatorship," in Blondel, *op.cit,* pp. 187-199.
13. *Ibid.,* p. 94.
14. Andrew Sindair, *An Anatomy of Terror : A History of Terrorism,* London: Macmillan, 2003, p. xv.
15. Arnold Brown, *The Threat of Thearchy,* Futurism, September-October, 2004, pp. 26-29.
16. See D.D. Basu, *Constitutional Law of India,* New Delhi : Prentice Hall, 1987, M.M. Sankhdher and K.K. Wadhwa (eds.), *National Unity and Religious Minorities,* New Delhi: Gitanjali Publishing House, 1991.
17. R. Shama Sastri, *Kautilya's Arthsastra,* Mysore : Raghuveer Press, 1951, pp. 19, 26, 68.
18. India, *Code of Criminal Procedure* (1973), Sec. 94 *et. al.*
19. J.S. Verma, "Rule of Law The Bedrock of Democracy", *Young Indian,* July 9-15. 2005.
20. *Ibid.,* part II, *Young Indian,* July 16-22.
21. L. Paul Bremer III, "Counter-terrorism : Strategies and Programs," *Terrorism,* Vol. 10, No. 4 (1987), p. 337.
22. *Ibid.,* p. 338.
23. *Ibid.,* p. 339.
24. Raj Chengappa and Prema Thakurdesai, "Why Can't we Get Dawood?" *India Today,* Sept. 25. 2006.
25. Abraham D. Sofaer, "Terrorism and International law," *The American Review,* 2, 1987, p. 3.
26. Richard Falkenrath, "Analytic Models and Policy Prescription : Understanding Recent Innovation in US Counter-terrorism," *Studies in Conflict and Terrorism,* 24: 2001, p. 164.

27. Quoted in Sofaer, *op.cit.,* p. 3. Till date there is no comprehensive draft of one convention on terrorism. See for details, Ajay K. Mehra and O.P. Sharma, *Terrorism and the Rule of Law : An Indian Perspective,* New Delhi: Konrad Adenamer Shiftung, 2006.
28. See *Hindustan Times,* 30.9.06.
29. Sofaer, *op.cit.,* p. 4.
30. See M. Mahmood, *An Encyclopaedic Dictionary of Politics,* New Delhi : Anmol Publisher 2006, pp. 318-19, also see Mehra and Sharma, *op.cit.,* pp. 67-131.
31. The Guardian's news published in *Hindustan Times,* "seven grilling ways the CIA wants," 20.09.06.
32. *Ibid.*
33. Jimmy Gurule, "The Global Effort to Stop Terrorist Financing," *US Foreign Policy Agenda,* e-Journal USA, Vol. 8, No. l, August 2003, p. 21.
34. Juan Carlos Zarate, "Bankrupting Terrorist," *e-Journal USA,* September, 2004.
35. Andrew Sullivan, "Is This a Religious War?" *Span,* March/April 2002, p. 42.
36. Susan E. Rice, "US National Security Policy Post-9/11 : Perilis and Prospectes," *The Fletcher Forum of World Affairs,* Vol. 28, No. 1, Winter 2004, p. 134.

Index

R

T